❧ The Ethos of History ❧

MAKING SENSE OF HISTORY
Studies in Historical Cultures
General Editor: Stefan Berger
Founding Editor: Jörn Rüsen

Bridging the gap between historical theory and the study of historical memory, this series crosses the boundaries between both academic disciplines and cultural, social, political and historical contexts. In an age of rapid globalization, which tends to manifest itself on an economic and political level, locating the cultural practices involved in generating its underlying historical sense is an increasingly urgent task.

For a full volume listing please see back matter.

THE ETHOS OF HISTORY

Time and Responsibility

Edited by Stefan Helgesson and Jayne Svenungsson

berghahn

NEW YORK · OXFORD

www.berghahnbooks.com

First published in 2018 by
Berghahn Books
www.berghahnbooks.com

© 2018 Stefan Helgesson and Jayne Svenungsson

Library of Congress Cataloging-in-Publication Data

A C.I.P. cataloging record is available from the Library of Congress

British Library Cataloguing in Publication Data

A catalogue record for this book is available from the British Library

ISBN 978-1-78533-884-7 hardback
ISBN 978-1-78533-885-4 ebook

Contents

Acknowledgements

We wish, first of all, to express our gratitude to Hans Ruin, without whose intellectual guidance as the research leader of the 'Time, Memory, and Representation' initiative, this volume would never have materialized. Thanks are also due to the Swedish Foundation for Humanities and Social Sciences, whose generous support facilitated this intellectual endeavour. As we conceptualized this volume, Stefan Berger's enthusiastic reception of our initial proposal was likewise essential in facilitating its genesis.

Situating the Ethos of History

STEFAN HELGESSON AND JAYNE SVENUNGSSON

History is no longer what it used to be. With the advent of poststructuralism in the 1970s, theorists of history would pay increasing attention to the forms, assumptions and disciplinary conditions of historiography, rather than the 'thing itself'. This differed from earlier twentieth-century debates between, for example, liberal and Marxist historians who struggled over the very content and truth of history – its ontology, one might say. Regardless of ideological orientation, and irrespective of any pragmatic difficulties in securing archival evidence, the actuality of history as that which 'really happened' – to allude to Leopold von Ranke's famous motto – was never really questioned in those earlier exchanges.

The poststructuralist turn unsettled this attachment to the real by reframing history as a regime of knowledge and mode of representation rather than an empirical science; epistemology, not ontology, took the front seat. History could now be theorized in terms of 'discourse' (Foucault) or 'metahistory' (White), which unmoored old truth-claims. Instead of being authorized as the science of the past, history could be defined as irreducibly involved in the construction, distribution and exercise of power. Contrary to earlier varieties of ideology critique – the notion of 'false consciousness', after all, presupposed the possibility of truth – there was, in the most extreme versions of poststructuralist theory, nothing 'behind' the narrative of the past. Nothing, that is, besides the conventions of genre and the will to power that governed these conventions.

The strongest thinker in this vein was Hayden White, whose mark on the field is impossible to ignore. By questioning the authority that historical

Notes for this section begin on page 12.

accounts can claim 'as contributions to a secured knowledge of reality', he opened the doors to an extensive interrogation of disciplinary procedures and assumptions.[1] Challenging the Aristotelian opposition between history and fiction, White argued in his seminal essay 'The Historical Text as Literary Artifact' that it was the cultural expectations shaped by literary culture that enabled the 'emplotment', or the meaningful configuration of events, in historiography:

> As a symbolic structure, the historical narrative does not *reproduce* the events it describes; it tells us in what direction to think about the events and charges our thought about the events with different emotional valences. The historical narrative does not *image* the things it indicates; it *calls to mind* images of the things it indicates, in the same way that a metaphor does. When a given concourse of events is emplotted as a 'tragedy', this simply means that the historian has so described the events as to *remind us* of that form of fiction which we associate with the concept 'tragic'. Properly understood, histories ought never to be read as unambiguous signs of the events they report, but rather as symbolic structures, extended metaphors, that 'liken' the events reported in them to some form with which we have already become familiar in our literary culture.[2]

In this reversal of the priority between fiction and reality, formulated in the early 1970s, we glimpse already the full-blown questioning of historiography in its established forms. We also see how drastically limited White was at this stage to a Western frame of reference (and, as is evident elsewhere in *Tropics of Discourse,* to a patriarchal one). As time passed, however, poststructuralist critique dovetailed in unanticipated ways with modes of inquiry grounded in social activism – notably feminism and anticolonialism. This would result in landmark studies by scholars such as Joan Scott and Dipesh Chakrabarty, among others, who argued that the discipline of history was shaped by – and, in turn, contributed to shaping – flawed patriarchal and/or Eurocentric conceptions of history, which rendered invisible the subaltern and the female gendered subject.

In her influential article 'Gender: A Useful Category of Historical Analysis', Scott, for instance, pointed to the inadequacy of existing bodies of theory for explaining persisting inequality between men and women. While 'women's history' certainly had had the effect of raising gender awareness among historians, it nonetheless left the basic tenets of patriarchal historiography unchallenged: gender was a useful tool for the study of things related to women, but seemed irrelevant to the thinking of historians concerned with issues of economics, politics and power. By contrast, Scott made a forceful claim for the importance of gender as an analytical category for all areas of history:

> The subject of war, diplomacy, and high politics frequently comes up when traditional historians question the utility of gender in their work. But here,

too, we need to look beyond the actors and the literal import of their words. Power relations among nations and the status of colonial subjects have been made comprehensible (and thus legitimate) in terms of relations between male and female.[3]

Chakrabarty would also occasionally incorporate gender in his analyses, but his main argument addressed the imperialist underpinnings of 'historicist' thinking. Famously, he maintained that histories of India, Kenya, China and so on, 'tend to become variations on a master narrative that could be called "the history of Europe"'.[4] Beholden to a European conception of modernity, with predetermined roles assigned to the bourgeoisie, the proletariat and/or the enlightened citizen of the liberal state, the unfolding history of the postcolonial state would always be found lacking. The historian's task was therefore as philosophical and theoretical as it was empirical: the excavation of the hidden history of India by the Subaltern Studies Group (to which Chakrabarty was affiliated) would court failure unless it was accompanied by a rigorous questioning of the basic categories and concepts of modernity.

Although neither Scott nor Chakrabarty were making strong claims about the unknowability or fictionality of history, it is notable that their studies were marked by the double bind of using the institutional site of the discipline in order to interrogate the discipline. At an early stage in his undertaking to 'provincialize Europe', this led Chakrabarty to speak of a 'politics of despair' born out of a realization of the project's very impossibility.[5] He would soon distance himself from such pessimism, but it is worth reexamining this moment of despair from where we stand today, almost two full decades into the new millennium.[6] Why, after all, did Chakrabarty feel that he could abandon the politics of despair? One explanation might be that the entire project of rethinking history was far more successful than he or anyone else had anticipated. Perhaps imperialist teleologies and patriarchal narratives now finally do belong in the past, championed by no one with an authoritative position in the discipline. And perhaps the very boundaries of the discipline are less clear-cut than before, with countless interdisciplinary and transdisciplinary overlappings between history, theology, philosophy, media studies, literary studies, memory studies and so on underway, productively enabling ever new forms of historical inquiry.

And so they lived happily ever after? Not quite: one of the great ironies of our age is that the fundamental gesture of questioning hegemonic narratives has proven to be perfectly adaptable to other, distinctly reactionary, political agendas. In the post-truth era of presidents Putin and Trump, 'alternative facts' (also known as lies) are brazenly presented as the thing-in-itself, as that which indeed happened, even when everyone knows that it did not.[7] When media reports fail to comply with their political interests, 'alternative media' step in to support them. Long-standing public agreements about the relationship between utterances and events have become tenuous, sometimes perilously so, in a distorted echoing of elements of poststructuralist theory. It would seem that current developments have confirmed the validity of the rhetorical question that Bruno Latour directed at the academic community already in 2004: 'While we spent years trying to detect the real prejudices hidden behind the appearance of objective statements, do we now have to reveal the real objective and incontrovertible facts hidden behind the *illusion* of prejudices?'[8]

We stand to be accused of comparing apples and oranges here: on the one hand advanced critique of academic historiography, on the other political demagoguery. Yet both developments force us to reflect on how the authority of the public truth-claim relates to the ethical commitment to justice. If postcolonial and feminist critique interrogated truth-claims in the name of justice, what we are witnessing with many current iterations of political populism is the undermining of justice through the manipulation of truth. The difference here is everything, and the shift we are experiencing today seems to restore to the question of truth some of the gravitas it had lost in the heyday of poststructuralism. Allow us at least to entertain this, optimistically, as one possible outcome of current events.

With the present volume, we invite the reader to engage more extensively, in our shared present, with complex relations between historiography, justice, gender, postcoloniality and notions of time. By the 'ethos of history', the title gestures towards both 'place' and 'character' as dimensions of history – recognizing thereby that such a place and character are caught up in a constant process of disciplinary and political renegotiations of the historian's responsibility. In the Greek tradition from which we derive the term, 'ethos' relates to something else than merely externally observable behaviour. Rather, it is to be understood as a disposition that makes certain types of behaviour more likely than others. Put differently, there is a *moral* dimension to both individual and collective forms of ethos that, insofar as it becomes an object of self-reflection, invites an interrogation also of the value of character. For Aristotle, 'excellence of character' is 'the settled condition we are in when we are well off in relation to feelings and actions', whereas with a vicious character this balance between feelings and external actions is disrupted.[9] Perhaps it is this notion of ethos as a complex relationality that we can transpose to the field of history and the labour of critique. An ethos of history can only form through a web of relations between an emplaced subject – the historian, the reader, the citizen – and a range of other phenomena: temporal, disciplinary, cultural, political. Such relations are never just voluntary; nor are they rigidly predetermined. Rather – and this is where the contributions to this volume all in their diverse ways speak to our theme – 'character' is formed precisely in the engagement with and resistance against those multiple relations. (In this regard, 'ethos' comes close to the 'structuring structure' of Bourdieu's notion of habitus.)[10] Hence, the critical projects outlined above could be described as moments when the ethos transforms as a consequence of its own reflexivity. A 'vicious character' – to remain with Aristotle's vocabulary – would simply reproduce old patterns of patriarchal and colonial thinking, whereas an ethos worth its salt also entails a preparedness for change. By the same token, however, a settled ethos of history will not accept change as a value in and of itself, but will gauge the worth and urgency of particular changes.

Emerging from a transdisciplinary research programme in Sweden that ran from 2010 until 2015 (and also, more specifically, the conference 'The Ethos of History', held in Sigtuna, Sweden, in September 2015), the contributions here engage in diverse ways with the disciplinary expansion and transformation of history and, more broadly, historical thought. They present in this way a sampling of how the ethos of history has become a concern in our day across a surprising range of academic fields. It should be noted that neither of the two editors are historians by training; of the contributors, only a few work within the strict disciplinary domain of history. This could be seen as a limitation. More importantly, however, it manifests the multiple ways in which history matters across diverse disciplines and intellectual traditions.

There are several ways of understanding this transdisciplinarity. The intersections between history, on the one hand, and literary, postcolonial and gender theory, on the other, have already been mentioned. But other developments, such as the burgeoning field of cultural memory studies, the renewed interest in the philosophy of history and the temporal turn in media studies, must also be mentioned.[11] Clearly, the globalized, postcolonial and mediatized present in which multiple 'we's' live has produced a need for numerous reconfigurations of the scholarly approach to the past.

One of the most significant developments, reflected in all the contributions to this volume, is the renewed interrogation of time. Taking its cue from such various sources as hermeneutics, phenomenology, psychoanalysis, the process-oriented philosophy of Gilles Deleuze and Jacques Derrida's deconstruction of past and present in *Specters of Marx* (an important point of reference for many contributors), the contemporary debate on historical time revolves mainly around three issues: nonlinearity, noncoincidence and immanence.[12] Moving away from the universal, public time of earlier conceptions of history, theoretical formulations today have moved decisively towards an understanding of time as embodied and experienced.[13] This emphasis, in turn, has enabled a thoroughgoing questioning of both assumed linearity and coincidence. History, we have learnt, does not move in a straight line, nor is it uniform. 'Progress' in one part of the world or for one sector of society will have another meaning for its 'others'. The relationship between what Reinhart Koselleck taught us to think of as the space of experience (the past) and the horizon of expectation (the future), has turned out to be far more multiform and changeable than the hegemonic narrative of modernity once allowed.[14]

A consequence of this interrogation is also that the ethical dimension of history has powerfully been brought to the fore. The bulk of the essays presented here locate themselves precisely at this nexus of time and (in)justice. In their various ways, they all demonstrate that it is the unfinished business of colonial conquest, racism, gender oppression and the Holocaust that make the past 'stick'. The after-effects of what had apparently been superseded by an enlightened liberal order – Francis Fukuyama's notion of the 'end of history' – have arguably become more palpable than ever and brought about a significant shift in the ethos of history.

Before exploring further the nature of this shift, however, we should remind ourselves that also history has a history. In the first chapter, Aleida Assmann returns to the beginning of Western historiography in early modernity and gives an overview of its major paradigms, from the 'critical ethos' of the Renaissance humanists, through the 'objectivist ethos' guiding the professionalization of historiography in the nineteenth century, and on to more recent shifts that have emerged in response to the violent pasts of European modernity. Changes in the historical ethos, Assmann suggests, 'happen whenever the relationship between history, politics and society is at stake and has to be readjusted'. The second chapter, coauthored by Claudia Lindén and Hans Ruin, can be read as an intriguing case study of this observation. The authors take us back to the late eighteenth century and point to the era's ambivalent relation to the past. This is the period when humanity grants itself a history in the sense of a temporal axis on which everything has its fixed chronological place. It is also, however, a period that is striving for the past to be not wholly past but in some sense still living, as can be seen in the era's fascination with classical antiquity, medieval legends, ruins and, last but not least, *vampires*. The thought-provoking thesis of this essay, explored through a close reading of three emblematic literary works, is that the vampire, as a creature that respects neither the boundary between life and death nor conventional historical chronology, in an essential way captures the period's inner tensions with regard to the past.

Not only vampires, but the past in general haunts us, as Derrida forcefully made us aware with his neologism 'hauntology' (*hantologie*), and it is in this ghostly guise that it places demands on the present.[15] This is one lesson to be learnt from the growing field of testimonial literature, but also from the more general urge to heed to victims' demand for justice through memory politics, truth and reconciliation commissions or even outright legal processes. As the past increasingly has become an arena for moral, political and even legal claims, historians have been faced with new challenges. These developments have called not only for a renegotiation of the detached posture traditionally ascribed to the responsible historian vis-à-vis the past, but also for a critical reflection on the sometimes strained relation between historical time, ethical time and the time of jurisprudence.

The two subsequent essays address these challenges in diverse ways. Taking her cue from the postwar debates in Germany and France about the applicability of statutory limitation to Nazi crimes, Victoria Fareld explores how the temporal space opened up by the legal notion of imprescriptibility has forced historians to raise questions about the relation between history and justice: 'Against a notion of the past as irreversibly and definitively gone, and which has been constitutive of conventional historical time, the idea of the imprescriptible has made visible another temporality in which the events of the past can be invoked as possible to act upon as if they were dimensions of the present.' Although legal definitions of crime, punishment and guilt should not determine the historian's relation to the past, the appearance of the principle of imprescriptibility has nevertheless contributed to a critical awareness among historians that their task is not primarily to reconstruct an absent past, but to deal with a past that lingers in the present and that can even be acted upon morally and legally.

That the idea of a past that can 'be acted upon' is not unambiguous is further explored by Berber Bevernage. Shifting the focus slightly, Bevernage turns to the increasingly influential idea (among policy makers, activists, therapists and academics) of 'historical dialogue' and 'shared histories' as ways to build peace and foster reconciliation in former or present conflict areas. As is revealed through an array of examples from the past decades, the various epistemic positions and narrative strategies of these endeavours differ essentially in their political motivation. Nevertheless, they all seem to rely on a specific philosophy of history: 'one in which historical conflict is not primarily caused by conflicting material interests or structural injustices but conflicting identities and perceptions.' The author asks whether this underlying antimaterialist approach does not in fact run the risk of diverting our attention from other causes of conflict – such as socioeconomic inequality, underdevelopment, economic exploitation or occupied territories – and calls for a more materialist approach, not in the sense of a return to a 'positivist or anti-narrativist approach', but rather in the form of 'a new political theory of narratives which indicates asymmetrical power relations in historical dialogue by focusing on narrative inequality and unequal control over means of narrative production'.

While a certain 'spirit' or 'spectre' of Marx – to refer once more to Derrida – may help us to navigate between positivist and relativist accounts of

history, Freud might offer the historian yet another way to steer a course between Scylla and Charybdis. Reflecting back on her own intellectual trajectory, Joan Scott relates how Freud's insistence on the ultimate indeterminacy
of all knowledge has been a lasting source of inspiration for her own critical
work as an historian. That being said, Freud himself was far from consistent
on this matter. As Derrida observed in *Archive Fever,* there is in Freud a
constant tension between the critical thinker who sought to undermine the
modern myth of the rational self and the *Wissenschaftler* who claimed to pin
down the truth behind the analysand's 'irrational' experiences and thereby
only reinforced the hubris of modern rationalism.[16] If there is a 'spirit' of
Freud worth preserving, then, it is rather the 'post-Freudian Freud' – Freud
read through the lenses of poststructuralism, feminism and postcolonialism,
but also through the inner tensions of his own thinking. Applied to historiography, Scott suggests, the critical role of psychoanalysis may consist in
attempting 'to account for the unconscious motives that play into and define
what counts as an event or a fact, and that colour the debates – on all sides –
about their meaning'.

Intriguingly, the detour through psychoanalysis has also refined Scott's
notion of gender as a 'category for historical analysis' (see above). If in her
earlier works 'gender' had the character of a fixed diagnostic category, in
her more recent work, while no less fundamental, it has mainly an *unsettling*
function, offering an approach that 'opens us to new readings of the past'
and 'also reminds us that those readings are never entirely definitive, never
the last word'. This destabilizing potential of the gender concept moves to
centre stage in the following chapter by Kristina Fjelkestam, which explores
a trajectory leading from first-wave feminism's preoccupation with gendered
temporalities to more recent notions of queer temporality, including a focus
on desire as an essential driving force behind all history writing. The answer
to the question in her title – Does time have a gender? – is emphatically
yes, and this needs to be factored into our historiographical critique. While
admitting that the promotion of 'affective historiography' is not without its
risks in an era of rising nationalism and concomitant ideological exploitation
of the past, Fjelkestam argues that 'desire' nevertheless allows us to gain a
conceptual foothold on the anachronistic, plural and multilayered nature of
temporality.

But what about the *undesirable* past, the repulsive parts of our 'own'
history and the painful history of others? In a trenchant reflection on how
the colonial past lives on in the Brazilian present, Patricia Lorenzoni reminds us of the limits of academic writing when it comes to doing justice
to the historical pain of others. Her essay is also, however, an exploration
of possible ways of expanding these limits through nonacademic practices
of narrating history. In the case of Brazil, one such practice is found in the

forceful tradition of liberation theology, channelled through the Catholic indigenist mission. In particular, Lorenzoni focuses on the 1973 document *Y-Juca-Pirama,* authored in the spirit of the Second Vatican Council and signed by a large group of Brazilian bishops and missionaries. While many historians, when addressing indigenous history in Brazil, have tended to reiterate the colonial impulse of viewing the *índio* as destined to disappear with the coming of colonial modernity, the document offers a relentless critique of colonial violence and emphasizes indigenous resistance. But it does not end there. On the last pages, the fate of the *índio* is juxtaposed with the suffering, death and resurrection of Christ, whereby a 'prophetic temporality' is activated, a temporality that not only disallows us from letting the victim perish into the past, but also in some way makes the missionary coeval with their own conqueror ancestors.

In ways that resonate strongly with Lorenzoni's essay, Stefan Helgesson also investigates the resistant – if not directly emancipatory – capacities of prophetic temporality, but now as a narrative rather than theological modality. Focusing on the work of three writers from Brazil and South Africa – Euclides da Cunha, Olive Schreiner and Thomas Mofolo – the guiding assumption in this chapter is that the European high-imperial moment around 1900 was marked by brutal contradictions between spaces of experience and horizons of expectation in the plural. Hence, the expectation of progress among segments of mainly European and/or white creole populations had its counterpart in the horizon of *extinction* for colonized and racialized others – either literally, through death, or figurally, through disenfranchisement and cultural assimilation. The larger question broached by this chapter concerns, therefore, how narrative form can contend with a hegemonic horizon of expectation. Helgesson's main claim is thus that the narrative ordering of time – particularly in the form of prophecy – has the capacity to exploit and expose the contradictions of the temporal regime of colonial modernity (particularly its narrativization of genocide and extinction) and allows a 'radical time' of decoloniality to be intimated.

The three concluding essays return us in various ways to some pressing issues in our present cultural condition. As already noted, this is not only an era in which lies are substituted for truth and serious news reporting is spurned as 'fake news'. It is also a time when the profoundly ethical impulses of the identitarian movements of the past decades are turned into aggressive assertions of 'superior' identities, be it in the form of white supremacist ideologies, violent Islamist groupings or the numerous nationalist movements on the rise in Europe and elsewhere. These developments confront historians – indeed, any scholar – with entirely new challenges. To put it sharply: all the good intentions of pluralistic historiography, memory politics and discussions about cultural heritage notwithstanding, is there a not risk that we play into the hands of segregating forces? How do we prevent that the replacement of a hegemonic notion of History with a plural vision of 'histories' only ends up reproducing the very idea of history it seeks to undermine?

It is in the light of such self-reflexive questions that Marcia Sá Cavalcante Schuback suggests that it has become time to interrogate the notion of 'engagement with history', current in many institutional, political, academic and aesthetic discourses. Faced with the challenges of an increasing ideological investment in the past, it is not enough to write history with political engagement. What is needed today is rather 'engaged history', a critical reflection on how even our best efforts to commemorate what history has destroyed constantly run the risk of ossifying the past in ways that ultimately disengage us from history. Inspired by Jean-Paul Sartre's notion of 'engaged literature', Cavalcante Schuback calls for a new relation between theory and practice, for a kind of critique that does not allow us to place ourselves at a safe distance from concrete situations and experiences: 'What I am proposing is that history is indeed a risk, a risk that history is perhaps nothing but engageability itself. As such, it is what refuses fixing in strong figures and fast determinations, for it is permanently passing.'

From these more general reflections, Alana Vincent proceeds in her essay to draw attention to a specific instance of how public acts of memorialization may in fact overshadow the complexity of concrete historical experiences. In the wake of tragedies such as the *Charlie Hebdo* attacks in Paris in 2015 or the New York grand jury's decision (at about the same time) not to indict white police officers who had been filmed choking a black man to death, the world has seen an outpouring of digital sentiments expressed in Facebook statuses, Twitter updates and hashtags. While admitting that such commemorative acts may indeed be expressions of true sentiments of solidarity, Vincent also points to the precariousness of the kind of collective identity assumed by digital utterances such as 'je suis Charlie' or #ican'tbreathe. Since online interaction is stripped of many of the identity markers (ethnic, gendered, religious or class related) that inform judgement offline, it tends to acquire a claim to neutrality eroding the individual identities upon which any substantial solidarity must rest. Rather than hailing the redemptive potential of digital culture, Vincent therefore expresses concern that the underlying assumption of homogeneity in social media leads to a retreat from the negotiations of difference required by public life, at worst causing actual victims to disappear from view.

If there is a common ethos of the essays presented so far, it might be summarized as an overarching attempt to reconsider the past in terms of justice, desire, pain or engagement. But if we are to understand our rapidly changing world, perhaps we ought to reconsider the very idea that history is – or should be – exclusively about the past (or the past's presence today).

This, at least, is the bold proposition of the final essay of this volume. In contrast to the prevailing focus among historians on the past or the past's presence, Zoltán Boldizsár Simon sets out to defend the thesis that history is equally as much about the future as about the past; 'that *we cannot even think historically without having a vision of the future in the first place*'. This is not a plea for a return to earlier theologies and philosophies of histories, which presupposed a rather fixed vision of the future and relied on a teleological conception of history. It is, however, an attempt to say that our present-day concept of history to some extent needs to tally with the vision of the future that is de facto influencing people's way of making sense of the world and of themselves as historical beings. This vision, Boldizsár Simon suggests, can today – at least in the Western world – above all be found in a radically unknowable technological future.

A time-traveller from the 1960s (to conclude by way of an anthropomorphic anachronism) would perhaps recognize this sublime, technological vision of the future as unknowable. They would be more surprised to confront our present-day preoccupation with philosophies of history and, above all, our persistent preoccupation with the past. To allude to Hamlet's famous lament, the time that we call ours is indeed out of joint, and the task of setting it right is far more precarious than the long parenthesis of the modernist ideology of progress once made it seem. The temporal, geographical and methodological range of the contributions to this volume is indicative of the scope of this challenge. We are living in an age when the ethos of history is being put to the test more insistently, and certainly on a more planetary scale, than perhaps ever before. Granted, the experienced urgency of the 'now' might be as old as historiography itself, but that does not make it any less salient as we contemplate the disorientating, literally un-settling, horizons of expectation of our present.

Stefan Helgesson is professor of English at Stockholm University. His work has dealt with southern African literature in English and Portuguese, Brazilian literature, postcolonial theory, translation theory and theories of world literature. He is the author of *Writing in Crisis: Ethics and History in Gordimer, Ndebele and Coetzee* (2004) and *Transnationalism in Southern African Literature* (2009), has edited volume four of *Literary History: Towards a Global Perspective* (2006) and is coeditor (with Pieter Vermeulen) of *Institutions of World Literature: Writing, Translation, Markets* (2015). He is currently leading the Swedish research initiative 'Cosmopolitan and Vernacular Dynamics in World Literatures'.

Jayne Svenungsson is professor of systematic theology at Lund University (Sweden). Her research is focused on philosophy and theology of history as well as on political philosophy and theology. She is the author of *Divining History: Prophetism, Messianism and the Development of the Spirit* (2016) and coeditor of *Jewish Thought, Utopia and Revolution* (2014) and *Monument and Memory* (2015).

Notes

1. H. White, *Tropics of Discourse: Essays in Cultural Criticism* (Baltimore: Johns Hopkins University Press, 1978), 81.
2. White, *Tropics*, 91.
3. J.W. Scott, 'Gender: A Useful Category of Historical Analysis', *The American Historical Review* 91(5) (1986), 1073.
4. D. Chakrabarty, *Provincializing Europe: Postcolonial Thought and Historical Difference* (Princeton: Princeton University Press, 2000), 27.
5. Chakrabarty, *Provincializing Europe*, 45.
6. Chakrabarty, *Provincializing Europe*, 46.
7. N. Fandos, 'White House Pushes "Alternative Facts". Here Are the Real Ones', *New York Times*, 22 January 2017.
8. B. Latour, 'Why Has Critique Run out of Steam? From Matters of Fact to Matters of Concern', *Critical Inquiry* 30 (2004), 227.
9. M. Homiak, 'Moral Character', *Stanford Encyclopedia of Philosophy*. Accessed 9 October 2017.
10. P. Bourdieu, *Distinction: A Social Critique of the Judgment of Taste,* trans. Richard Nice (Cambridge, MA: Harvard University Press, 1984), 170.
11. See M. Rothberg, *Multidirectional Memory: Remembering the Holocaust in the Age of Decolonization* (Stanford: Stanford University Press, 2009); C. Lorenz and B. Bevernage (eds), *Breaking up Time: Negotiating the Borders between Present, Past and Future* (Göttingen: Vandenhoeck and Ruprecht, 2013); A. Rigney, *The Afterlives of Walter Scott* (Oxford: Oxford University Press, 2012); L. Bond, S. Craps and P. Vermeulen (eds), *Memory Unbound: Tracing the Dynamics of Memory Studies* (New York: Berghahn, 2017); recent issues of *History and Theory*; J. Durham Peters, *The Marvelous Clouds: Toward a Philosophy of Elemental Media* (Chicago: Chicago University Press, 2015).
12. J. Derrida, *Specters of Marx: The State of Debt, the Work of Mourning and the New International,* trans. P. Kamuf (London: Routledge, 2006).
13. R. West-Pavlov, *Temporalities* (London: Routledge, 2013).
14. R. Koselleck, '"Space of Experience" and "Horizon of Expectation": Two Historical Categories', in *Futures Past: On the Semantics of Historical Time,* trans. K. Tribe (Cambridge, MA: MIT Press, 1985), 267–88.
15. Derrida, *Specters of Marx*.
16. J. Derrida, *Archive Fever: A Freudian Impression,* trans. Eric Prenowitz (Chicago: University of Chicago Press, 1995).

Bibliography

Bond, L., S. Craps and P. Vermeulen (eds). *Memory Unbound: Tracing the Dynamics of Memory Studies.* New York: Berghahn, 2017.
Bourdieu, P. *Distinction: A Social Critique of the Judgment of Taste,* trans. Richard Nice. Cambridge, MA: Harvard University Press, 1984.

Chakrabarty, D. *Provincializing Europe: Postcolonial Thought and Historical Difference.* Princeton: Princeton University Press, 2000.

Derrida, J. *Archive Fever: A Freudian Impression,* trans. Eric Prenowitz. Chicago: University of Chicago Press, 1995.

———. *Specters of Marx: The State of Debt, the Work of Mourning and the New International,* trans. P. Kamuf. London: Routledge, 2006.

Durham Peters, J. *The Marvelous Clouds: Toward a Philosophy of Elemental Media.* Chicago: Chicago University Press, 2015.

Fandos, N. 'White House Pushes "Alternative Facts". Here Are the Real Ones', *New York Times,* 22 January 2017.

Homiak, M. 'Moral Character'. *Stanford Encyclopedia of Philosophy.* Accessed 9 October 2017.

Koselleck, R. '"Space of Experience" and "Horizon of Expectation": Two Historical Categories', in *Futures Past: On the Semantics of Historical Time,* trans. Keith Tribe. Cambridge, MA: MIT Press, 1985.

Latour, B. 'Why Has Critique Run out of Steam? From Matters of Fact to Matters of Concern', *Critical Inquiry* 30 (2004), 225–48.

Lorenz, C., and B. Bevernage (eds). *Breaking up Time: Negotiating the Borders between Present, Past and Future.* Göttingen: Vandenhoeck and Ruprecht, 2013.

Rigney, A. *The Afterlives of Walter Scott.* Oxford: Oxford University Press, 2012.

Rothberg, M. *Multidirectional Memory: Remembering the Holocaust in the Age of Decolonization.* Stanford: Stanford University Press, 2009.

Scott, J.W. 'Gender: A Useful Category of Historical Analysis', *The American Historical Review* 91(5) (1986), 1053–1075.

West-Pavlov, R. *Temporalities.* London: Routledge, 2013.

White, H. *Tropics of Discourse: Essays in Cultural Criticism.* Baltimore: Johns Hopkins University Press, 1978.

CHAPTER 1

Towards a
New Ethos of History?

ALEIDA ASSMANN

Historiography has seen many developments, changes and experiments in its long history. Many things have affected the representation of the past and shaped a modern ethos of history: political transformations and historical ruptures, the shift of cognitive frames and emotional sensibility, together with new projects, values and methodologies. Changes in the ethos of history, however, are not to be confused with the ongoing search for new techniques, orientations and paradigms that are part of an inherent dynamic of an academic discipline. From its very beginning, (professional) historiography has also produced a specific ethos. Metaphorically speaking, this ethos may be called the conscience of the profession, a critical form of metadiscourse, self-reflexion and self-evaluation evolving in an ongoing process that is triggered by external issues and challenges, demanding new responses, reactions and changes. The ethos of history is therefore not (only) an intrinsic part of historiography but arises from an intersection between historiography, social reality, cultural history and political orientation.

The following contribution to this topic attempts to sketch some transformations of the ethos of history. It goes back to the beginnings of historiography in early modernity and its professionalization in the nineteenth century, but focuses mainly on more recent shifts that have emerged as new responses to the ongoing impact of violent pasts.

Notes for this section begin on page 28.

The Critical Ethos: Probing the Authenticity of Sources (Fifteenth Century)

As early as the fifteenth century, a new ethos of history was developed by sceptics and independent thinkers of early modernity. They were the first to challenge old historical records that had served sacrosanct institutions as a basis for their legitimation. The paradigmatic case illustrating this new spirit of rigorous analysis was the document of the Donation of Constantine that was scrutinized in 1440 by Lorenzo Valla, an Italian Catholic priest and Renaissance humanist, who exposed it as a forgery. This proved to be a revolutionary event for the political authority of papacy that had been built on this document, but also for the reputation and self-image of historians. While throughout the Middle Ages historians had acted as carriers and preservers of an age-old memory, they now turned into critics of ancient documents, carefully probing the validity of traditions. In his *History of the King Alfonso of Naples* (1445), Valla stressed the new empirical spirit of his profession when he compared the skills of the historian with those of a judge and a doctor. Valla was not the only one, but according to Peter Burke, his approach was 'the most elaborate and systematic', creating an effective critical tool for humanist historians by applying an elaborate tradition of rigorous philological standards to written sources.[1]

The Objectivist Ethos: Establishing the Rules of the Game (Eighteenth Century)

It took four more centuries before this new critical ethos of history was inscribed into an academic institution and protected against external influences. The modern universities of the nineteenth century created the new discipline of historiography on a set of rules that were henceforth transmitted, monitored and developed by a growing international community of scholars. The central aim was a commitment to truth underpinned by a new methodology. In this context, the value of 'objectivity' arose as the most important claim and standard, requiring the strict independence and distance of the researcher from the matter of his research.

Reinhart Koselleck has elaborated this definition by adding distance in time from the investigated event as an important factor of objectivity.[2] Seen from this perspective, historians of contemporary history are in a problematic position because they are still close and to some extent part of the events that they aim to describe and analyse. According to Koselleck, the historian has to wait for time to pass before they can start to study a historical event without being influenced by personal bias, stakes and issues. On this basis,

Koselleck distinguished between an impure and a pure past. The impure past is still mixed with elements of the present, such as 'moral concern, apologetic gestures, accusations and impositions of guilt', which he sums up by the term 'strategies of mastering the past' (*Vergangenheitsbewältigungstechniken*). Temporal distance, he hoped, would provide an undistorted view of the past, similar to the clear and transparent view of the bottom of a pool after the muddied waters of contemporary issues have settled.

It is quite obvious that in the humanities, rigorous standards of truth are much more difficult to define and apply than in the natural sciences. Historicism is a new kind of scholarship that was established in academia together with new disciplines in the wake of the Enlightenment. In these new contexts, historiography emerged as a new profession with its autonomous rules and independent methodological standards. The nineteenth century, however, was also the century of nation-building, with a high demand for reconstructions of the collective past and gripping narratives that served the new states and their societies. In this context, many historians embraced their political mandate and mixed scholarly erudition and literary style in order to shape the past for new imagined communities.[3] Outside the national framework, when relating to ancient states and foreign cultures, the scholarly tools of historicism were applied with more empirical rigour and self-effacing objectivity, filling the shelves of libraries with volumes and volumes of dry erudition, and the archives of knowledge with endless neutral data. Nietzsche intensely disliked this vast output of historicist scholarship, chiding it as a dangerous undermining of an affective relation to one's past that destroys the possibility of identifying with one's cultural heritage.

In his book *That Noble Dream,* Peter Novick has offered a remarkable metareflexion on the principle of objectivity from within the historical profession.[4] This is how he defines it: its assumptions

> include a commitment to the reality of the past, and to truth as correspondence to that reality; a sharp separation between knower and known, between fact and value, and, above all, between history and fiction. Historical facts are seen as prior to and independent of interpretation: the value of an interpretation is judged by how well it accounts for the facts; if contradicted by the facts, it must be abandoned. Truth is one, not perspectival. Whatever patterns exist in history are 'found', not 'made'. . . . One corollary of all of this is that historians, as historians, must purge themselves of external loyalties: the historian's primary allegiance is to 'the objective historical truth', and to professional colleagues who share a commitment to cooperative, cumulative efforts to advance toward that goal.[5]

In his analysis of objectivity, Novick does not use the term 'ethos' but speaks of a 'morale', of an 'objectivist creed'. An essential article of this creed is the promise of 'a unitary convergent history which would correspond to a unitary past'.[6] The unitary past corresponds to Koselleck's definition of modern 'history' as a term in the singular that replaces the plural of 'histories' in the sense of 'Geschichten' (narratives). In his discussion of objectivity, Novick introduces the word 'myth' in an interesting way. Drawing on the functional approach of anthropologists, he defines myth as the pragmatic charter of a social institution. In stark contrast to Roland Barthes' use of the term, Novick's approach 'implies nothing about the truth or falsity of what is being discussed. Rather, it is a device to illuminate the important functions which "historical objectivity" has served in sustaining the professional historical venture; and, since myths are by definition sacred, the tenacity, indeed, ferocity, with which it has been defended'.[7] In the words of Malinowski, a myth 'expresses, enhances and codifies belief; it safeguards and enforces morality; it vouches for the efficacy of ritual and enforces practical rules for the guidance of man'.[8] What Malinowski claims for the relationship between myth and ritual, Novick claims for the relationship between the 'myth of objectivity' and the notion of 'truth' within the academic discipline of historiography. This pragmatic charter allows to set up institutions of learning and to separate the professional historians from the unprofessional ones, such as partisans, amateurs, gentleman historians or pamphleteers.

While the 'noble dream' of objectivity serves to constitute the discipline as a whole, it remains among historians an essentially contested concept.[9] There are many that have raised doubts about the standards of objectivity; the sacrosanct dichotomy between 'truth' and 'fiction' has been deconstructed, and there is even the question whether the aims and standards of historical objectivity were ever truly fulfilled. Although many tenets of the objectivist credo have become untenable for many historians, it is unlikely that they would willingly part with the core vision of the concept. While 'positivism' has been dismissed as boring and even as a dead end for historical practice, the noble dream of objectivity – in the sense of distance, adherence to verified sources, arguments on the basis of evidence, balance and even-handedness – is still widely accepted as the basis of the historian's practice. This dream continues to organize the academic profession of historiography in a self-critical manner, producing new visions and revisions, new theses and their polemical contradictions, constantly calling in question established assumptions and introducing new perspectives. What is perhaps most important about the scholarly ethos of objectivity is the institutionalized doubt that keeps historiography in flow as a self-conscious process of self-correction.

The Social Ethos: Criticizing the Archive and Enlarging the Scope of the Past (1970s and Onwards)

Changes in historiography do not only occur silently in a continuous process of self-correction and readjustment, but also more conspicuously due to cultural ruptures and changes in political orientation. One example is a movement that started in the 1970s as an alternative approach to established academic historiography. This new ethos of history emerged together with a new generation of baby-boomers and 1968ers born at the end of or after World War II. Leftist movements reverberated not only in pop culture and political activism but found expression also in new approaches to history. These were grounded on the awareness that what was dealt with and transmitted as 'history' was but a 'miserable defective "shred"' of the reality and lived experience of the past.[10] The new generation of historians started to criticize the official sources as the sole and sacrosanct basis for historical research, showing that the archive is itself an historical institution that is severely limited, reproducing automatically the bias and power structure of the rulers and the hegemonic class as the agents of history.

Johan Galtung has created a term for this invisible motor of the reproduction of social injustice, calling it 'structural violence'. Structural violence finds its manifestations in various forms of institutionalized inequality such as elitism, nationalism, ethnocentrism, racism or sexism.[11] In patriarchal societies, for instance, women had little or no access to writing and printing, which led to their effective exclusion from archives and libraries. The same applies to rural populations, religious or racial minorities and other oppressed social groups who occupy the lower rungs of society. 'Structural violence' creates a political and cultural frame of power that allows some voices to be heard while others are notoriously silenced.

The new ethos of history called for a broadening of the knowledge of the past. An important new approach was the introduction of oral history in order to tap new sources and to access hitherto concealed and forgotten aspects of everyday life, the history of workers, women and the rural population.[12] This ethos was oriented towards inclusion and aimed at enlarging the scope of the past. By interviewing and giving a voice to people that had not been heard so far, the themes of historiographical research were radically enlarged and an important segment of the society was for the first time represented and presented as an actor of history.

Carlo Ginzburg and, later, the movement of 'new historicism' revolutionized historiography by discovering and digging up sources in the historical archive that had been ignored. 'Dig where you stand!' also became an influential slogan that stirred communal local history projects against the mainstream of academic history. Among the younger generation of historians, selecting and interpreting neglected sources of nondescript persons and telling their individual stories in an anecdotal manner became an important way to reconstruct forgotten worlds and to complement the historiography of great men and great events. Regina Schulte, for instance, has retrieved the legal documents of the circuit court in Munich to reconstruct the daily life and sorrows of the rural population in upper Bavaria in the second half of the nineteenth century. Up till then, such sources had not been part of historiography of mentalities and everyday life.[13] In the same year appeared the three-volume edition of interviews conducted by Schulte's husband, Lutz Niethammer, and Alexander von Plato, who reconstructed the recent past of the workers in the Ruhr area from the workers' point of view.[14] They found none of their sources in the archives but produced them themselves in long processes of interviewing, transcribing, publishing and interpreting. From the start, these historians met with strong objections against their alternative history of mentality and its methodology. Critics condemned this approach to history as subjective and rejected its theoretical foundation. The new search for 'ego-documents' (Winfried Schulze) and 'ego-history' (Lutz Niethammer) privileged the individual against larger collectives and structures, but now this individual was no longer a notable bourgeois 'subject' but one that had not yet had a chance to appear on the stage of history.[15]

The Postcolonial Ethos: Changing the Point of View (1980s and Onwards)

'How much past is needed to understand the present?'[16] When asking this question, Jürgen Osterhammel argued for enlarging the stretch of the past that is under investigation. Another variation of the question could be 'which forgotten or repressed history is needed to understand the present?'. This brings us to a fourth change of the ethos of history, which consists in a *change of perspective*. Not every change of perspective, of course, introduces a change in the ethos of history. Changes of perspective have occurred frequently and are obviously highly consequential for the writing of history. There is, for example, the difference between the point of view of the victor and that of the loser; their historical accounts will differ considerably, emphasizing contradictory aims, experiences and lessons. There is also the difference between bourgeois and Marxist historiography as institutionalized, for instance, in former East and West Germany during the period of the Cold War. In this case, two contradictory and rivalling perspectives existed side by side in a perpetual strife for supremacy.

A consequential change in perspective that ushered in a new ethos of history was the *postcolonial perspective*. This perspective was part of the process of decolonization after World War II and was developed by intellectuals such as Frantz Fanon who drew on Marxist and existentialist theories. When this discourse was taken up by a generation and adopted into mainstream Western historiography in the 1980s and '90s, it involved a radical transvaluation of values in response to the enduring aftermath of racism. This led to

Aleida Assmann

a self-critical reshaping of the hegemonic historical narrative. Step by step, former empires started to adopt the perspective of the colonized victim into their own self-image, and acknowledged racial structures of violence and exploitation in their national past. Instead of relegating the trauma of the colonized other to those who had been impacted by racial violence, the former colonizers worked through the pernicious cultural legacy of racism and its continuing effects in democratic societies, thus acknowledging and embracing their share in the traumatic past. The postcolonial ethos of history creates a 'dialogic memory' in which the experience of the colonized is integrated into the official narrative of the state and supported by self-critical historians, new history textbooks and museums.[17] A shift in the ethos of history is not only manifested in historical writings but also in the opening of museums. To illustrate how difficult and tormented such a project and process might be, I take as an example the attempts at establishing a national museum of slavery in England and the United States.

In 2007, England commemorated the bicentenary of the abolition of slave trade in England in 1807. This dark chapter of history focusing on racist violence and exploitation was presented to the general public in the International Museum of Slavery in Liverpool. The perceptions of this museum and its exhibition were mixed. John Darwin, for instance, renowned historian of the British Empire, and a vocal opponent of a 'new imperial history' that reduces the building of empire to 'a brutal, coercive, exploitative, racist and sometimes genocidal enterprise', was impressed by the museum. He affirmed that 'the central importance of slavery in Britain's global expansion before 1800 has begun to receive its proper share of attention.'[18] The message of the slave-trade museum in Liverpool is clear: it adopts the point of view of the former slaves, acknowledging their suffering under antihumanitarian circumstances. It tells a now shameful chapter of one's own history in clear words and striking images, thus demonstrating that this chapter has been closed and belongs now literally to the past. By telling the story, the museum confirms that it is 'history' and no longer exerting its influence on the present. The museum, in other words, is a public statement by the former colonial power that is distancing itself from this chapter of its racist past. In doing so, it also acknowledges that the fight for the abolition of slavery had been a political project that had united members of the colonizers and the colonized in a common cause. In other words: the Liverpool museum is also a monument to abolition as the joint victory over slavery. An important function of a museum is thus to confirm that historical events are no longer part of the present.

The situation is different in the United States that, to date, does not have a state-sponsored museum of slavery. The absence of such a central site of commemoration does not mean that the history of slavery is unmemorialized in the United States. There are a number of local places where the history of slavery is presented. A remarkable exhibition on the history of slavery, for instance, was opened by President Obama in 2016 in Washington at the National Museum of African American History and Culture. This federally funded museum, which is part of the Smithsonian Institution, exhibits the history of slavery alongside Black folklore and pop culture, including a trumpet played by Louis Armstrong and boxing gloves worn by Muhammad Ali. Paul Finkelman, historian of slavery, commented on the exhibition: 'It has to be said that the end note in most of these museums is that civil rights triumphs and America is wonderful. We are a nation that has always readily embraced the good of the past and discarded the bad. This does not always lead to the most productive of dialogues on matters that deserve and require them.'[19]

The first attempt at a national museum of slavery opened in 1984 under the name America's Black Holocaust Museum (ABHM). It was not a state enterprise but emerged from a private initiative in Milwaukee, Wisconsin. Dr James Cameron, the only known survivor of a lynching, acquired a spacious freestanding building, collected memorabilia, displayed exhibitions, employed staff and organized guided tours for local, national and international visitors led by 'griots' who interpreted the exhibits and facilitated dialogue. The backbone of the museum was the testimony of Dr Cameron himself, who shared his embodied experience with visitors from different countries, acting as an impressive witness and example of 'living history'. His death in 2006 and the economic crisis forced the museum to give up its building in 2008. But it did not disappear altogether. In 2012, the ABHM went online and was reinstalled as a virtual museum. 'This 21st century, cost-effective format makes ABHM available to people around the world who would otherwise have no access to its information and resources.'[20] In a video message, Dr Cameron presents the aim of the museum as an effort to promote and support 'the unity of our sacred nation'.[21] This mission statement is also expressed on the homepage: 'ABHM builds public awareness of the harmful legacies of slavery in America and promotes racial repair, reconciliation, and healing. We envision a society that remembers its past in order to shape a better future – a nation undivided by race where every person matters equally.'[22] As one of the white supporters of the virtual museum points out, the message of the museum conveyed to its visitors is 'gift', not 'guilt'. It is not an indictment but an appeal to empathy and thus a gesture enabling reconciliation. Another member refers to it as a safe place and a framework to talk about this troubled history for which there is as yet no common language available.

In 2001, another museum project on American slavery was started in Fredericksburg, Virginia, by Douglas Wilder, a former grandson of slaves and the first elected black governor in the nation. He bought the ground on which he hoped to build the first 'United States National Slavery Museum'. In spite of ambitious visions and initial support, the project crashed together with the economic crisis in 2008. Around the same time, another national slave museum project had been started on the Whitney Plantation in Louisiana, a 'genuine landmark built by African slaves and their descendants. As a site of memory and consciousness, the Whitney Plantation Museum is meant to pay homage to all slaves on the plantation itself and to all of those who lived elsewhere in the US South.'[23] This project is in the vigorous hands of two collaborating actors who work on the site together: John Cummings, a white neighbour, financial sponsor and committed organizer, and Ibrahima Seck, a black scholar from Senegal who works in close contact with sources and archives. The latter comments on the project of the former: 'If one word comes to mind to summarize what is in John's head in doing this, that word would be "reparations". Real reparations. He feels there is something to be done in this country to make changes.'[24]

David Amsden sums up his article on 'Building the First Slavery Museum in America' with the comment, 'One hundred and fifty years after the end of the Civil War, no federally funded museum dedicated to slavery exists, no monument honoring America's slaves.' Although not state-funded, the Whitney project comes closes to such a project. 'As Americans', writes historian Eric Foner, 'we haven't yet figured out how to come to terms with slavery. To some, it's ancient history. To others, it's history that isn't quite history.'[25]

The Post-Traumatic Ethos: The Testimonial Paradigm (1980s and Onwards)

The post-traumatic ethos entered history also in the 1980s and 1990s. It is similar to the postcolonial ethos in many ways and interacts with it frequently in a multidirectional framework.[26] It is also based on a change of perspective and the building up of a more inclusive dialogic memory, this time relating to the post-traumatic experience of the Holocaust. This new ethos is backed up by what I want to call the 'testimonial paradigm', which, in the meantime, has also been applied to other historical traumas such as slavery, the extermination of indigenous people, or to forced disappearance as perpetrated by Argentinian State terror. In all of these cases, the state archives do not yield any or not enough sources to arrive at a full account and understanding of these events, because they happened under the condition of 'normative violence' (Judith Butler), meaning political circumstances that had not only condoned but even legitimated them. We are dealing here with historical events that were reinterpreted in the 1990s in terms of gross violations of human rights. The new historical genre of testimony was created in this framework to compensate for repressive forgetting, ignorance and a lack of sources. Its amazing career in the 1990s was exacerbated by the awareness that the voices of the victims had remained outside the official archive and were muffled by the national narrative. The new ethos of history consisted in listening to these voices, recognizing their validity and establishing their authority.

The testimonial ethos generated much controversy in historiography. The core of the problem was the introduction of a new kind of witness. The witness had been a key figure in ancient historiographical discourse, as he (and never she) had been an indispensible source of information and, in transmitting it, had vouched for its evidence. Modern historiography has discarded the subjective testimony of the witness in favour of the more objective quality of written sources. The new type of the ('moral') witness (Avishai Margalit) was neither a neutral reporter nor a subjective observer, but himself the passive victim of traumatic violence and historic crimes. The ethos of history connected to the 'testimonial paradigm' focused on the Holocaust survivor as its paradigm and established the credibility and authority of these new witnesses. Beginning in the 1980s and 1990s, seventy thousand video testimonies were collected in various archives to document this experience from the embodied point of view of the survivors.

The amazing career of the (moral) witness and the testimonial paradigm has raised hot debates and criticism among historians who feared that the more and more sacrosanct status of the witness compromised another ethos of history, namely that of objectivity. But new forms of historiography have successfully been developed to document subjective perspectives within an objectivist framework. For his two-volume history on Nazi extermination policy and practices, Saul Friedlander earned not only international praise but also a Pulitzer Prize.[27] He did not use survivor testimonies, however, but 'ego-documents' such as diary entries and quotations from letters. In doing so, he reconstructed another history of 'everyday', which, in this case, were the highly overdetermined, accelerated and compressed years of the extermination of the Jews. In these books, Friedlander created space for the voices of both perpetrators and victims. This constellation not only creates a multivocal effect emphasizing the density of the time and the events, but also restores the humanity of individuals behind the abstract enemy-stereotype of 'the Jew'. In a controlled form this ethos willingly breaks down the self-imposed distance of the professional historian, assuming a committed position and showing that she or he does not stand outside of history.

The Post-Dictatorial Ethos: The Project of Historical Commissions (1990s and Onwards)

Historians have always been indispensible for the state to legitimize its existence and to support the ruling power. Dictatorships depend on historians who are commissioned by the state to produce official narratives and widely publicized images of the past. The new type of 'historical commissions' or 'truth commissions' invented in the 1980s and 1990s in South America and South Africa, however, had a very different function. They were created to channel the transition and transformation from dictatorships and autocratic regimes to democracies. This new type of historians' commissions boomed in the 1990s also in Europe after the collapse of the Soviet Union and the opening of Eastern European archives. The idea was that in order to enforce a break and to create a new future, it was not enough to just forget the past; on the contrary, it had to be faced and to be worked through. Historians' commissions worked in different contexts. In Germany, half a century after the capitulation of the National Socialist state, not only various democratic institutions of the successor state, but also commercial firms and banks decided to have their Nazi-past x-rayed by historical commissions in order to distance themselves from this past and to negotiate compensations with the claims of survivors. In neutral Switzerland, the Bergier commission (1996) was appointed to help state and society face their past and to come to terms with their collaboration with the Nazi regime. In other cases, historians' commissions are formed to settle controversial questions that agitate the society. In Dresden, the city council established a historians' commission to determine the number of civilians that died in the allied bombing in February 1945.[28]

Although sponsored by the state, these historians' commissions worked very differently from the former ones. They no longer legitimized the self-serving narrative of those in power but were, on the contrary, committed to a human rights paradigm and self-critically investigated and brought to light dark episodes of the national past. This self-critical approach to one's national past was a historical innovation based on a new ethos of history. It combined what had hitherto been considered irreconcilable: professional rigour and institutional autonomy with political authority and public impact.

Although historians were in great demand in the aftermath of violent pasts, and their image rose in public esteem, they themselves were not united in their assessment of their new political mandate. Some argued that these commissions violated the ethos of historical objectivity in various respects. They were formed and paid by the state, their object of investigation was defined by an external agenda, they had to work under time constraints and they had to come up with results that were received as compact 'truth'.

While the experts in the new historians' commissions were granted full autonomy in their search for truth, this search differed from their academic work in that it did not emerge from an open-ended process of scholarship that knows only partial and provisional answers. Truth in the context of a historical commission was more like the work of a trial: the historians had the obligation to establish evidence, to interpret the facts and to arrive at a common judgement that helps to solve pressing social and political issues.

In 1992 and 1995, the German Parliament voted to install two historical commissions with the mission 'to overcome the consequences of the Socialist Unity Party (SED)-dictatorship in the process of German unification'. Norbert Frei belonged to those historians who expressed considerable qualms concerning this procedure. He raised doubts about imposing an interpretation of history from above, asking, 'Is it really the task of parliament to write history?'.[29] He preferred a more democratic approach to the German Democratic Republic past, based on the society, on a public discourse and on a trust in the historical profession in general. It is certainly not the job of parliaments to write history, but to establish a frame within which a public discourse on the past can take shape. Especially at historical turning points, when a chapter of repressive and violent history is closed and a new democratic system is to be installed, there is the need to reassess the past, to condemn its crimes, to identify the perpetrators and to acknowledge the victims. In historical commissions, historians are given more responsibility than they usually have. Within academia, scholars talk mainly to each other; in a commission, they first talk to each other and then as a group to the general public.

The contestation among historians about the use and abuse of these commissions reveals different views about the respective ethos of history (or of historians). Christoph Cornelißen, for instance, considers the historians' commission as an autocratic instrument and criticizes their mission to create a politically authorized view of history as jarring with the values of a pluralistic modern democracy. Like Frei, he does not like to see historians in the role of official interpreters of history and rejects the authoritative gesture of their final reports.[30] While suspicious about the historical commissions in the service of nations, he praises the new development of bi- and tri-lateral historians' commissions working together on entangled histories of violence in order to promote more inclusive and more dialogic narratives of the past that can serve as a common ground for shared visions of the future.[31]

Moshe Zimmermann has countered many of Cornelißen's objections, making three important points. The first addresses the rigid separation between politics and scholarship. For Zimmermann, 'the totally neutral, apolitical historical scholarship is an illusion, since the mingling of politics and science starts in the faculty, in the university, in our academic everyday work.'[32] His second point is that these commissions mediate scholarship into the public sphere. The final reports of historians' commissions should never be seen as the last word on a subject, but rather as part of an ongoing debate. According to Zimmermann, an important function of the historians' commissions' work lies in bridging the gap between politics, professional expertise and public knowledge. His third point concerns their impact and output. Having himself served in the commission on the history of the German Foreign Office, he emphasizes the multiple impact of this group of experts: they put the topic for the first time on the agenda of historical scholarship, they initiated a broad public discussion on the topic and, last but not least, published the first comprehensive study on the subject.[33] Historians have always had the obligation in the venerable tradition of Valla to critically probe and deconstruct the self-glorifying myths of the state,[34] but that they are commissioned by the state and paid for it is a historically new phenomenon.

Conclusion

There is, no doubt, a great diversity of approaches comprised in the study and representation of history. As already emphasized at the start, I am not dealing here with the great variety of schools, academic orientations and intellectual paradigms. When speaking of the ethos of history, I am trying to retrace some of the nodal points in the history of the field when the profession as a whole had to face a new challenge that required a new answer. These answers, I want to argue, have affected the course and character of the field as a whole, leaving none of the various approaches untouched.

'History' in the professional sense cannot exist without documents. In order to distinguish between memory and history, Jay Winter coined the formula 'Memory has affect, history has footnotes' and commented on it in the following way: 'What I do is based upon research, and archives and the footnotes matter. Footnotes stop people from lying about the past, archives stop people from lying about the past. I have the references and that is why I can speak about the past.'[35] Many of the transformations in the ethos of history that were discussed in this chapter have to do with structural changes in the historical archive. They were brought about by historians who were facing the simple problem 'that a good new question cannot be answered because it lacks documentation from the past'.[36] Under these circumstances, they had to explore new territory in order to enlarge the understanding of their work, which they did by extending the range of accessible sources.

Winter has also pointed out that there is a direct correlation between the historical archive, the evolution of new technical media and a new historical ethos that emerged in the 1970s, which he described as the shift from a heroic to a post-heroic narrative:

The historical discipline has shifted its focus away from the heroes of war, away from men, to women and children, to those whose voices were not heard normally within the canon of the historical narrative. . . . This shift around 1970 was in part caused by technical developments. The ability to record voices and faces is one of the critical vectors of the transformation of the representation of the past. From 1970 onwards the videocassette, Betamax and then VHS, emerged alongside the audio cassette as cheap and easily portable forms of archiving the voices of anybody who went through historical experiences. This opened the door to the democratization of representations.[37]

Lutz Niethammer has made a similar point, stressing the subversive project of rescuing a repressed political 'counter-memory'. For him, the project of oral history involves much more than the documentation of a hitherto unwritten subculture. Instead, it is 'a contribution to the democratization and integration into historiography of parts of the population that had not produced sources. In this way, the perception of historians is enriched by counter-traditions to the hegemonic narrative. This project achieves its ultimate meaning when it restores and lifts to the rank of history a lost, torn or distorted counter-memory.'[38]

The transformation of the archive and the democratization of representation proved to be central goals that have fuelled important changes in the ethos of history. Other changes had to do with a new commitment of the discipline in addressing public issues in the present that relate to lingering effects of a negative legacy of the past. The recent transformations in the ethos of history pertain to this awareness of the wounds of the past in the present and the attempts of the profession to develop modalities to cope with them in the public sphere. Historians do not only recover documents, represent the past and establish the truth about it; in doing all of this, they are also coping with the past in the present by helping to compensate for losses, by providing clear orientation, by performing a therapeutic function – in short, by assuming a new public function that consists in mediating the past in the present.

A new ethos of history is not just a new paradigm that is quickly replaced by another one, but a deeper – and, I would even add, irreversible – change in historical consciousness and historical sentiment. If we generalize, we may say that changes in the historical ethos happen whenever the relationship between history, politics, culture and society is at stake and has to be readjusted. These changes are stimulated and shaped by encounters of professional historiography with public concerns and demands in the present. In this process, professional history becomes part of 'public history'.

Aleida Assmann studied English literature and Egyptology at the universities Heidelberg and Tubingen. From 1993 until 2014 she held the chair of English literature and literary theory at the University of Konstanz, Germany. She has taught as a guest professor at various universities (Princeton, Yale, Chicago and Vienna), and in 2014 she received the Heineken Prize for History. Two of her recent publications in English are *Cultural Memory and Western Civilization: Functions, Media, Archives* (2012) and *Shadows of Trauma: Memory and the Politics of Postwar Identity* (2016).

Notes

1. P. Burke, *The Renaissance*.

2. R. Koselleck, 'Afterword', in Charlotte Beradt, *Das Dritte Reich des Traums* (Frankfurt am Main: Suhrkamp, [1966] 1994), 117: 'Die moralische Betroffenheit, die verkappten Schutzfunktionen, die Anklagen und die Schuldverteilungen der Geschichtsschreibung – all diese Vergangenheitsbewältigungstechniken verlieren ihren politisch-existentiellen Bezug, sie verblassen zugunsten von wissenschaftlicher Einzelforschung und hypothesengesteuerten Analysen.'

3. E. Schulin, *Traditionskritik und Rekonstruktionsversuch. Studien zur Entwicklung von Geschichtswissenschaft und historischem Denken* (Göttingen: Vandenhoeck & Ruprecht, 1979).

4. P. Novick, *That Noble Dream: The 'Objectivity Question' and the American Historical Profession* (New York: Cambridge University Press, 1988). The 'objectivity question' in historiography differs radically from that in the empirical sciences which L. Daston and P. Galison have reconstructed in their outstanding book *Objectivity* (Chicago: Zone Books, 2007). Using atlas images from the eighteenth to the early twentieth century, they 'uncover a hidden history of scientific objectivity', by focusing not only on objects and their representations but also on the 'distinctive scientific self' that is cultivated in the process of observing and investigating. While Novick emphasizes 'a sharp separation between knower and known' as a prerequisite for historical objectivity, Daston and Galison stress the convergence between knowing and knower that is effected when the researcher acquires a collective stance and sees an image no longer as a separate individual but as a member of a particular scientific community. While Novick uses the term objectivity to denote a distanced, unbiased and impartial view, Daston and Galison use the term to describe an embodied scientific habitus.

5. Novick, *That Noble Dream*, 1–2.

6. Novick, *That Noble Dream*, 5.

7. Novick, *That Noble Dream*, 3.

8. B. Malinowski, 'Myth in Primitive Psychology' (1926), in *Magic, Science and Religion and Other Essays* (Glencoe, IL: The Free Press, 1948), 78–79.

9. Novick himself cannot fully subscribe to it, because it jars, as he admits, with his own historicism: 'My way of thinking about anything in the past is primarily shaped by my understanding of its role within a particular historical context, and in the stream of history' (Novick, *That Noble Dream*, 7).

10. T. Carlyle, 'On History Again', in G.B. Tennyson (ed.), *A Carlyle Reader: Selections from the Writings of Thomas Carlyle* (Cambridge: Cambridge University Press, 1984), 107.

11. J. Galtung, 'Violence, Peace, and Peace Research', *Journal of Peace Research*, 6(3) (1969), 167–91; see also J. Galtung, 'Cultural Violence', *Journal of Peace Research*, 27(3) (1990), 291–305.

12. P. Thompson, *The Voice of the Past: Oral History* (Oxford: Oxford University Press, 1978).

13. R. Schulte, *Das Dorf im Verhör. Brandstifter, Kindsmörderin und Wilderer vor den Schranken der bürgerlichen Gerichte Oberbayerns 1848–1910* (Reinbek: Rowohlt, 1989).

14. L. Niethammer and A. von Plato, *Lebensgeschichte und Sozialkultur im Ruhrgebiet,* 3 vols. (Bonn: Dietz Verlag, 1989); see also: L. Niethammer (ed.), *Lebenserfahrung und Kollektives Gedächtnis. Die Praxis der 'Oral History'* (Frankfurt am Main: Syndikat, 1985).

15. In an essay published in the *Frankfurter Allgemeine Zeitung* (9 July 1986, No. 155, 29) Mark Siemons provides an interesting assessment of the democratization of history, the craze for 'history from below' and the local 'securing of evidence' (*Spurensicherung*) at a very early stage of its development. He interprets this turn as a neoromantic (and conservative) movement of a generation that has lost its taste for grand theory and utopian visions, privileging active memory work, small contexts and the texture of grown life-worlds (*gewachsene Lebenszusammenhänge*).

16. J. Osterhammel, 'Vergangenheiten. Über die Zeithorizonte der Geschichte', in J. Osterhammel, *Die Flughöhe der Adler: Historische Essays zur globalen Gegenwart* (Munich: Beck, 2017), 186.

17. A. Assmann, 'Dialogic Memory', in P. Mendes-Flohr (ed.), *Dialogue as a Trans-Disciplinary Concept: Martin Buber's Philosophy of Dialogue and Its Contemporary Reception* (Berlin: De Gruyter, 2015), 199–214.

18. J. Darwin, 'Memory of Empire in Britain. A Preliminary View', in D. Rothermund (ed.), *Memories of Post-Imperial Nations: The Aftermath of Decolonization, 1945–2013* (Cambridge: Cambridge University Press, 2015), 31–32.

19. D. Amsden, 'Building the First Slavery Museum in America', *New York Times,* 26 February 2015.

20. 'Welcome to ABHM!', America's Black Holocaust Museum, accessed 7 March 2017, http://abhmuseum.org.

21. See 'Welcome to ABHM!', http://abhmuseum.org. The formula of the 'sacred nation' is much older than the nineteenth century and goes back to the Hebrew and Christian Bible. In Shakespeare's *Merchant of Venice,* Shylock refers to his Jewish community as 'my sacred nation'. In the Puritan tradition, this formula was taken over by the dissenting Puritans who created a new utopian vision of a new imagined community who understood itself as a Second Israel and thus as a 'sacred nation'.

22. See 'Welcome to ABHM!', http://abhmuseum.org.

23. See 'History', Whitney Plantation, accessed 20 February 2017, http://whitneyplan tation.com/history.html; see also Wall Street Journal, 'Whitney Plantation Museum to Focus on Slavery', YouTube, accessed 20 February 2017, https://www.youtube.com/watch?v=MR UcLLFMl3g&feature=youtu.be.

24. Amsden, 'Building the First Slavery Museum in America'.

25. Amsden, 'Building the First Slavery Museum in America'.

26. M. Rothberg, *Multidirectional Memory: Remembering the Holocaust in the Age of Decolonization* (Stanford: Stanford University Press, 2009).

27. S. Friedlander, *Nazi Germany and the Jews: The Years of Persecution, 1933–1939* (New York: HarperCollins, 1997) and *The Years of Extermination: Nazi Germany and the Jews, 1939– 1945* (New York: HarperCollins, 2007).

28. The number that had been publicized by David Irving in the 1950s had been three hundred thousand; the official number arrived at in 2004 is twenty-five thousand.

29. N. Frei, 'Der Erinnerungstisch ist reich gedeckt', *Die ZEIT,* 26 March 2009.

30. C. Cornelißen, 'Historie im politischen Alltag? Zur ambivalenten Rolle nationaler und internationaler Historikerkommissionen', *Jahrbuch für Politik und Geschichte* 3 (2012), 204.

31. Cornelißen, 'Historie im politischen Alltag?, 206.

32. M. Zimmermann, 'Historie im politischen Alltag? Zur ambivalenten Rolle nationaler und internationaler Historikerkommissionen', *Jahrbuch für Politik und Geschichte* 3 (2012), 216.

33. M. Zimmermann, 'Historie im politischen Alltag?, 212.

34. For a recent example, see the deconstruction of Swiss myths by T. Maissen, *Schweizer Heldengeschichten und was dahinter steckt* (Baden: Hier und Jetzt Verlag, 2015). The use of the term 'myth' in this context is that of Roland Barthes and not of Bronislav Malinowski.

35. Interview with J. Winter, in *Tarih* 1(1) 2009, 32.

36. L. Niethammer, 'Der Zeitzeuge – eine Schimäre?', retrieved 7 March 2017 from http://lernen-aus-der-geschichte.de/sites/default/files/attach/11028/ln-vortrag-prora-2012 _0.pdf.

37. Winter, [interview], 31.

38. Niethammer, 'Der Zeitzeuge', 17.

Bibliography

Amsden, D. 'Building the First Slavery Museum in America', *New York Times*, 26 February 2015.

Assmann, A. 'Dialogic Memory', in P. Mendes-Flohr (ed.), *Dialogue as a Trans-Disciplinary Concept: Martin Buber's Philosophy of Dialogue and Its Contemporary Reception.* (Berlin: De Gruyter, 2015), 199–214.

Burke, P. *The Renaissance.* Atlantic Highlands: Humanities Press International, 1987.

Carlyle, T. 'On History Again', in G.B. Tennyson (ed.), *A Carlyle Reader: Selections from the Writings of Thomas Carlyle* (Cambridge: Cambridge University Press, 1984), 104–112.

Cornelißen, C. 'Historie im politischen Alltag? Zur ambivalenten Rolle nationaler und internationaler Historikerkommissionen', *Jahrbuch für Politik und Geschichte* 3 (2012), 201–17.

Darwin, J. 'Memory of Empire in Britain. A Preliminary View', in D. Rothermund (ed.), *Memories of Post-Imperial Nations: The Aftermath of Decolonization, 1945–2013* (Cambridge: Cambridge University Press, 2015), 18–37.

Daston, L., and P. Galison. *Objectivity.* Chicago: Zone Books, 2007.

Friedlander, S. *Nazi Germany and the Jews: The Years of Persecution, 1933–1939.* New York: HarperCollins, 1997.

———. *The Years of Extermination: Nazi Germany and the Jews, 1939–1945.* New York: HarperCollins, 2007.

Frei, N. 'Der Erinnerungstisch ist reich gedeckt', *Die ZEIT*, 26 March 2009.

Galtung, J. 'Cultural Violence'. *Journal of Peace Research* 27(3) (1990), 291–305.

———. 'Violence, Peace, and Peace Research'. *Journal of Peace Research* 6(3) (1969), 167–91.

'History'. Whitney Plantation. Accessed 20 February 2018, http://whitneyplantation.com/history.html.

Koselleck, R. 'Afterword', in Charlotte Beradt, *Das Dritte Reich des Traums* (Frankfurt am Main: Suhrkamp, 1966/1994), 117–32.

Maissen, T. *Schweizer Heldengeschichten und was dahinter steckt.* Baden: Hier und Jetzt Verlag, 2015.

Malinowski, B. *Magic, Science and Religion and Other Essays.* Glencoe, IL: The Free Press, 1948.

Niethammer, L. (ed.), *Lebenserfahrung und Kollektives Gedächtnis. Die Praxis der 'Oral History'.* Frankfurt am Main: Syndikat, 1985.

———. 'Der Zeitzeuge – eine Schimäre?'. Retrieved 7 March 2017 from http://lernen-aus-der-geschichte.de/sites/default/files/attach/11028/ln-vortrag-prora-2012_0.pdf.

Niethammer, L., and A. von Plato, *Lebensgeschichte und Sozialkultur im Ruhrgebiet*, 3 vols. Bonn: Dietz Verlag, 1989.

Novick, P. *That Noble Dream: The 'Objectivity Question' and the American Historical Profession.* New York: Cambridge University Press, 1988.

Osterhammel, J. *Die Flughöhe der Adler: Historische Essays zur globalen Gegenwart.* Munich: Beck, 2017.

Rothberg, M. *Multidirectional Memory: Remembering the Holocaust in the Age of Decolonization.* Stanford: Stanford University Press, 2009.

Schulin, E. *Traditionskritik und Rekonstruktionsversuch. Studien zur Entwicklung von Geschichtswissenschaft und historischem Denken.* Göttingen: Vandenhoeck & Ruprecht, 1979.

Schulte, R. *Das Dorf im Verhör. Brandstifter, Kindsmörderin und Wilderer vor den Schranken der bürgerlichen Gerichte Oberbayerns 1848–1910.* Reinbek: Rowohlt, 1989.

Thompson, P. *The Voice of the Past: Oral History.* Oxford: Oxford University Press, 1978.

Wall Street Journal. 'Whitney Plantation Museum to Focus on Slavery'. YouTube. Accessed 20 February 2017, https://www.youtube.com/watch?v=MRUcLLFMl3g&feature=youtu.be.

'Welcome to ABHM!' America's Black Holocaust Museum. Accessed 7 March 2017, http://abhmuseum.org.

Winter, J. [interview], in *Tarih* 1(1) 2009, 29–36.

Zimmermann, M. 'Historie im politischen Alltag? Zur ambivalenten Rolle nationaler und internationaler Historikerkommissionen', *Jahrbuch für Politik und Geschichte* 3 (2012), 201–17.

CHAPTER 2

The Vampire, the Undead and the Anxieties of Historical Consciousness

CLAUDIA LINDÉN AND HANS RUIN

Philosophying was always a form of vampyrism!
—Nietzsche, *The Gay Science*

Capital is dead labour, that, vampire-like, only lives by sucking living labour, and lives the more, the more labour it sucks.
—Marx, *The Capital*

Introduction

The Shelleys spent the summer of 1816 with Lord Byron and their doctor friend John William Polidori on the shore of Lake Geneva. The ash plume of a massive volcanic eruption on an Indonesian island had reached Europe, causing 'the year without a summer', which brought famine in its wake. Confined to the beautiful Villa Diodati, the visitors devoted those dark June days to a series of literary experiments that was to result in two classics of Gothic literature: Mary Shelley's *Frankenstein* and Polidori's *The Vampyre*. At this historic juncture, the literary vampire took its modern form within a circle of antiquity-loving British Romantics in southern European exile.

Notes for this section begin on page 50.

As the name of an undead creature preying upon the blood of the living, 'the vampire' coincided with the era of Enlightenment, of European Hellenophilia, and of modern historical consciousness. Its previous incarnations can be traced back to the oldest strata of recorded culture, in the fear that the dead might walk again and in various ways harm the living. Bloodsucking demons have figured in the folklore of Christian Europe ever since the late medieval period. As a concept, a cultural and aesthetic trope, and a political and rhetorical figure, however, the vampire appears during the period we customarily refer to as modernity. Having arisen as the object of real panic at the start of the eighteenth century, it quickly establishes itself as one of the most powerful and almost incalculably polysemous cultural figures of the period.

As a cultural icon, the vampire is typically associated with Bram Stoker's 1897 novel *Dracula*. As a literary phantasm, however, it had already enjoyed a breakthrough a century earlier. The year 1797 saw the publication of Goethe's 'The Bride of Corinth' and Coleridge's 'Christabel', both of which depict female vampires who lure their lovers to an untimely death. The vampire is usually identified with Gothicism and, with it, a genre regarded as distinct from Romanticism proper. Yet this distinction between Romanticism and Gothicism, with their accompanying valuations as high and low literature, respectively, is a post hoc invention.[1] The fantastic, horror, transgressive sexuality and vampirism also caught the interest of Keats, Byron and Shelley.

The massive secondary literature on the vampire as a cultural formation invariably associates it on the one hand with questions of popular belief and superstition, and on the other with the ethical-political effects of modernization and changes in the gender system, particularly as regards sexuality. By contrast, an issue that hitherto has largely been ignored by scholars is the vampire as a temporal-historical figure, or, to be more precise, the vampire itself as an embodiment of the temporal-historical. The vampire is a creature that respects neither the boundary between life and death nor conventional historical chronology. Its refusal to die is also a refusal to allow itself to be localized and confined within a given temporal order. The vampire is someone who returns, who moves across and through time, and who thereby visualizes a past that does not rest peacefully in its grave but intrudes upon the present in order to simultaneously attract, threaten and exploit it for its own continued existence. In so doing, it breaks with what Elizabeth Freeman in her book *Time Binds* calls 'chrononormativity', by breaking with time as its own norm.[2]

The eighteenth century is the century of the emergence and reinvention of history. It is the period when humanity grants itself a history that can be visualized as a temporal axis, one that runs from a beginning to a victorious present and in which every event, object and life can be situated within a chronological matrix. It is also a period that sees as its foremost ambition to collate the remains of all the dead and to restore them to life – but now as historical entities. The science of history, like historical culture, with its archives and museums, might thus be described as characterized by a chronological anomaly accompanied by a latent chronological anxiety. On the one hand, by arranging everything in its chronologically structured place, it expresses a confidence in the possibility of distinguishing the living from the dead. On the other, it seeks to *breathe life* into that which has been, especially that period which, more than any other, represents its perceived home and origin: classical antiquity. Through cultural-historical research and archaeology, it seeks to restore and ultimately reanimate what it perceives as this greatest of humanity's incarnations.

In refusing to remain within the boundaries stipulated by such historical consciousness, the vampire can be viewed as a force that simultaneously defies and confirms this period's historical ethos, which could be defined as chronological desire. It works as a metonym for a historical-scientific culture for which nothing can repeat itself and for which everything has its chronological place, but which at the same time is ultimately striving for the past not to be wholly past but rather in some sense living. Like no other cultural icon, the vampire can in this way be said to capture the inner pathology of *the historical*. This line of thought recalls the argument of Michel de Certeau's *The Writing of History,* which identifies historical knowledge and modern historical consciousness as the necessary precondition for establishing the very boundary between the dead and the living. De Certeau describes how history writing takes for granted the impossibility of belief in the presence of the dead in the way that characterized previous civilizations. Historical science would accordingly operate at precisely this interstice, in the knowledge of having killed the past as well as the desire to keep it alive.[3]

That the first phase of the vampire's modern mythico-poetical existence should have coincided with the most exalted period of European philhellenism might therefore be seen as indicative of how this figure is more fundamentally tied up with historical breaks, intersections, trauma and anxiety. When the vampire subsequently appears in the United States, it is often in connection with the historical wound that, more than any other, continues to define the country's fate as a national formation, namely the Civil War and the postwar South. Also, the inability of post-Soviet society to manage its collective grief and many unburied dead shows inter alia that it is in the form of vampires that the past often reveals itself in popular culture and the national imaginary. Such is the thesis developed by Russian psychologist and literary scholar Alexander Etkind in his 2013 study *Warped Mourning.*[4] The book is partly inspired by Derrida's influential argument in *Specters of Marx,* which developed a typology for conceptualizing history as 'spectrality', that is, as various kinds of ghosts and uncanny visitations. Derrida does refer in passing to the vampire, but he does not develop how its metaphorical force can be said to complement his Gothicism-inflected typology, which concerns the different ways in which history refuses to lie quiescent but returns, particularly when the dead have not been mourned or been given justice.[5]

Limitations of space preclude a fuller justification of this thesis here. For now, we will concentrate upon how the relationship to classical antiquity acquires a special charge in conjunction with the vampire's arrival on the literary scene around 1800. The essay is organized as follows. First, we offer a summary description of the vampire in folklore, literature and cultural-theoretical scholarship. This is followed by a section dealing with historical consciousness and the historiographical culture that takes shape during the second half of the eighteenth century, with particular emphasis on the return of classical antiquity. Our aim is to highlight the way in which these phenomena actualize those anxieties about life, death, survival and disaster that pave the way for the vampiric as a poetic crystallization of these inner tensions. By means of a close reading of Goethe's 'The Bride of Corinth', Keats's 'Lamia' and finally Polidori's 'The Vampire', we seek to show how the vampiric lends itself to interpretation in terms of this historical-theoretical frame – as both a desire and a fear that history might refuse to keep to its place and instead begin to walk abroad in the present.

Tropes of the Vampiric

Like its etymology, the first occurrence of the word 'vampire' is debated. It appears in certain sources as early as the latter part of the seventeenth century. During the first half of the eighteenth century, undead and blood-drinking spectres begin to acquire a proper foothold in the European imaginary under this designation. Several spectacular cases of alleged vampirism and vampire panics were documented in the 1720s and became the object of interventions by the authorities.[6] The significance of this problem in public debate is evidenced by the fact that both Voltaire and Rousseau felt obligated to officially distance themselves from and argue against belief in vampires. In his *Encyclopedia,* published in 1772, Voltaire includes an entry on 'Vampires' that opens with the dismayed exclamation that there still be vampires in this eighteenth century, after which he proceeds to scoff at those who assert the existence of such creatures. As early as the 1740s, the vampire also begins to appear as an image of 'exploitation'. In the same entry, Voltaire remarks that vampires have been sighted in neither London nor Paris, adding that 'it is in these cities that there exist businessmen who daily suck the blood of other people but, while corrupt, they are hardly dead' and that 'the true

bloodsuckers live, not in churchyards, but in very pleasant palaces'.[7] A century later, Marx was to use the same metaphor in his description of capital as
a 'vampiric' force. Another eighty years and the vampire would be used as a
figure for the sinister 'exploiting Jew' in Nazi propaganda.[8]

Another transformation of the vampiric, which was to prove epoch-
defining for the cultural imaginary, was its appearance as an aesthetic-cultural
trope during the second half of the eighteenth century. The first poem to
identify a vampire by name is H.A. Ossenfelder's 'Der Vampir' (1748). It is
a short poem in two verses which introduces the vampire as a bloodsucker
who drinks young women's blood in a fashion that is rendered explicitly
erotic by virtue of the vampire being presumed to make nocturnal visits
while the girl is asleep. Gottfrid Bürger's 'Leonore' (1774) concerns a young
woman in mourning for her beloved William, who has failed to return from
the wars. When at last he does return, he persuades her to run off with him,
and the couple ride away at full gallop through the night. But their ride
ends in a churchyard, where William is turned into a skeleton and drags his
lover into the grave. Yet the real breakthrough year for the literary vampire
was 1797, when both Coleridge's 'Christabel' and Goethe's 'The Bride of
Corinth' were published, followed in 1819 by Polidori's *The Vampyre*. The
last of these created, in the figure of Lord Ruthven, the refined masculine vampire. Polidori's text marked the vampire's definitive transition from
high literary experiment to mass cultural phenomenon, and was disseminated widely by numerous editions and theatrical adaptations throughout the
nineteenth century.[9] By the time Bram Stoker published *Dracula* in 1897, the
genre and its basic tropes were thus already well established.[10]

Dracula nonetheless lends an explosive impetus to the vampire narrative,
particularly via the new medium of film, which quickly adopts the vampire,
from Murnau's *Nosferatu* (1922), Ted Browning's classic *Dracula* (1931), fea-
turing Bela Lugosi in the title role, and Dreyer's *Vampire* (based on Le Fanu's
Carmilla) (1932) right up to the present invasion of cinematic vampires. It is
as if the specific mediality of film – a sequential montage uniquely endowed
with the ability to breathe life and movement into the dead and the static –
were peculiarly suited to depicting the vampiric.

The vast scholarship on the vampire and the vampiric almost defies
summary. It ranges all the way from the openly superstitious and occult,
through the more fanzine-style publications, to a growing body of cultural-
theoretical scholarship that has applied the entire arsenal of psychoanalysis,
critical theory and gender theory to this multifaceted cultural icon. In the
mid-1990s, most studies of vampires were still focused upon their role in
myth and folklore. What research existed on literary vampires concentrated
principally on *Dracula*.[11] Many recent studies are focused on the vampire in
young adult and popular culture. The *Twilight* series alone is already the sub-

ject of several scholarly books and a considerable number of journal articles.[12] To the extent that the topic is treated historically, this tends to stop with *Dracula,* at best with Polidori's *The Vampyre* being mentioned as an early instance or tentative precursor.

Where earlier commentators saw the vampire as an eternal, ubiquitous figure, the last few decades have instead emphasized its cultural mutability.[13] Today the vampire is seen as both a reflection and a staging of contemporary concerns. In recent years, critics have increasingly emphasized questions of gender, ethnicity, race, xenophobia and colonialism. Media theorist Friedrich Kittler reads *Dracula* as attesting to the impact of new reproductive technologies of discourse around 1900, such as the typewriter and the wax phonograph cylinder. Analyses of contemporary vampire narratives have often focused on consumer culture.

Analysis of the vampire has above all centred upon sexuality, both as the expression of a taboo and as an instance of norm-defying behaviour. As Eric Butler has remarked, the vampire figure is not a symptom but rather an opportunity for transgression.[14] Nonetheless, it must be stressed that sexuality is not the vampire's only, or even its most central, quality. As noted earlier, a central aspect of the vampire that nonetheless has remained surprisingly unexamined concerns its relationship to *time.* The vampire's ability to transcend human, biological time is after all a fundamental aspect of its monstrosity. Understood as a temporal figure, the vampire might thus be seen as a monster that, more than any other, both defines and is produced by the time of chronological history. In her study *Time and Tradition,* Aleida Assmann has stressed how the conventional model of history leads us to regard the past as something alien and irreversible. This model of history, which forms the backbone of modern historiography, remains tied to a specific conception of time, namely that of the linear and irreversible. In the analysis that follows, we intend to show how the vampire can be understood as a cultural figure partly generated from within historical consciousness's own unconscious – combining its desire and its anxiety. In order to make such a reading credible, we now shift our focus to the emergence of historical culture and the rise of historical consciousness during the second part of the eighteenth century, and especially the rediscovery of ancient Greece and the rise of European Hellenophilia.

The Rise of Historical Consciousness and the Lure of the Greeks

The eighteenth century in Europe was not only the era of Enlightenment and critique of religion. It was also the era of history, for it was in this period that time and, indeed, history itself emerged as preeminent categories of knowledge. While Western subjectivity for most of the seventeenth century still interpreted world events through the filter of Judaeo-Christian eschatology on the one hand, and the circular view of change articulated by classical political philosophy on the other, a concept of *progress* as a historical reality was also emerging. Time itself acquired direction and motion, and questions of origin and development gained new dignity as objects of knowledge and investigation.

At the start of the eighteenth century, the word 'history' had no more specific philosophical-historical connotation than a representation of some event in the past. A hundred years later, human thought has been historicized to such a point that reason itself can be seen as a historical process, and historical reflection the highest form of knowledge, as expressed first in Herder and culminating in the philosophy of Hegel. In Herder's writings, *the historical* become a new theodicy, a redeeming possibility for a humanity about to cast off its Christological mythology.[15] Foucault and Koselleck represent two different historical-philosophical approaches to this transformation. In *The Order of Things* (1966), Foucault defined it as a decisive epistemological rupture in which a static and taxonomic knowledge was replaced by a historical-genealogical knowledge. For Koselleck, the issue was about differentiating and understanding the basis for the new temporal horizons and temporalities that follow upon this shift, one in which a new way of comprehending the future unites with the discovery of *the historical* as both humanity's entire realm of action and a boundless new domain for a novel kind of knowledge.[16]

In his earlier and classical study of the rise of 'historicism', Friedrich Meinecke traced its multifarious origins in part to a union between a fascination with the historically unique and individual, and an idealistic hope in an interconnected totality. Herder was seen as having established this new signification of *the historical,* while Goethe most fully embodied its spirit.[17] The universal subject was a human being who succeeded in gathering and sustaining the historical as a multivocal choir of individual expressions, someone to whom nothing was now foreign. A formulation by Ranke captures the ethos and attitude of the new historian as follows: 'To look at the world, past and present, and to absorb it into my being as far as my powers will enable me; to draw out and appropriate all that is beautiful and great, to see with unbiased eyes the universal progress of history, and in this spirit to produce beautiful and noble works; imagine what happiness it would be for me if I could realize this ideal, if only in a small degree.'[18]

The individual who perhaps more than any other represented historicism's desire to recreate a lost world, however, was Winckelmann, whose comprehensive excavation and systematizing of Greek and Roman art in

History of Ancient Art from 1764 laid the foundations of modern art history and classics. Ten years previously, he had published *Thoughts on the Imitation of Greek Works in Painting and Sculpture,* a work that was to become a paradigm not only for classicist aesthetics but for all subsequent attempts to articulate the notion of a 'return' to antiquity, particularly by German aesthetic-philosophical thinkers. Through his travels and detailed descriptions of what he had seen and experienced of classical culture in Southern Europe, Winckelmann also provided the model for a Grand Tour that would henceforth direct Northern Europeans in pursuit of learning. For Winckelmann, it was literally a case of rescuing the past from out of the earth in order to give it new life. Among the works he bequeathed to prosperity was a text from the 1750s on the restoration of classical sculptures, which showed how such work consisted of reconstituting fragmented bodies and body parts. In the Italian villas that used classical sculptures as ornaments, he found bodies with wholly mismatched hands and heads. It was upon these practices that he trained his historical gaze in an effort to restore to these sundered bodies from the past their original human form and names.[19]

The same concern informs his celebrated meditation upon the mutilated Belvedere Torso, whose impressive but fragmentary physical form is ultimately described as merely a 'receptacle' for an 'immortality' and a 'higher spirit' that occupy 'the space of mortal limbs'.[20] He places his hopes in a productive imitation that might be capable of recreating its life, only to return almost at once to the insight that it will remain a fragment, one that it is ultimately the task of art history to conserve. This double perspective recalls the melancholic closing passage of his great *History of Ancient Art,* in which he relates how in his quest to restore the art of antiquity he became a witness to its ruin and loss. Here he compares himself to a young girl standing on the shore of the sea with tears in her eyes, following the departure of her beloved without hopes of ever seeing him again.[21] The desire to hold on to classical art ultimately bears comparison with people who want to communicate with 'ghosts' and who believe that they can see them, even though there are none to be seen. Antiquity, he writes, has become a prejudice, but one that does not lack utility.

His reflection resonates strikingly with Nietzsche's statement a century later, where in one of his late notebooks he ironically characterizes all of German culture and its desire for an ideal Greece as a striving to 'have joined anew the bond that seemed to have been broken, the bond with the Greeks, the hitherto highest type of man'.[22] This line of reasoning concludes with an image of Germans as being hitherto more like 'Hellenizing ghosts' but who will ultimately be 'also in our bodies' more Greek. Once again, both statements give the impression of an anxiety about classical antiquity and the present: on the one hand, something dead whose renewal in the present is urgently desired; on the other, a selfsame entity that one day will reanimate the bodies of the present that have hitherto been as if dead in relation to that life which emanates from the past.[23]

Romantic Vampires and the Hellenophilic Imagination

The historical consciousness – the new culture of history – that begins to take shape in earnest during the second half of the eighteenth century was marked by a series of internal tensions. It sought to make all previous history into something that could be recovered and incorporated. At the same time, it sought to arrange history by means of an overarching genealogical-chronological system. Lastly, it viewed itself as an attempt to revivify the best of that past, namely classical antiquity and its unsurpassed aesthetic-ethical culture. The staging of this historical-temporal return took the form of the Grand Tour, that great educational journey to the ruined remains of antiquity, a ruin that was at the same time being accelerated by the desire to restore it. It was also in this exact moment, around 1800, and in these same circles that the vampire first appeared as an aesthetic construct.

There was a notion that the soul of the Greek people had been preserved intact since antiquity, a kind of essential Greekness sustained by proximity to its origin. In a study of the vampire myth and neo-Hellenism, Ken Gelder has noted how the latter clearly represented a projection onto the Greeks rather than a conception that they held of themselves. Even so, it led contemporary visitors to Greece to see 'the ancient become visible in the modern' and how Greece's resurrection as a modern nation state 'brought the ancient back to life – it demonstrated *the ability of antiquity to live again*'.[24] While not the conclusion drawn by Gelder, the formulation offers a glimpse into how modern Greece became a living death, or undeath, a form of existence that establishes a genealogical connection to a lost origin.

Written in 1797, Goethe's 'The Bride from Corinth' takes place in Corinth as it is in the process of being Christianized.[25] The poem concerns a young Athenian man who comes to Corinth to meet the woman to whom he has been betrothed since childhood. Arriving late at night, he does not meet the daughter but is instead given supper by her mother, who shows him to a bedroom where he exhaustedly tumbles into bed fully clothed. Scarcely has he closed his eyes when 'a youthful maiden . . . / Robed in white' glides into the room.[26] Surprised, the young man gets up, only to hear the maiden complain that she has now been promised to heaven: 'Joy is not for me, nor festive cheer.' She explains that her mother, following a period of illness, renounced Christianity and swore an oath:

'The old gods, that bright and jocund train.
One, unseen, in heaven, is worshipped only.
And upon the cross a Saviour slain.'

The young man now immediately asks whether this maiden is his intended bride. She then replies that her younger sister is instead now meant to marry him.

"'Tis not mine, but 'tis my sister's place;
When in lonely cell I weep and languish,
Think, oh, think of me in her embrace!
I think but of thee –
Pining drearily,
Soon beneath the earth to hide my face!'

The young man becomes enamoured of the girl and they arrange a wedding feast then and there, but she refuses to taste the bread and drinks nothing but 'Hasty draughts of purple-tinctured wine'. He implores her to let him embrace her, until he at last bursts into tears. Then she lies down beside him in bed and says,

'Dear one, still thee!
Ah, how sad am I to see thee so!
But, alas! these limbs of mine would chill thee:
Love! they mantle not with passion's glow;
Thou wouldst be afraid,
Didst thou find the maid
Thou hast chosen, cold as ice or snow.'

                                        XVII.
Round her waist his eager arms he bended,
. . . .
'Wert thou even from the grave ascended,
I could warm thee well with my desire!'

By now she is as cold as the grave, and even if 'His hot breath through all her frame is tingling',

There they lie, caressing and caressed.
His impassioned mood
Warms her torpid blood,
Yet there beats no heart within her breast!

At cockcrow they are obliged to part, to be reunited the following night. Hearing the noises, the mother hammers from the outside. Finally she gets the door open, only to see her daughter, newly arisen from the grave, in the Athenian's bed. The daughter then cries to her mother:

> 'Mother! mother! Wherefore thus deprive me
> Of such joy as I this night have known?
> Wherefore from these warm embraces drive me?
> Was I wakened up to meet thy frown?
> Did it not suffice
> That in virgin guise
> To an early grave you forced me down?'
> XXIV.
>
> . . . .
> 'From the dark-heaped chamber where I lay;
> Powerless are your drowsy anthems, neither
> Can your priests prevail, howe'er they pray.
> Salt not lymph can cool,
> Where the pulse is full.'

The daughter accuses her mother of having broken the vow she made to the ancient gods: 'To this youth my early troth was plighted, / Whilst yet Venus ruled within the land.' The poem then ends with the young man's death and the undead vampire daughter declaring that she has sucked his blood and will visit other young men and do the same to them:

> 'Nightly from my narrow chamber driven,
> Come I to fulfil my destined part.
> Him to seek to whom my troth was given,
> And to draw the life-blood from his heart.
> He hath served my will;
> More I yet must kill,
> For another prey I now depart.'

The maiden's cry to her mother can be understood as a cry coming from the real antiquity, from the other side of Christian modernity, and thus from a living death. The poem can thus also be read as giving expression to a desire for a genuine antiquity and an anxiety that it is, in fact, already dead.

According to the eighteenth-century vampire myths, the vampire would initially return to haunt his or her own family, as also described in Byron's 'The Giaour'. The vampiric woman in Goethe's poem goes beyond this when she refers to 'sacrificing other young men'. Her bloodsucking has no temporal boundary; it can continue forever, with countless new young men becoming her victims. The poem also suggests that the real antiquity has been unjustly excluded by Christianity, at the same time as it manifests itself as a vengeful spectre luring young men to their doom. The daughter begs her mother to light a non-Christian funeral pyre in order to let the lovers rest in peace:

> 'And in flames our souls to peace restore.
> When the ashes glow,
> When the fire-sparks flow
> To the ancient gods aloft we soar.'

It is unclear whether these closing lines mean that she will find peace and cease to be a vampire. The reference in the final verse to returning to the old gods would rather seem to imply that they still live and can grant peace to the daughter on condition that the mother performs the old burial rites that she is asking for. The vampire maiden becomes yet another image of antiquity as undead, a beautiful and alluring figure that haunts the living and that simultaneously carries both coldness and death, like a whitened marble statue. In exemplary fashion, it seems to grasp the anxiety underlying classicist historical consciousness and its blend of desire and terror.

Goethe got no further than Italy, where he especially admired the Greek temple at Paestum. Byron travelled to Italy and Greece. Keats had to content himself by going to the British Museum in order to admire its classical sculptures and the Elgin Marbles. Keats may well have read Polidori's *The Vampyre* by the time he came to write *Lamia* in 1819. In any event, he had almost certainly read Goethe's 'The Bride of Corinth'. The previous year he had composed another vampire poem, 'La Belle Dame Sans Merci', and he returned to the theme in *Lamia*, this time also setting it in classical Greece, specifically Corinth. Like Goethe's poem, *Lamia* thematizes the relation between old and new in ancient Greece. The opposition in *Lamia* is not between Christianity and classical ideals but between an enlightened Platonism and a pre-Platonic order governed by the old gods. Here, too, then, the question of the relation to history is central.

In *Lamia*, the vampire is initially a kind of goddess in the shape of a serpent who asks Hermes – mediator and messenger between gods and humans, but also exemplar of the art of interpretation – to be transformed into a beautiful maiden in order to forge bonds of love with a young man named Lycius. Like the vampire maiden of Goethe's poem, she is in despair at the way that physical circumstances prevent her from loving: 'When from this wreathed tomb shall I awake! / When move in a sweet body fit for life.' But Lamia's request is granted, and she meets Lycius when he is on his way back to Corinth from the island of Aegina, where he has made offerings to Zeus. Lycius is beguiled by Lamia's beauty in human form and she accompanies him to Corinth. Lamia calls Lycius a 'scholar', and the person they meet upon reaching Corinth is his old teacher Apollonius. Lamia understands that Apollonius, 'robed in philosophical gown', can see through her – that is, can see what she really is. Lycius, too, rejects him: 'And good instructor; but tonight he seems / The ghost of folly haunting my sweet dreams.'

Lycius is torn between praying to the old gods and putting his faith in the power of philosophy and reason as embodied in his teacher Apollonius. He can thus be said to stand on the historical threshold to enlightenment and science, looking back, like the Romantic poets, upon a past that he wishes to cherish and nurture. At their first meeting, both Lamia and even Lycius himself avoid Apollonius's gaze. Lycius and Lamia set up house and live happily until Lycius proposes to her. Although she does not want to marry, he convinces her. She agrees on condition that he does *not* invite his teacher to the wedding feast. But Apollonius turns up uninvited and reproaches Lycius with his folly: 'Fool! Fool! Repeated he.' The philosopher declares that he has not raised and protected Lycius for him to fall prey to a serpent. Clearly, Apollonius has come to expose Lamia. And, just as she had feared, she literally melts away under his gaze:

> Do not all charms fly
> At the mere touch of cold philosophy?
> . . . .
> as it erewhile made
> The tender-person'd Lamia melt into a shade.

Lamia, the ancient deity given human form by Hermes, becomes a shadow, returning to her serpentine semblance under the gaze of philosophy and science, but takes with her Lycius. The final lines of the poem describe him lying cold in his marriage robe. Apollonius thus fails in his attempt to save Lycius. Philosophy's efforts to neutralize the old gods result in the destruction of the young whom they have ensnared. Here, as in Goethe's poem, the desire to obliterate the ancient celestial order is juxtaposed with the love elicited by that order, with catastrophic consequences for all those involved. Lamia, too, becomes emblematic of the desire and temptation inherent in the Romantic longing for a lost ancient world, one that here takes the form of a seductive woman. For the romantic young man, she is both tantalizing promise and impending death. She is the undead in history that returns to tempt the living. She cannot endure the exacting gaze of science, which annihilates her, but when she resumes her true form, she takes with her the doomed Lycius.

We come at last to Polidori's *The Vampyre* (1819), the paradigm for the modern vampire myth, in order to assess to what extent it can be read as an allegory of Romantic historical consciousness and its philhellenism. Though barely twenty pages long, this novella has had an extraordinary impact upon the literature that has followed it. In 1818, Colburn, editor of *New Monthly Magazine,* had received an anonymous package containing a text said to be written by Byron but discovered by someone else.[27] Colburn saw a means of raising his journal's circulation and published *The Vampyre* as a narrative by Lord Byron. After its serial publication, *The Vampyre* was issued as a book and went through seven printings in 1819 alone. The following year it was adapted for the stage by J.R. Planché, and in France it inspired both a play and a long novel by Cyprien Bérard, *Lord Ruthven, or the Vampires* (1820), and was quickly translated into several languages.

Although Byron and Polidori soon rectified the authorial misattribution, the tale has come to be associated with Byron. The vampire Ruthven is the archetype of the demoniacal Byronic hero. Byron might not have written it, contemporaries reasoned, but Polidori's portrait of Ruthven had none-theless been inspired by Byron and the aura of decadence and wickedness that coloured his reputation. Byron strove to distance himself by publicly denouncing the portrait as slanderous, but only served to strengthen the as-sociation. As vampire, Lord Ruthven would thus permanently be connected with Byron.[28]

The frame narrative of 'The Vampyre' relates how the mysterious Lord Ruthven first appears in London and immediately fascinates those around him. He draws into his orbit the main protagonist of the story, the wealthy and orphaned Aubrey, who has recently arrived with his sister. Ruthven invites Aubrey to join him on a Grand Tour to Greece. En route, Aubrey gradually becomes aware of how Ruthven deliberately seeks out women in order to corrupt them. Aubrey accordingly leaves and instead spends a few happy weeks in Greece in the company of a young Greek maiden, Ianthe. She warns him about vampires, but one dark night she herself falls prey to someone with a suspicious resemblance to Ruthven. After Aubrey falls into a delirium of grief, Ruthven suddenly reappears in order to take care of him, and they resume their journey. One evening they are attacked, and Ruthven is mortally wounded. He extracts a promise from Aubrey not to tell anyone of his death for a year. Aubrey returns to London, only to learn that his sister is getting married – to Ruthven. Bound by his word of honour, Aubrey can say nothing. When at last, deeply disturbed, he tries to prevent the wedding, he is taken into custody as a madman and suffers a stroke after his sister falls victim to the vampire.

The frame narrative is thus a Romantic educational tour of Greece and the ruins of classical antiquity. When Ruthven first turns up in London, nothing is said of his origins, merely that he is a nobleman equipped with a 'dead' eye and with a penetrating gaze, a person both alluring and ominous. His face is said to wear a 'deadly hue' that remains unchanged by mental excitement, at the same time as his 'form and outline were beautiful'. Aubrey, by contrast, is a Romantic youth, who longs to realize the great historical adventure of his generation. He lives for poetry and the imagination: 'he cultivated his imagination more than his judgement'. He becomes Ruthven's companion on a journey to the fabled origins of antiquity, a journey back to the place from which – it will be revealed – Ruthven himself hails. When Aubrey, having first broken with Ruthven during the journey, reaches Greece, he finds in it two contradictory figures: on the one hand, the beautiful and living Ianthe; on the other, the dead sculptures, stone remains to which he is drawn in hopes of being able to elicit their secret life. The narrative describes how he occupies himself with these 'faded records of ancient glory' that relate what 'free men' once accomplished but that now shamefacedly hide themselves in the earth in a land of 'slaves'. The image reflects the Romantics' divided view of Greece under Turkish rule: antiquity lay hidden beneath the protecting earth, buried not like something dead but rather like something undead, awaiting resurrection. Directly after these lines there follows a description of the lovely Ianthe, 'so beautiful and delicate' that she is said to have been a possible model for a painter who wanted to portray the lovely maidens said to inhabit the 'Muslim paradise'.

Ianthe is represented as a natural creature who embodies the classical ideal of beauty, a Winckelmannesque dream of an eternally youthful Greece in the ephemeral form of a woman who herself has no interest in history. At three points in the text she is contrasted with other women, all of whom in different ways are presented as soulless and affected, at the same time as she herself is entirely lacking in education. She is as beautiful as a gazelle but lacks 'that sleepy luxurious look of the animal' that suits but 'the taste of the epikuré'. It is Ianthe's 'innocence, so contrasted with the affected virtues of the women among whom he had sought for his vision of romance' that wins his heart, even though he questions whether he, a young man 'of English habits', can marry an 'uneducated Greek girl'. The text juxtaposes Ianthe with the monuments, speaking of how the 'light step of Ianthe often accompanied Aubrey in his search after antiquities' and how 'the unconscious girl, engaged in the pursuit of a Kashmere butterfly', led him to forget 'the letters he had just deciphered upon an almost effaced tablet, in the contemplation of her sylph-like figure'.

Following an *a-b-a-b* pattern, the text twice repeats antiquity, Ianthe, antiquity, Ianthe in the same sentence. As Aubrey shifts back and forward, what at first glance might seem like a contradiction between half-buried monuments and a living woman becomes a fusion of antiquity and the female – of something dead and something living. Ianthe becomes a metonym of antiquity itself, which is feminized in the process. The description of the innocent, artless and natural Ianthe, in contrast to the affected women in London, recalls the bourgeoisie's critique of the upper class as artificial and depraved, in combination with a feminine ideal that foregrounds passivity and chastity. Juxtaposing the innocent Ianthe with the buried ancient monuments twice in the same sentence, Polidori's text creates an alloy of innocent woman and ancient monuments that thereby creates the image of antiquity as a natural, intrinsic part of the inhabitants of modern Greece, simultaneously vulnerable and threatened. Antiquity in the shape of Ianthe – beautiful, natural and eternal – is waiting there, like the stones in the ground, to be discovered by the English man. Ianthe is equated with a passive Greece, awaiting discovery and rescue in the same way as Lord Elgin had done with the Parthenon frieze.

When the past is coded as feminine-passive in the figure of Ianthe, it becomes like the monuments crouching under the moss, beautiful and enticing. But when the past makes an active appearance in 'The Vampyre', it instead becomes masculine, homoerotic and deadly. In the figure of Ruthven, the past becomes a deadly threat. Lord Ruthven is as Greek as Ianthe, just infinitely older and eternal in a different way to her. It is Ianthe and her family who warn Aubrey about vampires. Aubrey does not want to believe her, 'but Ianthe cited to him the names of old men, which had at least detected one living among themselves, after several of their near relatives and children had been found marked with the stamp of the fiend's appetite'.

After the girl is murdered by the unidentified vampire, Aubrey is struck by a violent fever. It is at this point that Ruthven appears again and takes care of him, the very same man whom he now suspects of being the vampire. But since Ruthven is now changed and in view of 'the attention, anxiety and care which he showed' him, Aubrey lets the nobleman become his companion once again. And yet Ruthven sometimes watches him, his 'gaze fixed intently upon him with a smile of *malicious exultation playing upon his lips*; he knew not why but this smile *haunted* him' (italics added). At this point, as the reader, like Aubrey, realizes that Lord Ruthven is the vampire, the description acquires an overtone that is both homoerotic and threatening. There is something about Ruthven's mouth that unsettles Aubrey. The early nineteenth century celebrated same-sex romantic friendships and was entirely lacking in the homophobia which developed towards the end of the century. While Ruthven's care for the invalid Aubrey and the trust he thereby elicits falls entirely within this paradigm of romantic friendship, the cruel and exulting smile that haunts Aubrey prefigures the homophobia that, according to Eve Kosfosky Sedgwick, became a defining feature of the late nineteenth century.[29] The mixing of romantic friendship with the fear of being bitten by the vampire, as staged in these scenes, invites an interpretation of the vampire as an ambivalent figure along the lines of what Sedgwick has called the homophobic 'paranoid Gothic'. This ambivalence in relation to Ruthven thus makes him, even more than Ianthe, into a figure that combines desire and dread.

Aubrey and Ruthven renew their classical investigations and, while travelling, are attacked by robbers. Ruthven is shot and, dying, draws Aubrey into the pact that ultimately seals both his own fate and that of the narrative, namely to promise not to reveal that Ruthven has died – and how. After Ruthven's death, his body is carried off by assistants who have been given the task of placing it atop a hill at full moon. When Aubrey goes there to bury the body, he finds it vanished. What Aubrey has witnessed, then, is how the undead can seemingly die, only to return to life.

Shaken, Aubrey returns to London, where it is time to introduce his sister into society. When Ruthven reappears, he forces Aubrey to keep his promise even though he realizes that Ruthven really is the vampire ('he could not believe it possible – the dead rise again!'). Burdened with the knowledge that he cannot tell what he knows, Aubrey suffers a mental collapse. He tries desperately to warn his sister to have nothing to do with Ruthven, but while he is recuperating from his psychological exhaustion, she nevertheless decides to marry him. Aubrey dies after suffering a stroke, and the novella closes, somewhat abruptly, with the words 'Lord Ruthven had disappeared, and Aubrey's sister had glutted the thirst of a VAMPYRE!'.

For a second time the demon of this tale has destroyed that which Aubrey loves most of all – his sister – and with her his own self. Aubrey himself is not bitten, but his cultural-historical and homoerotic pact with Ruthven proves his downfall. His desire to be united with Greek antiquity by means of studying its monuments, his love for Ianthe, and the pact to keep secret that he has seen 'the dead rise again' all lead him to death and annihilation. Step by step, we can see how the narrative captures the dark side of the Romantic historical consciousness's quest to bear witness to the resurrection of a lost antiquity. Its glorification of a past life also contained the threat of death. Behind the rosy image of a rediscovered ancient world, this early vampire narrative thus points towards the contradictory desires that informed these Romantic dreams.

Concluding Remarks

The vampire can be read as an exemplary image of the historical in its double manifestation as desire for something that can be resurrected and dread of something undead that threatens the living. The vampire's deathlessness and its rupturing of a chrononormative order attract the living but ultimately lead to their destruction. In the writings of Goethe, Keats and Polidori, the phil-hellenism of the eighteenth century and the Romantics can thus be seen to stage the representation of a vampiric force charged with erotic desires that result in death and annihilation. The central concern of each of the works considered here is the attraction to something that enables the living dead to attack the living, quite literally draining their life-blood.

The vampire cannot die. And yet it is a spectre that needs the living if its shadowy existence is to continue. It entices the living by its age, its refine-ment and its tragic depth, even while heralding their ruin. When the living cannot defend themselves against the undead, when they are lured into too close a proximity to those from another time, they risk themselves becoming living dead in the present.

The vampire encapsulates the historical as both temptation and terror, even more so than the 'ghost', the 'spectre', or the 'phantom', which were all mobilized by Derrida in *Specters of Marx* as a vocabulary for the historical imagination. Furthermore, as a literary-cultural figure, it not only appears at the chronological intersection of classicism's and Romanticism's joint pas-sion for antiquity, but is literally invented by some of the most important representatives of this movement, localizing it within an imagined Greece and the desire for its 'resurrection' in the present.

The vampire is a genuinely terrifying figure. It is a spectre who not merely returns like a shadowy ghost of the past to remind the living of per-petrated injustices. It is undead history itself, as anxiety and desire, as some-thing the living cannot control, as something they are lured into dealing with but that will thereby prove their undoing. On this view, the vampire presents itself as the figuration of time and the historical, a product of the chrononormative confidence of historical consciousness that the dead will stay in their graves even as other signs indicate that they now walk among the living, thirsting for their blood and, ultimately, their lives so that they themselves may continue to live.

Claudia Lindén is associate professor in comparative literature at Södertörn University (Sweden). Her research is focused on eighteenth-century litera-ture from gender and queer perspectives. She has published a monograph on the Swedish feminist Ellen Key (*About Love: Literature, Sexuality and Politics of Ellen Key*) and articles on, among other things, Emily Dickinson, masculin-ity in Wilhelm von Humboldt, and the *Twilight Saga*. She has also published several articles on gender theory and historiography on contemporary gen-der theory. She is currently working on a book about Isak Dinesen and the Gothic.

Hans Ruin is professor of philosophy at Södertörn University. He is the author of many articles and two monographs in phenomenology and hermeneutics. He has coedited fifteen books, the latest of which is a three-volume work in the theory of history and memory in Swedish, titled *Historiens hemvist I-III* (2016). He is the coeditor of Nietzsche's collected works in Swedish, and during the period 2010–2016 he directed the multidisciplinary research program Time, Memory, Representation (www.histcon.se). He is the author of *Being with the Dead: Burial, Ancestral Politics, and the Roots of Historical Consciousness* (Stanford University Press, forthcoming).

Notes

1. While the Gothic has also been considered a subgenre of Romanticism in Anglo-American scholarship, it has always been a presence. See F. Botting, *Gothic* (London: Routledge, 1996), 5.
2. As such, it might also be characterized as a 'queer temporality', as originally coined by J. Halberstam in a book of the same name, in which (s)he connects it to the dissolution of the bourgeois family, reproduction and inheritance. See also 'Theorizing Queer Temporalities: A Roundtable Discussion', *GLQ: A Journal of Lesbian and Gay Studies* 13 (2007), 177–95.
3. M. de Certeau, *The Writing of History*, trans. T. Conley (New York: Columbia University Press, 1988), 5–6.
4. A. Etkind, *Warped Mourning: Stories of the Undead in the Land of the Unburied* (Stanford: Stanford University Press, 2013), 211–13.
5. For a remark on the vampire in relation to Derrida, see also J. Castricano, *Cryptomimesis: The Gothic and Jacques Derrida's Ghost Writing* (Montreal: McGill University Press, 2001), 57–58. For a philosophical contextualization of the topic of spectrality in *Spectres of Marx*, see also H. Ruin, 'Spectral Phenomenology: Derrida, Heidegger and the Problem of the Ancestral', in K. Kattago (ed.), *The Ashgate Research Companion to Memory Studies* (Farnham: Ashgate, 2015), 61–74.
6. For good accounts of the cultural-historical background, see J. Twitchell, *The Living Dead: A Study of the Vampire in Romantic Literature* (Durham: Duke University Press, 1981); P. Barber, *Vampires, Burial, and Death* (New Haven: Yale University Press, 1988/2010); and E. Butler, *Metamorphoses of the Vampire in Literature and Film: Cultural Transformations in Europe, 1732–1933* (Rochester, NY: Camden House, 2010). In Swedish there is also Anna Höglund's impressive study of 300 years of Western vampire narratives, *Vampyrer. En kulturkritisk studie av den västerländska vampyrberättlsen 1700–2000* (Växjö: Växjö University Press, 2009).
7. Voltaire, *Œuvres complètes*, vol. 8 (Oxford: Voltaire Foundation, 2002), 252.
8. See S. Robinson, *Blood Will Tell: Vampires as Political Metaphors before World War I* (Boston: Boston Academic Studies Press, 2011).
9. For a description of Ruthven's stage career, see R. Stuart, *Stage Blood: Vampires of the 19th-Century Stage* (Bowling Green: Bowling Green State University Press, 1994).
10. Works that substantially impacted the genre include E. Grey's *The Skeleton Count or, The Vampire Mistress* (1828), M. Rymer's *Varney the Vampire or the Feast of Blood* (1840s) and S. Le Fanu's *Carmilla* (1871). There are obvious intertextual parallels between Polidori's, Grey's, Rymer's and Le Fanu's works, as there are between all four and Stoker. It seems highly likely that Grey had read *The Vampyre*. Rymer's text features, among other things, a Count Polidori.
11. Margaret Carter and David J. Skal have played a key role in extending our knowledge of this rich corpus in literature and film. The same goes for Carol A. Senf and Jean Ma-

rigny. Nina Auerbach paved the way for feminist readings of the vampire. James B. Twitchell has been particularly important for this article since he specifically addressed the vampire in Romanticism. See also M. Dennison, *Vampirism: Literary Tropes of Decadence and Entropy* (New York: Peter Lang, 2001).

12. See, for example, M. Larsson and A. Steiner (eds), *Interdisciplinary Approaches to Twilight: Studies in Fiction, Media and a Contemporary Cultural Experience* (Lund: Nordic Academic Press, 2011); and C. Lindén. 'Virtue as Adventure and Excess'.

13. See, for example, C. Frayling (ed.), *Vampires: Lord Byron to Count Dracula* (London: Faber and Faber, 1992).

14. E. Butler, *Metamorphoses of the Vampire in Literature and Film: Cultural Transformations in Europe, 1732–1933* (Rochester, NY: Camden House, 2010), 12.

15. See J. Zammito, 'Herder and Historical Metanarrative: What's Philosophical about History?', in H. Adler and W. Koepke (eds), *A Companion to the Works of Johan Gottfried Herder* (Rochester: Camden House, 2009), 65–85.

16. See in particular R. Kosselleck, 'Historia Magistra Vitae: The Dissolution of the Topos into the Perspective of a Modernized Historical Process', in *Futures Past: On the Semantics of Historical Time*, trans. K. Tribe (New York: Columbia University Press, 2004), 26–42.

17. F. Meinecke, *Historicism: The Rise of a New Historical Outlook*, trans. J.E. Anderson (New York: Herder & Herder, 1972/1936).

18. L. von Ranke, *The Secret of World History: Selected Writings on the Art and Science of History*, ed. and trans. R. Wines (New York: Fordham University Press, 1981); see in particular the short essay 'The Historian's Ideal'.

19. J. Winckelmann, 'Von der Restauration der Antiquen', in S. Bruer and M. Kunze (eds), *Eine unvollendete Schrift Winckelmanns* (Mainz: Verlag Philip von Zabern, 1996).

20. J. Winckelmann, 'Thoughts on the Imitation of Greek Works in Painting and the Art of Sculpture', in *Johan Joachim Winckelmann on Art, Architecture and Archaeology*, trans. D. Carter (Rochester: Camden House, 2013), 57–80.

21. J. Winckelmann, *History of the Art of Antiquity*, trans. H. Mallgrave (Los Angeles: Getty Research Institute, 2006).

22. F. Nietzsche, *The Will to Power*, trans. W. Kaufmann and R.J. Hollingdale (New York: Vintage Books, 1968), §419.

23. For an excellent account of German philhellenism and its development from utopia to decadence and, ultimately, a mere 'nostalgic memory', see S. Marchand, *Down from Olympus: Archaeology and Philhellenism in Germany, 1750–1970* (Princeton: Princeton University Press, 1996).

24. K. Gelder, *Reading the Vampire* (London: Routledge, 1994), 36.

25. The poem has dazzled readers and commentators ever since its appearance. For a review of previous interpretations, see M. Mayers, 'Goethes Vampirische Poetik. Zwei Thesen zur Braut von Corinth', in *Jahrbuch der Deutschen Schillergesellschaft* 43 (1999), 148–58, who also defends its status in Goethe's oeuvre, arguing that it ultimately represents a 'zwiespalt zwischen Antike und Christentum, zwischen Körperlichkeit och Spiritualitet' (dichotomy between antiquity and Christianity, between corporeality and spirituality) as well as capturing his 'Poetik der Distanz' (poetics of distance) (158).

26. For the English translation, see N. Haskell Dole (ed.), *The Works of Goethe*, vol. 9 (Boston: Francis & Niccolls, 1901), 152–53.

27. How this text came to be published in the first place is a fascinating story in its own right. Polidori likely left the text behind when he left Switzerland in autumn 1816. How it then reached the hands of the editor in London has never been established. As the preface states, 'Behind it lies some unknown scavenger of Byroniana, whose unwholesome curiosity led him or her to interrogate the servants in and around villa Diodati, with momentous results' (x). There also exists a draft of the frame narrative in Polidori's hand, which explicitly states that it was conceived by Byron. The narrative written by Byron has a plot frame that recalls

Polidori's text but that wholly lacks the vampire element. It is titled 'Augustus Darvell', in R. Morrison and C. Baldick (eds), *The Vampyre and Other Tales of the Macabre* (Oxford: Oxford World's Classics, 1997), 246–52.

28. It has been suggested that Polidori's story about Aubrey was also an attempt to tell his own story, particularly his destructive relationship with Byron. See P. Skarda, 'Vampyrism and Plagiarism: Byron's Influence and Polidori's Practice', *Studies in Romanticism* 28 (1989), 249–69. And Erik Butler has argued that the accusations of plagiarism, his involvement with Byron, and the intense media attention were factors in Polidori's suicide in August 1821; see Butler, *Metamorphoses,* 85–86.

29. E. Kosfosky Sedgwick, *The Coherence of Gothic Conventions* (London: Methuen, 1986).

Bibliography

Assmann, A. *Zeit und Tradition: Kulturelle Strategien der Dauer.* Cologne: Böhlau, 1999.

Auerbach, N. *Our Vampires, Ourselves.* Chicago: Chicago University Press, 1995.

Barber, P. *Vampires, Burial, and Death.* New Haven: Yale University Press, 1988/2010.

Botting, F. *Gothic.* London: Routledge, 1996.

Butler, E. *Metamorphoses of the Vampire in Literature and Film: Cultural Transformations in Europe, 1732–1933.* Rochester, N.Y.: Camden House, 2010.

Byron. *The Poetical Works of Lord Byron.* London: Oxford University Press, 1957.

———. 'Augustus Darvell', in R. Morrison and C. Baldick (eds), *The Vampyre and Other Tales of the Macabre* (Oxford: Oxford World's Classics, 1997), 246–52.

Castricano, J. *Cryptomimesis: The Gothic and Jacques Derrida's Ghost Writing.* Montreal: McGill University Press, 2001.

de Certeau, M. *The Writing of History,* trans. T. Conley. New York: Columbia University Press, 1988.

Dennison, M. *Vampirism: Literary Tropes of Decadence and Entropy.* New York: Peter Lang, 2001.

Derrida, J. *Specters of Marx: The State of Debt, the Work of Mourning and the New International,* trans. P. Kamuf. London: Routledge, 2006.

Etkind, A. *Warped Mourning: Stories of the Undead in the Land of the Unburied.* Stanford: Stanford University Press, 2013.

Foucault, M. *The Order of Things: An Archaeology of the Human Sciences,* trans. unknown, London: Routledge, 2002.

Frayling, C. (ed.). *Vampires: Lord Byron to Count Dracula.* London: Faber and Faber, 1992.

Gelder, K. *Reading the Vampire.* London: Routledge, 1994.

Goethe. *The Works of Goethe,* vol. 9, ed. N. Haskell Dole. Boston: Francis & Niccolls, 1901.

Halberstam, J. *Skin Shows: Gothic Horror and the Technology of Monsters.* Durham: Duke University Press, 1995.

———. 2007. 'Theorizing Queer Temporalities: A Roundtable Discussion'. *GLQ: A Journal of Lesbian and Gay Studies* 13: 177–95

Höglund, A. *Vampyrer. En kulturkritisk studie av västerländska vampyrberättelsen från 1700-talet till 2000-talet.* Växjö: Växjö University Press, 2009.

Khair, T., and J. Höglund (eds). *Transnational and Postcolonial Vampires: Dark Blood.* Basingstoke: Palgrave Macmillan, 2013.

Kosofsky Sedgwick, E. *The Coherence of Gothic Conventions.* London: Methuen, 1986.

Kosselleck, R. 'Historia Magistra Vitae: The Dissolution of the Topos into the Perspective of a Modernized Historical Process', in *Futures Past: On the Semantics of Historical Time,* trans. K. Tribe (New York: Columbia University Press, 2004), 26–42.

Larsson, M., and A. Steiner (eds). *Interdisciplinary Approaches to Twilight: Studies in Fiction, Media and a Contemporary Cultural Experience*. Lund: Nordic Academic Press, 2011.

Lindén, Claudia. 'Virtue as Adventure and Excess: Intertextuality, Masculinity, and Desire in the *Twilight* Series', *Culture Unbound: Journal of Current Cultural Research* 5 (2013), 213–37. Retrieved 9 March 2017 from http://www.cultureunbound.ep.liu.se/v5/a15/cu13v5a15.pdf.

Marchand, S. *Down from Olympus: Archaeology and Philhellenism in Germany, 1750–1970*. Princeton: Princeton University Press, 1996.

Marigny, J. *Sang pour sang: le réveil des vampires*. Paris: Gallimard, 2010.

Marx, K. *Capital: A Critique of Political Economy*, vol. 1, trans. B. Fowkes. Harmondsworth: Penguin, 1990.

Mayers, M. 'Goethes Vampirische Poetik. Zwei Thesen zur Braut von Corinth'. *Jahrbuch der Deutschen Schillergesellschaft* 43 (1999), 148–158.

Meinecke, F. *Historicism: The Rise of a New Historical Outlook*, trans. J.E. Anderson. New York: Herder & Herder, 1936/1972.

Nietzsche, F. *The Will to Power*, trans. W. Kaufmann and R.J. Hollingdale. New York: Vintage Books, 1968.

Polidori, J.W. *The Vampire and Other Tales of the Macabre*. London: Oxford World's Classics, 1997.

Ranke, L. von. *The Secret of World History: Selected Writings on the Art and Science of History*, ed. and trans. R. Wines. New York: Fordham University Press, 1981.

Robinson, S. *Blood Will Tell: Vampires as Political Metaphors before World War I*. Boston: Boston Academic Studies Press, 2011.

Ruin, H. 'Spectral Phenomenology: Derrida, Heidegger and the Problem of the Ancestral', in K. Kattago (ed.), *The Ashgate Research Companion to Memory Studies* (Farnham: Ashgate, 2015), 61–74.

Senf, C. *The Vampire in Nineteenth-Century English Literature*. Bowling Green: Bowling Green State University Popular Press, 1988.

Skarda, P. 'Vampyrism and Plagiarism: Byron's Influence and Polidori's Practice', *Studies in Romanticism* 28 (1989), 249–69.

Stuart, R. *Stage Blood: Vampires of the 19th-Century Stage*. Bowling Green: Bowling Green State University Press, 1994.

Twitchell, J. *The Living Dead: A Study of the Vampire in Romantic Literature*. Durham: Duke University Press, 1981.

Voltaire. *Œuvres complètes*, vol. 8. Oxford: Voltaire Foundation, 2002.

Winckelmann, J. 'Von der Restauration der Antiquen', in S. Bruer and M. Kunze (eds), *Eine unvollendete Schrift Winckelmanns* (Mainz: Verlag Philip von Zabern, 1996).

———. *History of the Art of Antiquity*, trans. H. Mallgrave. Los Angeles: Getty Research Institute, 2006.

———. 'Thoughts on the Imitation of Greek Works in Painting and the Art of Sculpture, in *Johan Joachim Winckelmann on Art, Architecture and Archaeology*, trans. D. Carter (Rochester: Camden House, 2013), 57–80.

Zammito, J. 'Herder and Historical Metanarrative: What's Philosophical about History?', in H. Adler and W. Koepke (eds), *A Companion to the Works of Johan Gottfried Herder* (Rochester: Camden House, 2009), 65–85.

CHAPTER 3

History, Justice and
the Time of the Imprescriptible

Victoria Fareld

Traditionally, the core of the historian's ethos – *ethos* understood in its major twofold sense: place and responsibility – has been articulated as an effort to arrive at a truth concerning the past. Today, as truth is not seen as a purely epistemological or linguistic concern, the virtue of being true to the past also involves ethical considerations, which necessarily have social and political dimensions. The recent existential turn within the historical sciences can be seen against this background, visible in the increased scholarly interest in lived experience, individual testimonies and questions of memory.[1] The concern for how historians deal with the haunting memories of victims and their demand for justice has also moved to the very centre of historical de-bate as a growing site of popular interest and of political struggle, notably through the work of truth and reconciliation commissions and discussions of transitional justice. These changes have called for a renegotiation of the critical, distant relationship traditionally ascribed to the responsible historian vis-à-vis the past. How this critical relation is to be understood, not only epistemologically, but also ethically, has become a major concern.[2]

Hand in hand with this turn to ethics goes an effort to reconceptualize fundamental temporal categories as the basis of historiography. The con-ception of linear and irreversible time is being challenged by experiential categories of multilayered or entangled temporalities, informed by an idea of the persistence of the past, whether in terms of memory, trauma, mourning or spectrality. The current changes not only influence our understanding of what it means to stand in a historical relation to the past, but they also affect our sense of the present. How are we to define the boundaries of the contemporary in relation to a past that persists in the present? Is there an ethical, as distinct from a historical, understanding of this boundary?

Invoking the Past

In 2011, the 91-year-old John Demjanjuk, at the time an American citizen, was convicted by a German criminal court for crimes he committed as a 23-year-old in 1943. Based on a service record showing that he had worked as an SS guard at the Nazi extermination camp in Sobibór in occupied Poland during World War II, he was convicted as an accessory to the murder of about twenty-eight thousand persons in the camp.[3] Two years later, in 2013, German judicial authorities announced that fifty former guards at Auschwitz-Birkenau would stand trial for complicity in mass murder during the war based on similar service records. The first former guard to be arrested, the 93-year-old Hans Lipschis, was later deemed by the court to be unfit for trial due to increasing dementia.[4]

Due to the imprescriptibility of the Nazi crimes – meaning the punishability of the crimes cannot expire – the perpetrators remain contemporary with, and can be prosecuted for, the crimes for as long as they live. Their guilt does not diminish with the passage of time, nor does the social importance of prosecution and punishment. Or put in temporal terms, chronological time is set aside in favour of a moral and juridical regulation of time in which the criminal events of the past are treated as if they were part of the present.

In recent decades, we have seen many examples of how the past has become an arena for political claims, confessions and accusations, as well as for legal actions in the present. In historical works about painful pasts, history has to a large extent taken the form of a retrospective working-through of crimes and oppression that occurred in the past, together with a growing sensibility for and interest in the fate of the victim. When states deal increasingly with their violent past, judges enter the domain of history, and historians often end up, as expert witnesses, at the centre of adjudication processes.[5]

One important aspect of the current intertwinement of historiography and jurisprudence is, I argue, the temporality of international law and its effects on the writing of history. For many historians today, their task is not primarily to reconstruct or represent an absent past, but to deal with a past that remains and is even *acted upon* in the present.

In this essay, I argue that the legal notion of imprescriptibility has introduced a new temporal figure not only within the domain of the law but also within the field of history. Against a notion of the past as irreversibly and definitively gone, and which has been constitutive of conventional historical time, the idea of the imprescriptible has made visible another temporality in which the events of the past can be invoked as possible to act upon as if they were dimensions of the present. This invocation of the past is therefore something more, and other, than simply looking back at and remembering what has happened. It is an act which turns the past into something upon which one can act morally and legally, by letting it coincide with the present in an extended contemporaneity.

The Debate on the Statute of Limitations

A decisive event for the appearance of the new temporal figure of the imprescriptible is the so called *Verjährungsdebatte,* the debate on the statute of limitations for Nazi war crimes in West Germany in the 1960s. It concerned whether the statute of limitations on crimes committed by the Nazi regime would expire in May 1965, twenty years after the end of the war and the fall of the Third Reich.

Historian Caroline Sharples points out that the statute of limitations is a relatively uninvestigated subject in historical research. There are some studies from a legal perspective and a few which focus on the political dimensions of the debates with regard to the Nazi war crimes.[6] The consequences of the debates for the writing of history, however, are largely unexplored.[7] The temporal figure of imprescriptibility has, I argue, made serious impact also on the writing of history and has forced historians to discuss the relation between historical and ethical time.

In the autumn of 1964, when the first Frankfurt Auschwitz trial was running, hundreds of the witnesses were survivors from the camp. The twentieth anniversary of the end of the war awaited the following year. On this day, 8 May 1965, the crimes committed during the Nazi era would be subject to prescription in accordance with paragraph 67 in the West German penal code. The deadline for war crimes investigations came closer. In November 1964, the West German government announced that there would be no prolongation of the statute of limitations for the Nazi crimes. No special adjustment to the current legal framework in the face of those crimes would be made.[8]

Massive international reactions were not long in coming in the form of letters, petitions, resolutions and demonstrations organized by Jewish groups. Among the two thousand people gathered in Paris in January 1965 was the French philosopher Vladimir Jankélévitch.[9] Shortly after the demonstration, Jankélévitch published an article in *Le Monde* called 'L'imprescriptible', in which he vehemently attacked the idea of applying a statute of limitations for the Nazi crimes.[10] I will return to Jankélévitch's article in greater detail below, as it highlights the conflictual temporalities of the debate as well as, I argue, its consequences for the writing of history.

Although more acidly articulated, Jankélévitch's personal position was completely in line with the French official response. Already in December 1964, a month after the West German government's announcement, the French National Assembly voted unanimously for a new law stating that crimes against humanity, following the 1946 UN resolution, are 'imprescriptibles par leur nature'.[11] When Jankélévitch gathered with a great number of French intellectuals to condemn the statute as a 'legal and moral scandal, but also a political scandal', they directly addressed the West German government and argued for an internationalization of the new French law on crimes against humanity.[12] In 1968, a convention declaring the 'Non-applicability of Statutes of Limitations to War Crimes and Crimes against Humanity' was passed in the United Nations, which reflected a change in several national legislations, among them in France and the United States.[13]

In West Germany, however, the public responses were altogether different. The international debates generated by the government's announcement were described as an expression of 'incomprehension' by then Minister of Justice Ewald Bucher, belonging to the liberal Free Democratic Party (FDP).[14] Not only did Bucher consider himself as conveying the result of a vote in the government, but also as representing a majority of the West German citizens.[15] It was agreed that the final decision about the statute should be postponed until all documents of interest to the investigators had been registered, in particular material held in Eastern Europe. In March 1965, a seven-hour-long debate took place in the Bundestag, which is considered one of the most important parliamentary debates in the history of the country.[16]

The reasons put forward in the debate by Ewald Bucher and others for upholding the statute of limitations were mainly judicial. A retrospective change of the closing date for the statute was considered incompatible with the main principle of the West German constitutional law.[17] A change in the law that would affect people retrospectively would, it was argued, be a threat to the rule of law and undermine the public faith in the judicial system. The prohibition of retrospective legislation is part of the so-called principle of legality requiring that one cannot be convicted and punished for an act that was not prohibited by law at the time it was committed.[18]

Whether an extension of the statute of limitations would run counter to the principle of legality and thus oppose the very foundation of the modern constitutional state was, however, disputed by lawyers. The strongest proponent for an extension of the statute, Ernst Benda, a lawyer and the Bundestag politician for the Christian Democratic Union and later interior minister, asserted that extending the statute required only a revision of the penal code, by no means any changes in the constitutional law.[19] A defence of the constitutional state should moreover imply, Benda argued, an effort to reach greatest possible justice rather than a loyalty to formal aspects of current legislation.[20]

Shortly before the Bundestag debate the journal *Der Spiegel* published a dialogue between the journal's editor Rudolf Augstein and the philosopher Karl Jaspers, in which Jaspers forcefully argued in favour of a special legislation based on the legal notions of genocide and imprescriptibility; the crimes of the Nazis are fundamentally different from crimes committed by individual persons.[21] The Bundestag debate about the statute of limitations did not, however, result in any amendments of the law. In spite of the fact that 'genocide' and 'crimes against humanity' were legal notions that had entered the West German penal code in the mid-1950s, the resistance was too strong to give them any retrospective effect. The Bundestag debates and voting resulted in a compromise arrangement which postponed the time limit five years to 1970. Only in 1979 was the issue finally settled by a Bundestag decision about the annulment of the statute of limitations for murder generally.[22]

The debate on the statute exposed opposing understandings of the law: a formal judicial perspective focussing on the rule of law clashed with an outlook calling for justice and moral *Wiedergutmachung* (reparation) for the victims.[23] Legal and moral arguments were set against each other. Moreover, different temporalities collided. The principle of the nonapplicability of the statutory limitations marks a new temporal figure within the domain of the law. An idea of time as irreversible, in which the past is seen as irrevocably gone came into conflict with an idea of ethical time in which events of the past can be acted upon as if they were taking place in an expanding present.

The Importance of Forgetting, the Need to Remember

Time is a fundamental motive for effecting a statute of limitation. The need of a statute is often motivated by a reference to common sense ideas of the flow of time. The saying 'time heals all wounds' is frequently present in the argumentation. The urge to investigate, prosecute and punish an act that took place in the past is supposed to decrease as time goes by, as is the social turbulence generated by it.[24]

The time limit also corresponds to the general assumption that the availability and reliability of evidence gradually decreases, which endangers the right of the defendant to a fair hearing.[25] A recurrent argument for the statute is moreover 'the need to forget' in order to maintain social stability.[26] Statutes of limitations are often referred to as a socially ratified or institutionalized forgetting.[27] At the time of the debate about the statute of limitations for Nazi crimes, it was emphasized that social cohesion is dependent upon an ability to turn the page on the past and face the future, as well as the importance of not letting younger generations inherit the conflicts of their parents and grandparents.[28]

In Vladimir Jankélévitch's forceful criticism against an approaching deadline for investigating and prosecuting Nazi perpetrators, he rejects the main arguments in favour of a statute one by one. The arguments, he claims, do not apply to systematic crimes committed by a regime against part of its own population.[29] The crimes have put the principle of effecting a statute of limitations out of play. Later generations are standing at an abyss – morally, legally and temporally. The belief in a time that heals all wounds is forever lost: 'Pardoning died in the death camps', he writes.[30] Jankélévitch points out that the amount of evidence has significantly increased during the twenty years passed since the end of the war, contrary to the general assumption of a gradual loss of reliable evidence.[31] He stresses the informative and emotional backlog characteristic of the camp experiences, which overrules the conventional time of justice. The knowledge of what happened is still growing after twenty years, as well as the realizations of the effects, Jankélévitch continues. The emotions among the affected do not gradually decline, but rather grow in strength. Those who did not want to see are slowly realizing the immense proportions of what happened. And the survivors, he notes, 'rub their eyes in amazement, they learn every day what they already knew – knew, but not fully . . . they look at one another in silence'.[32]

Jankélévitch sharply criticizes the fact that the question of the statute of limitations for Nazi crimes is to be decided by West German legislators. The crimes are international, he stresses, and should not be judged by a national court. They are, he continues, crimes against humanity rather than crimes against individuals.[33] For these 'metaphysical' crimes, a statute of limitations would not only be immoral but moreover lead to a repetition of the crime: 'When an act denies the essence of a human being as a human being, the statutory limitations that in the name of morality would lead one to absolve that act itself contradict morality. . . . To forget this gigantic crime against humanity would be a new crime against the human species.'[34]

Jankélévitch is here articulating several of the arguments that later constituted the international principle of the nonapplicability of the statute of limitation, and which is an axiomatic point of reference in today's discussions of crimes against humanity and war crimes. He articulates, sometimes literally, the arguments from the French parliamentary debates. And he repeats a sentence that can be found in the political discussions precipitating the new bill in France: 'Crimes against humanity are *imprescriptible,* that is, the penalties against them *cannot* lapse; time has no hold on them.'[35] Jankélévitch articulates this sentence – time has no hold on the crimes – as a call to us, living in the future, to change our common sense understanding of the relation between time and justice; if time has no hold on these crimes, it means that we all have to assume responsibility in order not to retrospectively become accomplices of crimes already committed in the past. There is no moral statute of limitations for us either; the responsibility is never ending for us all – also for the ones later to come.

Justice as Reversible Time

Strikingly, Jankélévitch's intervention reveals the tacit temporal assumptions about time in the debate about the statute. The idea of a statute of limitations rests heavily upon a conception of linear time in which the past is seen as automatically disappearing into the present and which makes society's administration of justice less and less urgent as time goes by. Time sweeps everything away in its relentless onward march, and the statute of limitations is thus simply an acceptance of its omnipotence.

Jankélévitch emphasizes that time is no moral instance. He points to the absurdity that time *as such* would regulate the moral and legal questions of guilt and responsibility: 'It is in general incomprehensible that time, a natural process without normative value, could have a diminishing effect on the unbearable horror of Auschwitz.'[36] His critique shows that the statute of limitations is not a response to a natural course of things but a social institution that uses the flow of biological time as an argument for advancing a certain moral and political standpoint. Through society's reference to time as a neutral and natural phenomenon, the time of the victims appears as a deviation from an unspoken temporal normativity. Jankélévitch thus reveals that a statute of limitations is a manifestation of a certain time politics, which favours the perpetrators rather than the victims.[37]

Jankélévitch's texts are a frontal attack against the concept of time that has modelled the principle of a statute – against the tacit assumption that events occurring in time are automatically transformed into past events – and ask why the importance of a legal administration of justice gradually diminishes: 'Twenty years are enough, it would seem, for the unpardonable to become miraculously pardonable: by right and from one day to the next the unforgettable is forgotten. A crime that had been unpardonable until May 1965 thus suddenly ceases to be so in June – as if by magic.'[38] He calls attention not only to the arbitrariness of the statute's time frame; by describing the statute of limitations as 'the official or legal forgetting', he argues that it is a way for society to legally sanction its desire to forget, to leave the past as well as the victims behind.[39] By turning forgiveness, forgetting and the law into aspects of the same phenomenon, forgiveness appears as the moral equivalent to the statute of the law.[40] He relates both to a desire to forget. The statute, he writes sarcastically, is nothing else but a society's way of sanctioning this desire: 'Forgetfulness had already done its work before statutory limitations; after statutory limitations forgetfulness would become in a sense official and normative. Our epoch is indeed lighthearted. From here on we would have the *right* to be lighthearted; we would have a juridically light heart.'[41]

Against society's time – a time which passes, which heals all wounds, which makes us forget and forgive – Jankélévitch makes visible another time, the time of the victim – a time that does not pass, that incessantly relives the horrors – and he points to the fundamental conflict between them. His accounts of a past that does not pass have much in common with what later research calls 'trauma time', which Jankélévitch himself expressed with an ironic twist as 'our inability to settle the past [*liquider le passé*]'.[42] It would be misleading, however, to understand Jankélévitch's attack on the silent primacy of chronological time as an expression of trauma time. Such an understanding would risk losing sight of the social and political edge of his critique, which broadly understood is a questioning of the entire modern regime of temporality, underpinning the dominant time of modern society.[43]

Time has no hold on the crimes – that is why we cannot range them in a chronological space according to an idea of the irreversible flow of time. Within ethical time or the time of justice, institutionalized as a legal principle of imprescriptibility, the chronological temporal scheme that situates the crime as something belonging to the past is simply ruled out in favour of a moral turning back of time. The past is reclaimed as an ethical space where past, present and future coincide. In the debate on the statute of limitations, and particularly through Jankélévitch's intervention, time appears as a cultural convention, a social institution, a legal category, a political phenomenon, a moral instance and, above all, not merely a natural process.

Temporal Intertwinements

What are we to make of the current intertwinement of historiography and the law? What does it mean that historians today, to an ever larger extent, have to deal with 'the new temporality of imprescriptibility'?[44]

The assumption about the relation between time and justice that shaped the idea of a statute of limitations – that social cohesion rests upon an ability to forget and let go of a violent past – has in the time of imprescriptibility been inverted to a duty to remember. The past as a growing arena for present claims, confessions and accusations is made visible by the UN articulated "right to the truth" in international law, which is motivated by the assumption that a society with a violent past has to get to the bottom of what happened and gain clarity about the events of the past in order to ensure long-term stability.[45] The right to the truth offers victims of crimes against humanity, war crimes and genocide the right to know the truth about the circumstances of the crimes – even in those cases where the perpetrators have not been prosecuted or have been given amnesty. The right can be claimed by victims during their entire lives. This is also the case for their families in the first and second generations, which means that the right can be expanded across two centuries. This right thus affects in important respects the work of the historian, as it is, in the words of historian Antoon de Baets, a 'right to *historical* truth' or even a 'right to history'.[46] De Baets describes the recent developments by emphasizing the appearance of an 'historical imprescriptibility' as an effect of the expansion of the legal principle to the domain of historiography.[47]

The appearance of the notion of imprescriptibility 'means concretely that the time of justice and the time of history no longer are separated', states historian and Vichy specialist Henry Rousso.[48] Even if Rousso emphasizes the ambiguous relation between history and justice present since the institutionalization of history as a scientific discipline, he sees a danger in their current intertwinement. He emphasizes that the task of the historian is to understand, not to judge, the past.[49] This is true and important. The judge and the historian relate to time and the past very differently. The judge always has the final say; her task is to close the case, settle the conflict. The task of the historian is rather to keep the case open. The binary logic of legal justice (the judgement either grants discharge or gives the benefit of the doubt; the prosecuted is either released or convicted), does not apply to historical justice, which remains open-ended and in a way always undecided. The verdict is set; history changes.[50] Against this background, historians are understandably the sharpest critics of the so-called memory laws that many European countries have passed in recent decades, which legally prescribes a society's collective memory by criminalizing certain interpretations of emotionally and politically charged historical events.[51]

The debate about the memory laws reveals different understandings of the task of the historian. It also exposes our ambiguous relation to the past as something not-absent, something which in spite of its pastness, of its not-being-there-anymore, still exists to be recalled and claimed.[52] The disagreement can thus also be seen as an expression of a temporal conflict that constitutes our very relation to the past *as history* – between, on the one hand, a time that is forever gone and that we through the doing of history can make present again in its absence by representations of material traces, and, on the other, a time that is still with us as a dimension of the present and that we for different reasons cannot leave behind. In contrast to conventional history understood as representations, this past is present to us in often unrepresented ways, or rather, in ways that are not so easily representable – a past in the form, one might say, of a historical *un*conscious. The writing of history thus appears not only as an effort to represent what no longer is, but as much an effort to capture a past that dwells in the present without making its presence easily representable. Historians' current interest in the present would, in this regard, is possible to understand as a way to expose 'the unrepresented way the past is present in the present', in the words of historian Eelco Runia.[53]

Vladimir Jankélévitch situated his critique against the irreversibility of time within the domain of the law. But legal justice was for him secondary. He fought for historical justice in relation to human suffering. He wanted history to take the form of a wound painful also for the ones later to come, arguing for an imprescriptible past that does not cease to morally call upon the present and the future.

The appearance of the principle of imprescriptibility has without doubt made it more difficult to separate the time of jurisprudence from the time of history. It has also, however, helped us to more clearly distinguish between different temporalities and their political significance and to question time as a unidirectional phenomenon. The letter of the law, the legal definition of crime, punishment and guilt, should not determine the historian's ethical relation to the past. Nevertheless, the temporal space opened up by the principle of imprescriptibility has forced historians to raise questions about the relation between history and justice. It has given them new possibilities to self-critically examine the temporal norms silently active at the core of their own writing, to expose the chrononormativity of historical time.[54]

Today, we can see a rapidly growing interest among historians to examine the temporal assumptions governing academic historiography.[55] The current rethinking of historical temporality questions the presumed and naturalized idea of past, present and future as separate and objective entities. In so doing, it surely challenges the dominant idea of time within conventional historiography. This rethinking, however, should not be seen as a threat to the discipline of history, but rather as ways to develop and even intensify the important work of Reinhart Koselleck, François Hartog and others who gather in their effort to historicize historical time. Against this background, the ongoing temporal explorations among historians are indeed expressions of a changing *ethos*, of a renegotiation of what constitutes the core of the historian's enterprise: how the transition between past, present and future, indeed how historical time, should be discursively understood and epistemically and ethically regulated.

Victoria Fareld is associate professor of intellectual history at Stockholm University (Sweden). Her research interests focus on historical time, ethics, memory and historical justice. Among her recent publications are '(In) Between the Living and the Dead: New Perspectives on Time in History' (2016) and '*Ressentiment* as Moral Imperative: Jean Améry's Nietzschean Revaluation of Victim Morality' (2016).

Notes

1. For an illuminating discussion of the ethical demands of a historiography dealing with these issues, see G.M. Spiegel, 'The Future of the Past: History, Memory and the Ethical Imperatives of Writing History', *Journal of the Philosophy of History* 8 (2014), 149–79. Some important works in this field are M. Roth and C. Salas (eds), *Disturbing Remains: Memory, History and Crisis in the Twentieth Century* (Los Angeles: Getty Research Institute, 2001); M. Roth, *Memory, Trauma and History: Essays on Living with the Past* (New York: Columbia University Press, 2012); F.R. Ankersmit, *Sublime Historical Experience* (Palo Alto: Stanford University Press, 2005); B. Bevernage, *History, Memory and State-Sponsored Violence: Time and Justice* (New York: Routledge, 2012); E. Runia, *Moved by the Past: Discontinuity and Historical Mutation* (New York: Columbia University Press, 2014).

2. This article is a revised version of an article previously published in Swedish, 'Tiden har inget grepp om brotten: Om historien och det icke-preskriberbara', in P. Lorenzoni and U. Manns (eds), *Historiens hemvist II: Etik, politik och historikerns ansvar* (Stockholm: Makadam, 2016), 271–93.

3. For a thorough analysis of the Demjanjuk case, see L. Douglas, *The Right Wrong Man: John Demjanjuk and the Last Great Nazi War Crimes Trial* (Princeton: Princeton University Press, 2016).

4. F. Bohr, 'Late Case Raises Questions about Justice System', *Spiegel Online International*, 30 September 2013, retrieved 18 December 2016 from http://www.spiegel.de/international/germany/former-auschwitz-worker-hans-lipschis-faces-trial-a-925247.html; 'Ehemalige KZ-Wachmann: Gericht erklärt Hans Lipschis für verhandlungsunfähig', *Spiegel Online*, 6 December 2013, retrieved 18 December 2016 from http://www.spiegel.de/panorama/justiz/gericht-erklaert-kz-wachmann-hans-lipschis-fuer-verhandlungsunfaehig-a-937660.html.

5. See, for instance, historian H. Rousso's discussions of why he refused to testify in the Papon and Touvier trials in France, in idem, *Haunting Past: History, Memory and Justice in Contemporary France* (Philadelphia: University of Pennsylvania Press, 2002); see also S. Löytömäki, *Law and the Politics of Memory: Confronting the Past* (New York: Routledge, 2014).

6. C. Sharples, 'In Pursuit of Justice: Debating the Statute of Limitations for Nazi War Crimes in Britain and West Germany during the 1960s', *Holocaust Studies* 20(3) (2014), 82, note 3.

7. An exception is the work of A. de Baets, see his *Responsible History* (New York: Berghahn, 2009); idem, 'Historical Imprescriptibility', *Storia della Storiografia*, 59–60 (2011), 128–49.

8. The time limit for the worst Nazi crimes was set at the time of Germany's surrender and the end of the Third Reich and not, in accordance with legal praxis, from the time when the crime was committed.

9. About the international responses to the statute, see Sharples, 'In Pursuit of Justice', 90–95, 103, note 43. See also C. Moisel, *Frankreich und die deutschen Kriegsverbrecher: Politik und Praxis der Strafverfolgung nach dem Zweiten Weltkrieg* (Göttingen: Wallstein, 2014), 175–77.

10. V. Jankélévitch, 'L'Imprescriptible', *Le Monde*, 4 January 1965.

11. *Le Code pénal. Livre II, Des crimes et delits contre les personnes,* Article 213-5, Loi no. 64-1326, décembre 1964, retrieved 18 December 2016 from http://www.legifrance.gouv .fr/affichCode.do?cidTexte=LEGITEXT000006070719; see also Moisel, *Frankreich,* 169–70.

12. 'Ni prescription, ni oubli!', *Droit et liberté* 239 (January 1965); 'Des crimes hitleriens! L'ardente soirée de l'Hôtel Moderne', *Droit et liberté* 239 (January 1965), 5: 'Un scandale judiciaire et morale, mais aussi un scandale politique'. See also G. Levasseur, 'Les crimes contre l'humanité et le problème de leur prescription', *Journal du droit international,* 2 (1966), 259–84.

13. M.C. Bassiouni, *Crimes against Humanity in International Criminal Law* (Dordrecht: M. Nijhoff Publishers, 1992). See also *Convention on the Non-applicability of Statutory Limitations* (New York: United Nations, 1968).

14. See Bucher's address in '1964/65 – Die grossen Debatten in der 4. Wahlperiode des Bundestages. Die erste Beratung von Regierungsbericht und Anträgen. 170. Sitzung des 4. Bundetages am 10.3. 1965', in *Zur Verjährung nationalsozialistischer Verbrechen. Dokumentation der parlamentarischen Bewältigung des Problems 1960–1979,* vol. 1 (Bonn: Deutsche Bundestag, 1980), 147: 'Unverständnis'. Bucher himself had, as many others in leading positions in post war German society, a history as a member of NSDAP and SA. He was even rewarded with a distinction in gold for a major achievement by the Hitler Jugend, see 'NS-Verbrechen, Verjährung: Gesundes Volksempfinden', *Der Spiegel,* 11 (1965), 33.

15. In March 1965, the result of an opinion poll was published showing that 63 per cent of the male and 76 per cent of the female West German population were in favour of upholding the statute; see 'NS-Verbrechen, Verjährung', 31.

16. Moisel, *Frankreich,* 178. For a thorough analysis of the political debates, see M. von Miguel, *Ahnden oder amnestieren? Westdeutsche Justiz und Vergangenheitspolitik in den sechziger Jahren* (Göttingen: Wallstein, 2004).

17. In accordance with article 103, section 2 in the German constitutional law, see *Grundgesetzt für die Bundesrepublik Deutschland: GG – Einzelnorm, Art. 3,* retrieved 18 December 2016 from http://www.gesetze-im-internet.de/gg/art_103.html. See also *Zur Verjährung nationalsozialistischer Verbrechen. Dokumentation der parlamentarischen Bewältigung des Problems 1960–1979,* vol. 1 (Bonn: Deutsche Bundestag, 1980), 12, 15, 19, 36–37.

18. See Bucher's address in '1964/65 – Die grossen Debatten in der 4. Wahlperiode des Bundestage', 35–39; A. Weinke, *Die Verfolgung von NS-Tätern im geteilten Deutschland: Vergangenheitsbewältigungen 1949–1969, oder, Eine deutsch-deutsche Beziehungsgeschichte im Kalten Krieg* (Paderborn: Ferdinand Schöningh, 2002), 187–88.

19. See Benda's address in '1964/65 – Die grossen Debatten in der 4. Wahlperiode des Bundestage', 152–66; D. Strothmann, 'Bleiben die Mörder unter uns? Das Ende der Verjährungsfrist – eine Streit ohne Ende', *Die Zeit,* 27 November 1964; Weinke, *Die Verfolgung,* 193.

20. Benda's address in '1964/65 – Die grossen Debatten in der 4. Wahlperiode des Bundestage', 157.

21. K. Jaspers, 'Für Völkermord gibt es keine Verjährung', in *Die Schuldfrage; Für Völkermord gibt es keine Verjährung* (Munich: Piper, 1979), 97–123.

22. About the 1979 debate, see *Zur Verjährung nationalsozialistischer Verbrechen. Dokumentation der parlamentarischen Bewältigung des Problems 1960–1979,* vol. 2–3 (Bonn: Deutsche Bundestag, 1980), 439–819; Moisel, *Frankreich,* 180.

23. P. Reichel, *Vergangenheitsbewältigung in Deutschland: Die Auseinandersetzung mit der NS-Diktatur in Politik und Justiz,* 2nd ed. (Munich: C.H. Beck, 2007), 188.

24. R.A. Kok, *Statutory Limitations in International Criminal Law* (The Hague: T.M.C. Asser Press, 2007), 239, 269.

25. Kok, *Statutory Limitations,* 246, 257.

26. F. Desportes and F. Le Gunehec, *Droit pénal général,* 9th ed. (Paris: Economica, 2002), 942: 'La première justification de la prescription est la nécessité d'oublier'.

27. Levasseur, 'Crimes contre l'humanité', 276: 'l'oubli (ce fondement capital de l'institution de la prescription)'. See also P. Ricoeur, 'À l'horizon de la prescription: l'oubli', in F.

Barret- Ducrocq (ed.), *Pourquoi se souvenir?: Forum international mémoire et histoire UNESCO, 25 mars 1998, La Sorbonne, 26 mars 1998* (Paris: Bernard Grasset, 1999), 95.

28. Cf. J. Georgel, *Le Monde*, 28 December, 1964.

29. Jankélévitch's text, originally published in *Le Monde*, was extended and published as a longer article, also with the title 'L'Imprescriptible', in February 1965 in *Revue administrative* 18(103) (1965), 37–42. Another extended version, with the title 'Pardonner?', was originally published in 1971; see V. Jankélévitch, *L'Imprescriptible: Pardonner? Dans l'honneur et la dignité* (Paris: Seuil, 1986). In this article, I refer exclusively to the English translation of 'Pardonner?', in V. Jankélévitch, 'Should We Pardon Them?', trans. A. Hobart, *Critical Inquiry* 22(3) (1996), 552–72.

30. Jankélévitch, 'Should We Pardon Them?', 567.

31. Jankélévitch, 'Should We Pardon Them?', 557. His arguments have been confirmed by later research: see Kok, *Statutory*, 244–45; R.G. Teitel, *Transitional Justice* (Oxford: Oxford University Press, 2000), 65.

32. Jankélévitch, 'Should We Pardon Them?', 553.

33. Jankélévitch, 'Should We Pardon Them?', 553–54.

34. Jankélévitch, 'Should We Pardon Them?', 556.

35. Jankélévitch, 'Should We Pardon Them?', 556–57. Cf. 'Imprescriptibilité des crimes contre l'humanité: Discussion d'une proposition de loi', in *Journal Officiel de la République Française Assemblée Nationale*, 17 December 1964, 6141–66, retrieved 18 December 2016 from http://archives.assemblee-nationale.fr/2/cri/1964-1965-ordinaire1/082.pdf.

36. Jankélévitch, 'Should We Pardon Them?', 557.

37. B. Bevernage has similarly to Jankélévitch emphasized 'the temporal antagonism between history and justice' in terms of irreversible versus reversible time, in idem, *History, Memory, and State-Sponsored Violence*, 2–3.

38. Jankélévitch, 'Should We Pardon Them?', 553.

39. Jankélévitch, 'Should We Pardon Them?', 553.

40. For a critique of the blurring between forgiveness and prescription in Jankélévitch, see J. Derrida, *On Cosmopolitanism and Forgiveness*, trans. M. Dooley and M. Hughes (London: Routledge, 2001), 33–38. About Jankélévitch's contradictory concept of forgiveness, see J. Hansel, 'Forgiveness and "Should We Pardon Them?": The Pardon and the Imprescriptible', in A. Udoff (ed.), *Vladimir Jankélévitch and the Question of Forgiveness* (Lanham: Lexington Books, 2013), 111–25.

41. Jankélévitch, 'Should We Pardon Them?', 566.

42. Jankélévitch, 'Should We Pardon Them?', 572; idem, 'L'Imprescriptible', 42.

43. For the concept of temporal regimes, see F. Hartog's *Regimes of Historicity: Presentism and Experiences of Time*, trans. S. Brown (New York: Columbia University Press, 2015).

44. F. Hartog, 'Time and Heritage', *Museum International* 57(227) (2005), 8.

45. General Assembly Resolution 68/165: *Right to the Truth*, A/RES/67/97, Resolution adopted by the General Assembly on 18 December 2013, United Nations official document, 21 January 2014, retrieved 18 December 2016 from http://www.un.org/en/ga/search/view_doc.asp?symbol=A/RES/68/165.

46. De Baets, *Responsible History*, 155.

47. De Baets, 'Historical Imprescriptibility', 128–49.

48. H. Rousso, 'Juger le passé? Justice et histoire en France', in F. Brayard (ed.), *Le génocide des Juifs: entre procès et histoire, 1943–2000* (Paris: Editions complexes, 2001), 265: 'Cette notion . . . signifie concrètement que le temps de la justice et le temps de l'histoire ne sont plus séparés'.

49. Rousso, 'Juger le passé?', 261.

50. Cf. A. Garapon, 'La justice et l'inversion morale du temps', in F. Barret-Ducrocq (ed.), *Pourquoi se souvenir?: Forum international mémoire et histoire UNESCO, 25 mars 1998, a Sor-*

bonne, 26 mars 1998 (Paris: Bernard Grasset, 1999), 122–23; P. Ricoeur, *Memory, History, Forgetting*, trans. K. Blamey and D. Pellauer (Chicago: University of Chicago Press, 2004), 314–33.

51. See the French movement *Liberté pour l'histoire*, established by P. Nora in 2005 with the aim of abolishing the memory laws in France, accessed 18 December 2016 from http://www.lph-asso.fr; see also R. Rémond, *Quand l'État se mêle de l'Histoire* (Paris: Stock, 2006).

52. E. Domanska, 'The Material Presence of the Past', *History and Theory* 45 (2006), 345–46.

53. E. Runia, 'Spots of Time", *History and Theory* 45 (2006), 305–6.

54. The concept of 'chrononormativity' is taken from E. Freeman's *Time Binds: Queer Temporalities, Queer Histories, Perverse Modernities* (Durham, NC: Duke University Press, 2010), 3.

55. See, for instance, B. Bevernage, 'The Past is Evil/Evil is Past: On Retrospective Politics, Philosophy of History, and Temporal Manichaeism', *History and Theory* 54 (Oct 2015), 333–52; B. Bevernage and C. Lorenz (eds), *Breaking Up Time: Negotiating the Borders between Past, Present and Future* (Göttingen: Vandenhoeck & Ruprecht, 2013); A. Assmann, *Ist die Zeit aus den Fugen? Aufstieg und Fall des Zeitregimes der Moderne* (Munich: Hanser, 2013); S. Tanaka, 'History without Chronology', *Public Culture* 28(1) (2015), 161–86.

Bibliography

'1964/65 – Die grossen Debatten in der 4. Wahlperiode des Bundestages. Die erste Beratung von Regierungsbericht und Anträgen. 170. Sitzung des 4. Bundetages am 10.3. 1965', in *Zur Verjährung nationalsozialistischer Verbrechen. Dokumentation der parlamentarischen Bewältigung des Problems 1960–1979*. Bonn: Deutsche Bundestag, 1980.

Ankersmit, F.R. *Sublime Historical Experience*. Palo Alto: Stanford University Press, 2005.

Assmann, A. *Ist die Zeit aus den Fugen? Aufstieg und Fall des Zeitregimes der Moderne*. Munich: Hanser, 2013.

Bassiouni, M.C. *Crimes against Humanity in International Criminal Law*. Dordrecht: M. Nijhoff Publishers, 1992.

Bevernage, B. *History, Memory, and State-Sponsored Violence: Time and Justice*. New York: Routledge, 2012.

———. 'The Past is Evil/Evil is Past: On Retrospective Politics, Philosophy of History, and Temporal Manichaeism'. *History and Theory* 54 (Oct 2015), 333–52.

Bevernage, B., and C. Lorenz (eds). *Breaking Up Time: Negotiating the Borders between Past, Present and Future*. Göttingen: Vandenhoeck & Ruprecht, 2013.

Bohr, F. 'Late Case Raises Questions about Justice System'. *Spiegel Online International*, 30 September 2013. Retrieved 18 December 2016 from http://www.spiegel.de/international/germany/former-auschwitz-worker-hans-lipschis-faces-trial-a-925247.html.

Le Code pénal. Livre II, Des crimes et delits contre les personnes, Article 213–5, Loi no. 64–1326, décembre 1964. Retrieved 18 December 2016 from http://www.legifrance.gouv.fr/affichCode.do?cidTexte=LEGITEXT000006070719.

Convention on the Non-applicability of Statutory Limitations. New York: United Nations, 1968.

de Baets, A. *Responsible History*. New York: Berghahn, 2009.

———. 'Historical Imprescriptibility'. *Storia della Storiografia* 59–60 (2011), 128–49.

'Des crimes hitleriens! L'ardente soirée de l'Hôtel Moderne'. *Droit et liberté* 239 (January 1965).

Derrida, J. *On Cosmopolitanism and Forgiveness*, trans. M. Dooley and M. Hughes. London: Routledge, 2001.

Desportes, F., and F. Le Gunehec. *Droit pénal général*, 9th ed. Paris: Economica, 2002.

Domanska, E. 'The Material Presence of the Past'. *History and Theory* 45 (2006), 337–48.

Douglas, L. *The Right Wrong Man: John Demjanjuk and the Last Great Nazi War Crimes Trial.* Princeton: Princeton University Press, 2016.

'Ehemalige KZ-Wachmann: Gericht erklärt Hans Lipschis für verhandlungsunfähig'. *Spiegel Online,* 6 December 2013. Retrieved 18 December 2016 from http://www.spiegel.de/panorama/justiz/gericht-erklaert-kz-wachmann-hans-lipschis-fuer-verhandlungsunfaehig-a-937660.html.

Freeman, E. *Time Binds: Queer Temporalities, Queer Histories, Perverse Modernities.* Durham, NC: Duke University Press, 2010.

Garapon, A. 'La justice et l'inversion morale du temps', in F. Barret- Ducrocq (ed.), *Pourquoi se souvenir?: Forum international mémoire et histoire UNESCO, 25 mars 1998, La Sorbonne, 26 mars 1998* (Paris: Bernard Grasset, 1999), 113–24.

General Assembly Resolution 68/165: *Right to the Truth.* A/RES/67/97. Resolution adopted by the General Assembly on 18 December 2013. United Nations official document, 21 January 2014. Retrieved 18 December 2016 from http://www.un.org/en/ga/search/view_doc.asp?symbol=A/RES/68/165.

Georgel, J. 'Libres opinions'. *Le Monde,* 28 December 1964.

Grundgesetz für die Bundesrepublik Deutschland: GG – Einzelnorm, Art. 3. Retrieved 18 December 2016 from http://www.gesetze-im-internet.de/gg/art_103.html.

'Imprescriptibilité des crimes contre l'humanité: Discussion d'une proposition de loi', in *Journal Officiel de la République Française Assemblée Nationale,* 17 December 1964, 6141–66. Retrieved 18 December 2016 from http://archives.assemblee-nationale.fr/2/cri/1964-1965-ordinaire1/082.pdf.

Jankélévitch, V. 'L'Imprescriptible'. *Le Monde,* 4 January 1965.

———. *L'Imprescriptible: Pardonner? Dans l'honneur et la dignité.* Paris: Seuil, 1986.

———. 'Should We Pardon Them?', trans. A. Hobart. *Critical Inquiry* 22(3) (1996), 552–72.

Jaspers, K. 'Für Völkermord gibt es keine Verjährung', in *Die Schuldfrage; Für Völkermord gibt es keine Verjährung* (Munich: Piper, 1979), 97–123.

Hansel, J. 'Forgiveness and "Should We Pardon Them?": The Pardon and the Imprescriptible', in A. Udoff (ed.), *Vladimir Jankélévitch and the Question of Forgiveness* (Lanham: Lexington Books, 2013), 111–25.

Hartog, F. *Regimes of Historicity: Presentism and Experiences of Time,* trans. Saskia Brown. New York: Columbia University Press, 2015.

———. 'Time and Heritage'. *Museum International* 57(227) (2005), 7–18.

Kok, R.A. *Statutory Limitations in International Criminal Law.* The Hague: T.M.C. Asser Press, 2007.

Levasseur, G. 'Les crimes contre l'humanité et le problème de leur prescription'. *Journal du droit international* 2 (1966), 259–84.

Liberté pour l'Histoire (website). Accessed 18 December 2016 from http://www.lph-asso.fr.

Löytömäki, S. *Law and the Politics of Memory: Confronting the Past.* New York: Routledge, 2014.

Moisel, C. *Frankreich und die deutschen Kriegsverbrecher: Politik und Praxis der Strafverfolgung nach dem Zweiten Weltkrieg.* Göttingen: Wallstein, 2014.

Miguel, M. von. *Ahnden oder amnestieren? Westdeutsche Justiz und Vergangenheitspolitik in den sechziger Jahren.* Göttingen: Wallstein, 2004.

'Ni prescription, ni oubli!'. *Droit et liberté* 239 (January 1965).

'NS-Verbrechen, Verjährung: Gesundes Volksempfinden'. *Der Spiegel,* no. 11, 10 March 1965.

Reichel, P. *Vergangenheitsbewältigung in Deutschland: Die Auseinandersetzung mit der NS-Diktatur in Politik und Justiz,* 2nd ed. Munich: C.H. Beck, 2007.

Rémond, R. *Quand l'État se mêle de l'Histoire.* Paris: Stock, 2006.

Ricoeur, P. 'À l'horizon de la prescription: l'oubli', in F. Barret-Ducrocq (ed.), *Pourquoi se souvenir?: Forum international mémoire et histoire UNESCO, 25 mars 1998, La Sorbonne, 26 mars 1998* (Paris: Bernard Grasset, 1999), 92–95.

————. *Memory, History, Forgetting*, trans. Kathleen Blamey and David Pellauer. Chicago: University of Chicago Press, 2004.

Roth, M. *Memory, Trauma and History: Essays on Living with the Past*. New York: Columbia University Press, 2012.

Roth, M. and C. Salas (eds). *Disturbing Remains: Memory, History and Crisis in the Twentieth Century*. Los Angeles: Getty Research Institute, 2001.

Rousso, H. *Haunting Past: History, Memory and Justice in Contemporary France*. Philadelphia: University of Pennsylvania Press, 2002.

————. 'Juger le passé? Justice et histoire en France', in F. Brayard (ed.), *Le génocide des Juifs: entre procès et histoire, 1943–2000* (Paris: Editions complexes, 2001), 261–87.

Runia, E. *Moved by the Past: Discontinuity and Historical Mutation*. New York: Columbia University Press, 2014.

————. 'Spots of Time', *History and Theory* 45 (2006), 305–16.

Sharples, C. 'In Pursuit of Justice: Debating the Statute of Limitations for Nazi War Crimes in Britain and West Germany during the 1960s'. *Holocaust Studies* 20(3) (2014), 81–108.

Spiegel, G.M. 'The Future of the Past: History, Memory and the Ethical Imperatives of Writing History'. *Journal of the Philosophy of History* 8 (2014), 149–79.

Strothmann, D. 'Bleiben die Mörder unter uns? Das Ende der Verjährungsfrist – eine Streit ohne Ende'. *Die Zeit*, 27 November 1964.

Tanaka, S. 'History without Chronology'. *Public Culture* 28(1) (2015), 161–86.

Teitel, R.G. *Transitional Justice*. Oxford: Oxford University Press, 2000.

Weinke, A. *Die Verfolgung von NS-Tätern im geteilten Deutschland: Vergangenheitsbewältigungen 1949–1969, oder, Eine deutsch-deutsche Beziehungsgeschichte im Kalten Krieg*. Paderborn: Ferdinand Schöningh, 2002.

Zur Verjährung nationalsozialistischer Verbrechen. Dokumentation der parlamentarischen Bewältigung des Problems 1960–1979. Bonn: Deutsche Bundestag, 1980.

CHAPTER 4

Narrating Pasts for Peace?

A Critical Analysis of Some Recent Initiatives of Historical Reconciliation through 'Historical Dialogue' and 'Shared History'

BERBER BEVERNAGE

Introduction

An increasing number of policy makers, activists, therapists and academics support the idea of historical dialogue and shared histories as a way to build peace and foster reconciliation in (post)conflict situations or to combat extremism and xenophobia. In January 2014, the role of historical narratives and memory in peacebuilding and reconciliation was even chosen as a central theme for a debate in the UN Security Council under the presidency of Jordan. In a preparatory note, the representative of Jordan, Prince Zeid Ra'ad Al-Hussein, argued that the UN would fail in fully forging reconciliation among ex-combatants as long as it did not see that an 'authentic, irreversible peace' should be based on 'a shared historical understanding'. According to Al-Hussein, lingering historical grievances and 'unresolved' historical narratives pose a major treat for international peace. Divergent historical narratives should be recognized as one of the 'leading causes' of war. Since the 'prerequisite for any shared narrative is the availability of the documents of State', Jordan asked the Security Council to 'consider mandating a small United Nations historical advisory team' that could assist states in recovering archives or setting up historical commissions once the guns go quiet.[1]

Notes for this section begin on page 85.

It is uncertain whether the idea of a UN historical advisory team will ever materialize. The idea seemed sensitive for many delegations, and, in the discussion that followed, historical reconciliation seemed far off: China and the People's Republic of Korea charged Japan of not fully repenting for its crimes during World War II; Armenia and Turkey accused each other of twisting historical facts, and other countries put the continuing debt of colonialism on the table. In contrast, some countries warned against the dangers of revisiting old historical narratives. Others supported the notion of creating shared narratives but seemed to have radically different ideas about what this would mean. Still others – such as Kenya and Chad – argued that inequality, social injustice, poverty and impunity are the prime global causes of conflict. Finally, the representative of France argued that 'it is not history that causes or fuels conflicts. It is conflicts that fashion history in their own image.'[2]

I have long kept myself from engaging with the theme of historical reconciliation because I find it a very enigmatic notion that sometimes clashes with my sense of justice – especially when it happens top-down or is forced upon victims. Due to debates such as the one just described, however, I have become convinced that the question of historical reconciliation deserves critical attention. I should immediately remark, however, that I will not consider the questions of the impact or feasibility of using historiography and historical narratives for reconciliatory purposes in this chapter. These questions are very important ones, and the fact that very few empirical studies exist about this subject is a serious problem.[3] But measuring scales of reconciliation and the impact of reconciliatory initiatives is a very difficult task for which I do not see myself fit. The aim of this chapter, in contrast, is rather modest: I merely want to illustrate the great diversity of existing discourses and practices that aim to promote reconciliation through historiography and give some preliminary reflections on their contradictions, possibilities and challenges. Readers will not find a full-fledged theory on the relation between history and reconciliation in this chapter. Yet I hope that it can serve as a preliminary study that can inspire others to work towards a more profound theoretical analysis of this relation.

Who Uses the Concepts of Historical Dialogue, Shared History and Historical Reconciliation?

The discourse on historical reconciliation is widespread. It has not only popped up in the Security Council but recently also features centrally in other spheres of the UN. In 2013 and 2014, two reports on 'historical and memorial narratives in divided and post-conflict societies' were written by

UN Special Rapporteur in the field of cultural rights, Farida Shaheed, and submitted to the General Assembly and the Human Rights Council.[4]

In the UNESCO, the idea of promoting shared history for reconciliation and peace has been around a long time. Recently, the idea has, for example, been made very explicit in the 'Routes of Dialogue' program and 'Slave Route' project based on the notion that 'ignorance or concealment of major historical events constitutes an obstacle to mutual understanding, reconciliation and cooperation among peoples'.[5]

Another international organization that strongly promotes the idea of historical reconciliation is the Council of Europe.[6] This intergovernmental body has made several recommendations on how to turn history and its teaching into a 'tool to support peace and reconciliation in conflict and post-conflict areas as well as tolerance and understanding when dealing with such phenomena as migration, immigration and changing demographics'.[7] The Council of Europe has recently put its concept of shared history into practice in the project Shared Histories: For a Europe without Dividing Lines, which ran from 2010 to 2014 and resulted in an electronic publication aiming primarily at teachers and pupils.[8]

There are also several bilateral governmental initiatives of historical dialogue or shared history. One noticeable recent example is the Chinese-Japanese joint history research committee. This committee was created in 2006 by an agreement between Japanese Prime Minister Shinzo Abe and Chinese President Hu Jintao. After a difficult negotiation process, the committee published its research results in January 2010. However, for political reasons the parallel histories produced by the Japanese and the Chinese members were published in their respective languages only. Moreover, the committee could find only the minimal necessary consensus for the publication to appear by agreeing not to discuss postwar history.[9]

The notions of historical dialogue and shared history are also strongly promoted by several NGOs and organizations of academics. One of the best-known among these organizations is the Peace Research Institute in the Middle East (PRIME), which coordinated the project Learning Each Other's Historical Narrative. This project brought together Jewish and Palestinian teachers and promoted the technique of dual or parallel narratives.[10] Other examples of recent reconciliatory textbook initiatives by historians and history teachers are the Franco-German and Chinese-Korean-Japanese ones. The Franco-German Histoire/Geschichte project resulted in the publication (between 2006 and 2011) of a series of officially recognized (yet not widely used) textbooks in French and German that aim to offer a shared vision of the history of Europe since antiquity.[11] In 2005, a nongovernmental initiative of some fifty historians, teachers and members of civil society from Japan, Korea and China led to the publication of the first joint history 'textbook' in East Asia. The same book was simultaneously published in Japanese, Korean and Chinese, but it was not recognized as an official textbook in any of the three countries where it appeared.[12]

One of the most extensive historical reconciliation projects in terms of the number of participants has probably been the Scholars' Initiative, which ran from 2001 to 2011 and focused on 'the Yugoslav Controversies'. The project coordinators (Charles W. Ingrao and Thomas Allan Emmert) gathered over three hundred scholars from thirty countries. They aimed to 'publish new, original research that exposes at least some of the myths and resolves at least some of those controversies that have foreclosed meaningful transnational communication between scholars and mutual understanding among peoples of the former Yugoslavia'.[13]

A series of smaller scale initiatives have been supervised by the Institute for Historical Justice and Reconciliation (IHJR), which was established in 2004 and in its own words is 'committed to promoting reconciliation, tolerance, and understanding in historically divided societies' by using 'the innovative and effective methodology of shared narratives'.[14] The work of the IHJR has up to now mostly resulted in a series of primarily scholarly publications focusing on the regions of Israel and the Palestinian territories, the former Yugoslavia and Armenia-Turkey.

Is the Current Focus on Historical Reconciliation, Historical Dialogue and Shared History New?

The use of shared history and historical dialogue for international reconciliation has many antecedents. The notion that a certain 'sharing' of history was needed to create a common identity for Europe and to combat extreme nationalism, for example, was a central feature of the European Cultural Convention of 1954, in which the signatories pledged to promote among their own nationals the study of 'the languages, history, and civilization' of the other European countries.[15] Similar ideas on the need for a sharing of history shortly after World War II also led UNESCO to set up or coordinate several bilateral initiatives to revise history textbooks.[16] Even earlier, during the interbellum, international textbook revision was pioneered by the League of Nations and by Föreningen Norden, the association of Nordic countries.[17]

Another set of important institutional carriers of the idea of reconciliation through history are the truth (and reconciliation) commissions (TRCs) that were first developed in the early 1980s and have in the meanwhile been established in more than thirty countries all around the world. Especially after the establishment of the South African TRC, many of these commissions have claimed that the revelation of (historical) truth can lead to political, social and even psychological reconciliation (that is, personal 'healing').[18]

These examples seem to suggest that there is nothing new about the current discourses and practices of historical reconciliation. This conclusion is misguided however: the current discourses and practices on historical reconciliation do have some new features on a quantitative as well as qualitative level. On a quantitative level, there seems to be an ever increasing number of initiatives aiming at historical reconciliation, and in the discursive realm the idea is spreading more and more broadly. In this context, the introduction of the relatively soft notion of historical reconciliation in the traditionally hard international security sector is quite remarkable. On a qualitative level, too, there are some relatively new aspects: first, the idea of reconciliation through history is increasingly seen as an exercise in sharing or reimagining historical and memorial narratives; second, and related to this, the older idea that reconciliation would mainly be served by objective truth or knowledge has increasingly been mixed with or even replaced by a stress on the importance of acknowledgement and multiperspectivity as sources of reconciliation.

To be sure, already Desmond Tutu, as president of the South African TRC, claimed that not only objective (factual or forensic) truth mattered for reconciliation, and pleaded for the inclusion of more subjective notions of truth (e.g., personal, social and healing truths). Likewise, some commentators already at the time of the South African TRC considered it misguided to conceive the revelation of truth itself as a cause of reconciliation and stressed instead the importance of narratives and storytelling.[19] Nevertheless, those focusing on narratives were a minority, and TRCs clearly obtained their rhetorical power and popularity due to their close association in popular imagination with objective truth. Moreover, several commentators have argued that truth commissions often rhetorically engage with alternative notions of truth during their public hearings but fall back on classic positivist notions of truth when writing their final reports.[20]

In the context of textbook revision and peace education, too, the stress on narratives and multiperspectivity seems to be a relatively new feature that replaces or at least fiercely challenges the older stress on a single objective historical truth. Classic textbook revision practices, as Georg Stöber remarks, aimed to objectify, de-emotionalize and demythologize textbooks and saw the academic state of the art as the model to be followed – even if they de facto created compromise narratives. Classic textbook revision was based on a practice whereby national experts would review each other's national textbooks and clear them of controversial or insulting claims or names but would not alter the national perspectives of the books; neither did they attempt to create common textbooks that would be multiperspectival and shared by two or more nations.[21]

Due to new evolutions in the thinking about the relation between history and reconciliation, current discourses and practices seem to revolve around an ambiguous conceptual mix of neopositivist and postmodernist (or post-postmodernist[22]) concepts – with some projects leaning much more to the one or the other side.

Reconciliation Historiography: A New Genre?

Can we then speak about the rise of a new historiographical genre or practice – that of reconciliation historiography or shared history? And what would be its theoretical basis? In a minimalist way, one could speak about the rise of a reconciliation historiography in the sense of a collection of histories that are written with the common aim of promoting reconciliation. Yet, if one expects this historiography to be based on a substantial level of shared epistemology, shared visions of what reconciliation means or the use of common narrative techniques to bring the latter into existence, then the answer is negative. Discourses and practices of historical reconciliation are certainly not uniform.

On the one hand, there are initiatives that believe in the power of objective scientific truth, the 'unmasking' of myths and the 'resolving' of contradictory historical narratives as a means to bridge cultural divisions. Often these initiatives consider the very divergence of historical narratives as a central problem and as one of the main causes of conflict. This approach can, for example, be found in the project Political Myths in the Former Yugoslavia and Successor States: A Shared Narrative, which was supervised by the historians Darko Gavrilovic and Vjekoslav Perica and sponsored by the IHJR and the Center for History, Democracy and Reconciliation in Serbia. A similar approach is found in The Scholar's Initiative: Confronting the Yugoslav Controversies. The problem in the former Yugoslavia, according to the organizers of this initiative, is that 'unfortunately, each national group employs a different array of facts, many of which are either distorted or blatantly untrue. The resulting, divergent recitations of history have divided nations by sowing mistrust, resentment and hatred between people who coexisted with one another for long periods of time'.[23] The objective of the Scholars' Initiative therefore is 'to bridge the gap that separates their knowledge of the tragic events of the period 1986–2000 from the proprietary interpretations that nationalist politicians and media have impressed on mass culture'. The organizers stress that they cannot resolve all issues, yet they hope to 'narrow the parameters within which opposing sides can still engage in reasoned debate'. This can be done, they claim, on the basis of the 'indisputable scientific credentials' of the involved scholars, the 'transparent impartiality' of their

shared methodology and the 'dispassionate' examination of 'key documen-
tary evidence'. The initiative wants to 'de-emphasize the importance of subjective differences in emphasis or interpretation in favor of making objective
judgments about the admissibility and validity of evidence that can establish
a single, incontrovertible factual matrix'. One of the project leaders explicitly
describes the approach as positivist.[24]

On the other hand, there are projects that primarily stress the importance of highlighting multiperspectivity and argue that narrative differences
mainly reflect subjective differences in interpretation that are often equally
legitimate. These initiatives generally have little faith in the feasibility or
usefulness of resolving narrative contradictions or bridging cognitive gaps.
Rather, they try to promote reconciliation by illustrating the different existing narratives and making them known to each of the conflicting parties in
a reflexive way. A clear example of this approach is found in the PRIME
booklets *Learning Each Other's Historical Narrative*[25] and the reworked publication *Side by Side: Parallel Histories of Israel-Palestine*,[26] supervised by Sami
Adwan, Dan Bar-On and Eyal Naveh. This project was innovative because
it presents two narratives side by side in two columns, which in the textbook
version are separated by a white column for the pupil's notes. The two narratives – of which it is claimed that they are the Palestinians' and Israelis'
national narratives and represent the perspective of 60 per cent to 70 per
cent of these societies[27] – resulted from a project that ran from 2002 until
2009, involved Palestinian and Israeli teachers and was supervised by two
professional historians. Despite, or rather because of, the fact that the project
ran during a very tense phase of the Israeli/Palestinian conflict, no attempts
are made to 'bridge' the narratives or judge their truthfulness. The authors
painstakingly attempt to give each of the narratives equal space and stress
their equal legitimacy. They call this a method of dual or parallel narratives
and posit that it could 'allow both peoples . . . to move beyond the one-
dimensional identification with their own narrative and become equipped
to acknowledge, understand, and respect (without having to accept) the
narrative of the other'.[28] Yet, they immediately warn that this process can
be very painful because 'learning to respect the narratives of the other may
be seen as a coping process, similar to a mourning process: one must learn
to give up those parts of one's narrative which are essential to maintaining
a negative and morally inferior collective image of the other (and a positive
narrative for one's own group)'.[29] Given the deep psychological structure of
people's attachment to historical narratives in (post)conflict situations, it is
stressed that emotions can and should play a central role in history teaching.
In order to be effective, multiperspectivist teaching should not be done in
a detached objectivist way but emotionally engage pupils with the parallel
narratives.

The above examples are situated at the two opposing sides of the continuum from neopositivist approaches to more postmodern, multiperspectival approaches. There are also historical reconciliation initiatives that can be situated in-between. A good example is the IHJR-sponsored book *Two Sides of the Coin: Independence and Nakba 1948,* published in 2011 by historians Motti Golani and Adel Manna.[30] Much like PRIME's Learning Each Other's Historical Narrative project, Golani and Manna stress the significance of narratives for conflict resolution and similarly represent two competing narratives on the same events – in this case primarily the Israeli/Arab war of 1948 – without trying to make judgments about their truthfulness.

There are, however, also remarkable differences between the two projects. Instead of presenting two narratives side by side, Golani and Manna choose to mix the narratives and write one text in which they constantly shift from one narrative to another. They point out that this results in a text that is occasionally internally contradictory, but they choose not to indicate these contradictions and not to mark from which perspective they are speaking at this or that moment. It should be noted that Golani and Manna have more freedom to experiment because, in contrast to the PRIME authors, they are not writing a textbook for pupils but primarily aim at an audience of adults or even fellow historians.

Yet there also seem to be other reasons for their choice to present one mixed and internally contradictory narrative rather than two parallel narratives that are diverging and yet internally coherent. While the PRIME authors empathically try as much as possible to treat the Palestinian and Israeli historical narratives as different yet equally legitimate (at least the more moderate among them),[31] Golani and Manna see these narratives as thoroughly unhistorical and treat them as equally illegitimate – even despite their argument for a fruitful and constructive discussion about the narratives.[32] Although they recognize that professional historians sometimes use narrative elements in their work, Golani and Manna make a strict (and in my opinion problematic) differentiation between 'historiography' – which should be 'research based', 'precise' and directed exclusively at the past – and 'historical narrative', which 'like memory . . . makes use of the past in light of the needs of the present for the sake of aspirations for the future'.[33] Because historical narrative is 'about the present and the future', it radically differs, according to the authors, from academic historiography. Historians may consider historical narrative as a legitimate source of study, but 'only if it was present during the period under examination'.[34] Historical narrative should, therefore, according to Golani and Manna, never be seen as a substitute for historiography.[35] Consistent with this view, Golani and Manna stress that they did not try to correct one narrative or another and 'found it unnecessary to confront the narratives . . . as historians'.[36]

The authors' vision is clearly reflected in the composition of *Two Sides of the Coin*, which is subdivided in 'historical' and 'narrative' chapters (with one chapter described as 'semi-narrative'). The 'historical' chapters do not contextualize the 'narrative' ones in the sense of reflecting about them but rather describe the chronological periods that come before and after the period treated in the 'narrative' chapters – that is, the violent events of 1947 and 1948. The 'historical' chapters thus, so to speak, chronologically isolate or contain the 'narrative' ones.[37]

In terms of epistemic positions and narrative strategies, we can thus analytically differentiate between those reconciliation historiographies that try to 'bridge' cognitive gaps and 'resolve' narrative contradictions and those that make no such claims but instead try to present diverging narratives, including their paradoxes, and try to make them known to the different parties. Bridging can happen negatively through levelling attempts to expose myths of conflicting parties, or it can happen through the construction of so-called positive histories that stress common traditions, shared values and cultural exchanges in the past. Bridging reconciliation historiographies are also often referred to as shared histories. Yet, the term 'shared history' is often used more broadly among scholars and practitioners focusing on reconciliation and can refer to at least three potential aspects of reconciliation historiographies: shared methodological procedures or shared authorship; a focus on shared events, values or actions in the past; or the construction of a single 'common' narrative that claims to evenhandedly represent the different perspectives of conflicting parties. Just as different approaches can be found in bridging narratives, so too can analytical differentiations be made among the narratives that do not make any bridging claims. As we have seen, one can, for example, differentiate between dual or parallel narratives and what I called mixed narratives.

These different epistemic positions and narrative strategies are not politically neutral. Specific approaches can be based on practical considerations but also on implicit or explicit political ones. It is doubtless no coincidence that, of the examples given above, the two bridging and to a certain extent interventionist approaches concern the case of the former Yugoslavia, while the parallel and mixed (noninterventionist) approaches concern the case of Israel/Palestine.[38]

The authors of PRIME's *Learning Each Other's Historical Narrative*, for example, make a profoundly political claim when explaining why they opted for parallel narratives rather than a single bridging narrative: 'We feel at this point of historical and political development of our societies that both sides need first to establish a two State solution and the Palestinian State, and therefore present their own narrative separately to feel secure and to give the other side the opportunity to know it.'[39] In this context it is important to note that PRIME chose to work with Palestinian teachers from the occupied territories and deliberately excluded the ambiguous perspective of the Palestinians living within the borders of the State of Israel.[40] Achim Rohde criticizes this choice, and the related idea of two ethnically homogenous nation-states living side by side, as out of touch with the much more complex empirical reality. He argues that the inclusion of the hybrid perspective of Palestinians of Israeli citizenship (numbering over one million, or one fifth of Israel's population) would have decisively altered the bipolar structure of the textbook.[41]

The authors of 'Two Sides of the Coin', Golani and Manna – who describe themselves as a Jewish-Israeli and a Palestinian of Israeli citizenship respectively – make a slightly different political claim: they also favour a two-state solution, but the primary goal of their book seems to be to stress the importance of 'mutual compromise' and the need to aim for 'equal and respectful co-existence' rather than 'justice' – 'all other options', they add, 'are a recipe for disaster'.[42] The authors' choice for a nonbridging or noninterventionist mixed narrative and their use of specific narrative techniques seem closely related to this stance. If one takes a closer look at the narrative techniques used by Golani and Manna, it can be noticed that they are often stressing the absence of choice for contemporary actors and the eternal repetition of violence and counterviolence: the tragic 'once again' dominates over the hopeful 'never again'.[43] In classic Whitean terms one can indeed call the overall narrative structure of 'Two Sides of the Coin' tragic[44] – tragic rather than satirical because the book seems to build towards a profound insight offered in a short epilogue, where it is claimed that Palestinians and Israelis actually have no choice but to reconcile and, one might add, to reconcile with the idea of giving up on the struggle for historical justice.

Up to now we have been focusing on relatively concrete political motives and effects of specific epistemologies and narrative strategies. On a more profound level however, I believe, these differences should also be considered in relation to different philosophical and legal ways of thinking as they, for example, can be found in human rights discourses. Historiography and the notion of historical truth have made an important entrance in human rights discourse in the context of the development of the so-called right to know or right to truth which was conceived as a part of the international fight against impunity. This notion was pioneered in the Inter-American Court of Human Rights with cases on forced disappearance. Yet, the idea made important headway in legal thinking when it was included in two reports by UN special rapporteurs Louis Joinet and Diane Orentlicher.[45] The right to know, Joinet explains, is not simply the right of any individual victim or closely related persons to know what happened, a right to the truth. The right to know is also a collective right, drawing upon history to prevent violations from recurring in the future. Its corollary is a 'duty to remember', which the State must assume, in order to guard against the perversions of history that go under the names of revisionism or negationism; the knowledge of the oppression it has lived through is part of a people's national heritage and as such must be preserved.[46]

The keywords in the legal documents on the right to know are indeed 'truth', 'knowledge', 'history' and the fight against 'revisionism' and 'negationism'.

History or, rather, historical and memorial narratives also enter human rights discourse through another entry point, namely that of cultural rights. Some remarkable evolutions can be found in two recent reports by UN special rapporteur Farida Shaheed. Shaheed wrote one report on the research, writing and teaching of history and another on memorialization and memorial policies with a special focus on conflict prevention, reconciliation and the danger of ideological indoctrination. One of the most remarkable features of these reports is that they do not primarily stress truth and historical knowledge (truth is barely mentioned, except negatively) but shift the emphasis to historical narratives and interpretation. In her discussion of the importance of historical and memorial narratives for the fields of cultural rights and cultural-dialogue, Shaheed especially stresses the alleged critical and emancipatory potential of multiperspectivism.

The teaching of history, according to Shaheed, should be based on academic historiography and should offer critical resistance against the stereotypes that can sometimes be found in collective memory. Yet she stresses one should start out from

> an acknowledgment that history is always subject to differing interpretations. While events may be proven, including in a court of law, historical narratives are viewpoints that, by definition, are partial. Accordingly, even when the facts are undisputed, conflicting parties may nevertheless fiercely debate moral legitimacy and the idea of who was right and who was wrong. . . . History is continuously interpreted to fulfil contemporary objectives by a multiplicity of actors. The challenge is to distinguish the legitimate continuous reinterpretation of the past from manipulations of history for political ends. The Special Rapporteur's recommendations are therefore based on the principle that history teaching should promote critical thinking and adopt a multiperspective approach, taking into account the right to freedom of opinion and expression, the right to information and education, academic freedoms and the rights of individuals and groups to have access to their cultural heritage and that of others.[47]

Shaheed comes to a conclusion that would be hard to digest for more positivist-inclined historians or history teachers: namely, that 'the right of children to develop their own historical perspective throughout education is to be considered an integral part of the right to education'.[48]

Some Challenges and Dilemmas

Let me return to the context that I described in the introduction: the emergence of the concept of historical reconciliation in the UN Security Council. There is a considerable risk that this notion will be appropriated for geopolitical purposes. This is especially the case when diverging narratives are identified as the root cause of conflict. Such an analysis can indeed take our attention away from other causes of conflict such as socioeconomic inequality, underdevelopment, economic exploitation, failing states, occupied territories, etc.

Some initiatives of historical reconciliation indeed seem to be underpinned by an antimaterialist ontology. To put it provocatively, one could argue that these reconciliation initiatives are based on a particular substantive or speculative philosophy of history: one in which historical conflict is not primarily caused by conflicting material interests or structural injustices but conflicting identities and perceptions. This idea is not new, of course. The Constitution of UNESCO of 1945, for example, opens with the claim that 'ignorance of each other's ways and lives has been a common cause [of war]' and that 'since wars begin in the minds of men, it is in the minds of men that the defences of peace must be constructed'.[49] Since roughly the end of the Cold War these particular philosophies of history and theories of (historical) conflict seem to have become increasingly popular among intellectuals in different segments of the political spectrum. Think for, example, of Samuel Huntington's idea of an imminent clash of civilizations, Francis Fukuyama and Peter Sloterdijk's related theories that human history, conflict and resentment are driven by *thymos* (i.e. a human pride and need for recognition) and Charles Taylor's argument that the non- or mis-recognition of identity claims can create a particular type of wound among individuals and communities and that a 'politics of recognition' is therefore needed to create peaceful and stable societies. Among the practitioners and theorists working on conflict transformation on reconciliation, one of the most explicitly idealist and antimaterialist conceptualizations of the nature of conflict and peace-building can be found in the highly influential work of John Paul Lederach. Lederach acknowledges that 'we must be careful not to push a single theoretical approach as the only mechanism for understanding social conflict'. Yet, he describes his own approach as the opposite of the historical materialist analysis of conflict and claims that 'conflict emerges through an interactive process based on the search for and creation of shared meaning'. Conflict transformation should therefore, according to Lederach, primarily focus on the relation between conflict and culture and privilege the construction of new forms of 'meaning' and 'knowledge'.[50]

When idealist analyses are used to enrich our understanding of conflict, and thus are seen as complementary to materialist analyses, this is, of course positive. Part of the problem with unequivocally antimaterialist approaches, however, is that they tend to gloss over the troubling question whether the demand for historical reconciliation is just (in a legal as well as in a more substantial sense). This question is of key importance if one places the demand for peace and reconciliation against a background of continuing injustice and inequality. Here we could mention the parable that the controversial film maker Lars von Trier told at the occasion of being awarded the UNI-CEF Cinema for Peace prize, which he refused. Von Trier said the people on earth can be compared to two tribes living in a desert – one living in a country with a well, the other without it. 'The desert tribe around the well wants "peace". The desert tribe on the outside doesn't want "peace" . . . it wants water!'[51] By referring to von Trier's provocative parable I certainly do not mean to belittle reconciliation initiatives. I do, however, believe that it can function as a reminder that reconciliation need not be politically desirable in any and all contexts.[52]

Even beyond the context of continuing injustice and inequality one can pose questions about the ethico-political implications of some of the basic concepts and approaches in discourses on historical reconciliation. Take, for example, the tension between the notions of multiperspectivity and the right to historical perspective on the one hand and the right to truth or the right of victims to be recognized or acknowledged on the other. Even beside the difficult question whether narrative differences are primarily an asset or a threat to societies, the narrative approach hardly seems to deliver on its promise of acknowledgement or recognition. Victims or survivors generally do not want their testimony to be acknowledged as narrative or as a perspectival account, even if this is done with empathy and respect, but as truth. Similarly, victims and survivors generally do not just want their suffering to be recognized but rather the fact that they suffer(ed) due to particular and real injustices. In this context, one could for example think of the South African Khulumani Support Group's rebellion against the psychologizing and pathologizing perspective of the truth and reconciliation commission and its associated therapists and psychologists.

We should, moreover, ask the puzzling question of how certain strands of reconciliation discourse can do without the concept of truth, which is so important to many truth commissions. I think there are several reasons. First, I think this should indeed be related to a specific set of dominant metahistorical ideas or a particular philosophy of history. Much like a speculative philosophy of history can never entirely be substantiated by historical facts or 'truth', equally so the promotion of such a speculative philosophy of history does not need to be entirely based on factual statements of truth claims.

The sense that history is tragic, that violence always begets more violence and that reconciliation is the only answer, can from this perspective be created equally well through narratives – or what narrativist philosophers call explanation by emplotment – as through truth claims or formal arguments.[53]

Second, it should be remarked that the notion of 'truth' is seldom entirely discarded but rather substituted by that of 'authenticity'. Many practitioners and theorists of historical reconciliation argue that narratives do not necessarily 'accurately' or 'objectively' represent the historical past but assume that narratives can authentically represent (individual or collective) identities and subjective experiences of the past. In this sense, the discourse on narrative reconciliation is not thoroughly postfoundationalist and rather loosely inspired by postmodernism. To put it in classical 'narrativist' terminology: there is indeed, in this view, still a specific congruence between 'word' and 'world'; stories are not just told but also lived (although in subjective experience).[54] As Mark Tessler puts it,

> Narratives are real and deserve attention regardless of the degree to which they are historically accurate. . . . That they are authentic is enough. The Palestinians' narrative is a product of their experience, just as the Zionists' is a product of theirs. It reflects how they perceived, interpreted, and evaluated the events and circumstances of their lives. Put differently, it is a community's own story – how the community understands and gives meaning to what it has endured. It is neither accurate nor inaccurate in a larger or more objective sense. It is simply one's story, subjective but real in the sense that it is the version of life and times that one not only tells but also believes. And to those who doubt this rendering of history, it may be said: if you had experienced what this community has experienced, it would be your narrative as well.[55]

The importance of this notion of authenticity for many reconciliation practices and theories can hardly be overestimated because it is this notion that renders it possible to speak about a form of acknowledgement in the absence of (factual) 'truth' and that legitimizes the attempts to listen to, and take seriously, each other's narratives in the first place.[56]

Third, I believe part of the attractiveness of the concept of narrative for scholars and practitioners aiming at reconciliation is that this concept can function as a model for an idealist and voluntarist notion of historical change.[57] Although historical narratives are often seen as authentic or existentially embedded and hence stubborn, they can, according to many reconciliation practitioners and theorists also be subjected to historical revisionism and undergo a thorough and sudden gestalt switch if small constitutive elements of their plot are changed. If this is the case for historical narratives, so the reasoning goes, likewise it can be the case for the identities and identity conflicts that are based on these narratives.

Fourth, and more disconcertingly, the increasing popularity of the notions of narrative and perspective could be related to a changed political context in which current reconciliation discourse mostly functions. Truth commissions are typically set up in contexts of so-called negotiated revolutions or transitions. An important political function of truth-discourse in such a context, as Robert Meister puts it, is that it should enable a compromise in which one of the parties (or even all of them) gives up on its claims to political or military victory (e.g. the ANC in South Africa) in exchange for a compensatory 'moral victory'.[58] By stressing the moral righteousness of the struggle or at least the innocence of the victims, 'truth telling' is then said to deliver a certain kind of justice or compensation. Current narrative reconciliation discourse, in contrast, often belongs to a more recent generalized application of transitional justice practices and generally operates in political contexts in which not even a negotiated transition has taken place or can be expected to take place in the future.[59] Whereas South Africa was the Mecca of 'truth telling', the Mecca of 'narrative reconciliation' is the Israeli–Palestinian conflict. To put it somewhat provocatively, my hypothesis is that the stress on truth is most heavily challenged and in some cases even replaced by a stress on narrative and perspective in situations where power balances are such that not even a moral victory or compensation can be, or must be, granted.[60]

Finally, there are some prevailing values or (cultural) conventions within most reconciliation historiographies that render them unneutral even when different narratives are carefully given equal space and attention.[61] The authors of the PRIME's *Side by Side* have a clear insight into this problem when they remark that

> the Israeli and the Palestinian narratives are not symmetrical in their internal construction, and cannot be expected to be so at the current stage. The Palestinian narrative is much more monolithic in its internal structure, representing Palestinians' need to develop their independent statehood, similar to the way the Israeli Jewish narrative was framed when Israel struggled for its independence. The Israeli narrative, after fifty-five years of statehood, is a bit more self-reflective and self-critical concerning some of the traditional 'Zionist' historical narratives. Since October 2000, however, the narrative incorporates a neo-monolithic turn. . . . In addition, the Israeli Jewish narrative reflects more of the Western cultural values of formal morality while the Palestinian narrative reflects more Eastern values of interpersonal morality.[62]

Elsewhere the PRIME project leaders also remark that the teams of teachers had many discussions about the way in which to describe painful events, and the level of detail to go into. These differences can indeed clearly be observed if one reads the two parallel narratives in *Side by Side*: the Israeli narrative, for example, much more often makes use of reflexive distancing and the inclusion of the other's perspective as perspective, and generally sticks more closely to a factual language or what Hayden White would call the literary genre of realism.[63] Both issues are of course highly relevant. Given the great stress in reconciliation historiographies on the metavalues of reflexivity and multiperspectivity, the success or failure to live up to these ideals delivers significant advantage or disadvantage in getting one's narrative recognized or making it rhetorically convincing. Similarly, reconciliation historiographies often exhibit a particular taboo on all too vivid and emotionally charged literary and visual evocations of suffering and violence – the controlling of emotions is sometimes explicitly mentioned as an objective of reconciliatory history teaching.[64]

It should be kept in mind that the writing of history in the name of the democratic values of dialogue and openness or in the service of reconciliation, peace and stability constitute a new instrumentalization of historiography. One can welcome this instrumentalism – certainly in the struggle against other nationalist or xenophobic instrumentalisms – but I think we should be careful with it. I am certainly not pleading for a return to a positivist or anti-narrativist approach. Rather, I believe we need to develop a new political theory of narratives that indicates asymmetrical power relations in historical dialogue by focusing on narrative inequality and unequal control over means of narrative production (to end with some Marx).

Berber Bevernage is associate professor of historical theory at the Department of History at Ghent University (Belgium). His research focuses on the dissemination, attestation and contestation of historical discourse and historical culture in postconflict situations. He has published in journals such as *History and Theory, Rethinking History, Memory Studies, Social History* and *History Workshop Journal*. Berber is (co)founder of the interdisciplinary research forum TAPAS/Thinking About the PASt, which focuses on popular, academic and artistic dealings with the past in a large variety of different cultural and social areas. Together with colleagues, he established the International Network for Theory of History (INTH), which aims to foster collaboration and the exchange of ideas among theorists of history around the world.

Notes

1. Letter dated 14 January 2014 from the Permanent Representative of Jordan addressed to the Secretary-General of the United Nations (UN Security Council S/2014/30).

2. UN Security Council S/PV.7105.

3. For some of the few empirical studies on the impact of reconciliation initiatives, see J. Gibson, 'Does Truth Lead to Reconciliation? Testing the Causal Assumptions of the South African Truth and Reconciliation Process', *American Journal of Political Science* 48(2) (2004), 201–17; K. Brounéus, 'The Trauma of Truth Telling: Effects of Witnessing in the Rwandan Gacaca Courts on Psychological Health', *Journal of Conflict Resolution* 54(3) (2010), 408–37; and D. Backer, 'Victims' Responses to Truth Commissions: Evidence from South Africa', in M. Ndulo (ed.), *Security, Reconciliation and Reconstruction: When the Wars End* (London: University College of London Press, 2007), 165–97.

4. F. Shaheed, 'Report of the Special Rapporteur in the Field of Cultural Rights: The Writing and Teaching of History (History Textbooks)' (A/68/296) (2013), 5, retrieved 6 January 2017 from https://documents-dds- ny.un.org/doc/UNDOC/GEN/N13/422/91/ PDF/N1342291.pdf?OpenElement; F. Shaheed, 'Report of the Special Rapporteur in the Field of Cultural Rights: Memorial Processes' (A/HRC/25/49). Retrieved 14 December 2014 from http://www.ohchr.org/EN/Issues/CulturalRights/Pages/AnnualReports.aspx.

5. UNESCO, 'The Slave Route' Retrieved 20 October 2014 from http://www.unesco .org/new/en/culture/themes/dialogue/the-slave-route/.

6. The Council of Europe was founded in 1949, currently has forty-seven member states and promotes cooperation between European countries. It should not be confused with the Council of the European Union.

7. Parliamentary Assembly of the Council of Europe, 'Recommendation 1880 (2009) History Teaching in Conflict and Post-Conflict Areas'; see also Parliamentary Assembly of the Council of Europe, 'Recommendation 1283 (1996) on History and the Learning of History in Europe'.

8. Council of Europe, *Shared Histories: For a Europe without Dividing Lines* (Strasbourg: Council of Europe Publishing, 2014). Another shared history project sponsored by the Council of Europe was the Tbilisi Initiative, which aimed to produce a common history textbook for Armenia, Georgia and Azerbaijan. However, due to political tensions, the textbook was never published. See K. Korostelina, 'The Tbilisi Initiative: The Story of an Unpublished Textbook', in K. Korostelina and S. Lässig (eds), *History Education and Post-Conflict Reconciliation* (New York: Routledge, 2014), 192–208.

9. S. Kitaoka, 'A Look Back on the Work of the Joint Japanese-Chinese History Research Committee', *Asia-Pacific Review* 17(1) (2010), 6–20.

10. Peace Research Institute in the Middle East (PRIME), 'Dual-Narrative History Project'. Retrieved 10 November 2014 from http://vispo.com/PRIME/index.htm.

11. For a discussion on this project see C. Defrance and U. Pfeil, 'Symbol or Reality? The Background, Implementation and Development of the Franco-German History Textbook', in Korostelina and Lässig, *History Education and Post-Conflict Reconciliation*, 52–68.

12. Z. Wang, 'Old Wounds, New Narratives: Joint History Textbook Writing and Peacebuilding in East Asia', *History & Memory* 21(1) (2009), 101–26.

13. The citation on the goals of the project comes from a document called 'prospectus' that was retrieved 10 November 2014 from C. Ingrao's personal page on Perdue University's website. See also C. Ingrao, 'Forging a Common Narrative in Former Yugoslavia: The Design, Implementation and Impact of the Scholars' Initiative' in Korostelina and Lässig, *History Education and Post-Conflict Reconciliation*, 120–39.

14. See the Institute for Historical Justice and Reconciliation' (IHJR) website. Accessed 19 October 2014 from http://historyandreconciliation.org/.

15. European Cultural Convention (1954). Retrieved 6 January 2017 from http://con ventions.coe.int/Treaty/en/Treaties/html/018.htm.

16. On these bilateral textbook commissions, see A. Karn, 'Depolarizing the Past: The Role of Historical Commissions in Conflict Mediation and Reconciliation', *Journal of International Affairs* 60(1) (2006), 31–50; M. Cattaruzza and S. Zala, 'Negotiated History? Bilateral Historical Commissions in Twentieth Century Europe', in H. Jones, K. Östberg and N. Randeraad (eds), *Contemporary History on Trial: Europe since 1989 and the Role of the Expert Historian* (Manchester: Manchester University Press, 2007), 123–43.

17. H.A. Elmersjö, 'History beyond Borders: Peace Education, History Textbook Revision, and the Internationalization of History Teaching in the Twentieth Century', *Historical Encounters* 1(1) (2014), 62–74.

18. See, for example, K. Asmal, L. Asmal and R.S. Roberts, *Reconciliation through Truth: A Reckoning of Apartheid's Criminal Governance* (Cape Town: David Philip Publishers, 1996).

See also T.A. Borer (ed.), *Telling the Truths: Truth Telling and Peace Building in Post-Conflict Societies* (Notre Dame, IN: University of Notre Dame Press, 2006).

19. C. Villa-Vicencio, 'Telling One Another Stories: Toward a Theology of Reconciliation', in H. Wells and G. Baum (eds), *The Reconciliation of Peoples: Challenge to the Churches* (Maryknoll, NY: Orbis Books, 1997), 105–21; see also A. Norval, 'Truth and Reconciliation: The Birth of the Present and the Reworking of History', *Journal of Southern African Studies* 25(3) (1999), 499–519.

20. See, for example, C. Bundy, 'The Beast of the Past: History and the TRC', in W. James and L. Van de Vijver, *After the TRC: Reflections on Truth and Reconciliation in South Africa* (Athens, OH: Ohio University Press, 2000), 9–20; R.A. Wilson, *The Politics of Truth and Reconciliation in South Africa: Legitimizing the Post-Apartheid State* (Cambridge: Cambridge University Press, 2001); R. Meister, 'Ways of Winning: The Costs of Moral Victory in Transitional Regimes', in A.D. Schrift (ed.), *Modernity and the Problem of Evil* (Bloomington: Indiana University Press, 2005), 81–111; G. Grandin, 'The Instruction of Great Catastrophe: Truth Commissions, National History, and State Formation in Argentina, Chile, and Guatemala', *American Historical Review* 110(1) (2005), 46–67.

21. G. Stöber, 'From Textbook Comparison to Common Textbooks? Changing Patterns in International Textbook Revision', in Korostelina and Lässig, *History Education and Post-Conflict Reconciliation*, 26–51.

22. N. Partner, 'Narrative Persistence: The Post-postmodern Life of Narrative Theory', in F. Ankersmit, E. Domanska and H. Kellner (eds), *Re-figuring Hayden White* (Stanford: Stanford University Press, 2009), 81–104.

23. Citations taken from the project description on the website of the 'Scholars Initiative', retrieved 21 November 2014 from https://www.cla.purdue.edu/si/scholarsprospectus.htm.

24. C. Ingrao, 'Introduction', in C. Ingrao and T.A. Emmert (eds), *Confronting the Yugoslav Controversies: A Scholars' Initiative* (Washington: United States Institute of Peace Press, 2009), 4.

25. This booklet was published in two parts in 2002 and 2006. They can be downloaded from the website Peace Research Institute in the Middle East (PRIME), http://vispo.com/PRIME/index.htm. For a detailed description of the project, see D. Bar-On and S. Adwan, 'The Prime Shared History Project: Peace-Building under Fire', in Y. Iram (ed.), *Educating toward a Culture of Peace* (Greenwich: Information Age Publishing, 2006), 309–23.

26. S. Adwan, D. Bar-On and E. Naveh (eds), *Side by Side: Parallel Histories of Israel-Palestine* (New York: The New Press, 2012).

27. S. Adwan and D. Bar-On, *Learning Each Other's Historical Narrative: Palestinians and Israelis (Part Two)* (Beit Jallah: Peace Research Institute in the Middle East, 2006), 3.

28. Adwan, Bar-On and Naveh, *Side by Side*, x.

29. Adwan, Bar-On and Naveh, *Side by Side*, xiii.

30. M. Golani and A. Manna, *Two Sides of the Coin: Independence and Nakba 1948. Two Narratives of the 1949 War and Its Outcome* (Dordrecht: Republic of Letter Publishing, 2011). This book was simultaneously published in an English-Hebrew and an English-Arabic version.

31. The PRIME authors are certainly not alone when stressing the need for a mutual acknowledgement and legitimation of the competing narratives as an essential tool to obtain peace and reconciliation. A survey among Jewish and Israel Palestinian peace educators in Israel, of which the results were published in 2002, indicated that these educators saw the creation of a deeper understanding and appreciation of the other side's collective narrative as one of the primary goals of peace education. See B. Nevo, G. Salomon and I. Brem, *Worthwhile Goals for Peace Education: Bottom-up Approach* (Haifa: Center for Research on Peace Education, 2002).

Gavriel Salomon concludes on the basis of this survey 'that the ultimate goal of coexistence education ought to be mutual legitimization of the other side's collective narrative and its implications'. G. Salomon, 'A Narrative-Based view of Coexistence Education', *Journal of Social Issues* 60(2) (2004), 278.

32. Golani and Manna, *Two Sides of the Coin*, ix.

33. Golani and Manna, *Two Sides of the Coin*, 1.

34. Golani and Manna, *Two Sides of the Coin*, 4.

35. Golani and Manna, *Two Sides of the Coin*, 4.

36. Golani and Manna, *Two Sides of the Coin*, 5.

37. The few times Golani and Manna do decide to intervene as historians in the narrative chapters (for example, to provide chronological markers), they do this in a different typographic font in order to make sure there can be no confusion.

38. The bridging approach seems to have very few supporters in Israel. See, for example, the volume edited by R. Rotberg, *Israeli and Palestinian Narratives: History's Double Helix* (Bloomington: Indiana University Press, 2006), in which the possibility of bridging narratives is rejected by most contributors. One important exception is the Israeli historian Ilan Pappe, who defends bridging narratives, although he has a very specific understanding of this notion; see I. Pappe, 'The Bridging Narrative Concept', in Rotberg, *Israeli and Palestinian Narratives*, 194–204.

39. Adwan and Bar-On, *Learning Each Other's Historical Narrative*, 4.

40. D. Bar-On and S. Adwan, 'The Psychology of Better Dialogue between Two Separate but Interdependent Narratives', in Rotberg, *Israeli and Palestinian Narratives*, 208.

41. A. Rohde, 'Learning Each Other's Historical Narrative: A Road Map to Peace in Israel/Palestine?', in Korostelina and Lässig, *History Education and Post-Conflict Reconciliation*, 181.

42. Golani and Manna, *Two Sides of the Coin*, 155. In their introduction, Golani and Manna argue that 'more than achieving justice, our goal should be living together side by side'. Golani and Manna, *Two Sides of the Coin*, 21. Elsewhere in the book, too, the authors stress that 'this book is not an attempt to achieve justice' (ix).

43. The events leading up to and during the Nakba and war of 1948 are predominantly presented as a vicious circle of actions and reactions whereby the involved actors' 'hands were tied', whereby they were 'helpless', 'unable', 'forced to respond' or whereby they often had 'no choice' but to act as they did. In the epilogue of the book, it is stressed that 'in some ways, the Nakba of 1948 is still going on today'. The history of the region since 1948 and especially since 1967 on a political level (in contrast to a military one) is presented as one of virtual standstill or even relapse, and according to the authors there is no way out unless both camps make a resolute choice for 'a more sophisticated political discussion', which can be facilitated by 'mutual recognition of the narratives of the 1984 war'. The authors are very optimistic about the power of narrative reconciliation to break the vicious circle of the conflict: 'Whoever is able to hear the other's narrative regarding the formative period of 1947–1949 will ultimately be capable of overcoming the many other inhibitions preventing a historic compromise resulting in two sustainable, independent states. The choice is in our hands.' Golani and Manna, *Two Sides of the Coin*, 155.

44. Hayden White claimed that historical narratives could be analytically divided according to the specific modes of emplotment that they used. Taking his inspiration from Northrop Frye, White identified four such modes of emplotment: romance, comedy, tragedy and satire. H. White, *Metahistory: The Historical Imagination in Nineteenth-Century Europe* (Baltimore: Johns Hopkins University Press, 1973).

45. The right to truth was eventually included in a resolution adopted by the General Assembly on 16 December 2005: 'Basic Principles and Guidelines on the Right to a Remedy and Reparation for Victims of Gross Violations of International Human Rights Law and Serious Violations of International Humanitarian Law.' Retrieved 7 March 2017 from http://www.ohchr.org/EN/ProfessionalInterest/Pages/RemedyAndReparation.aspx.

46. 'Question of the Impunity of Perpetrators of Human Rights Violations (Civil and Political)', Final report prepared by L. Joinet pursuant to Sub-Commission decision 1996/19 (26 June 1997), retrieved 6 January 2017 from https://documents-dds-ny.un.org/doc/UNDOC/GEN/G97/129/12/PDF/G9712912.pdf?OpenElement.

47. F. Shaheed, 'Report of the Special Rapporteur in the Field of Cultural Rights: The Writing and Teaching of History (History Textbooks)' (A/68/296) (2013), 5, retrieved 6 January 2017 from https://documents-dds-ny.un.org/doc/UNDOC/GEN/N13/422/91/PDF/N1342291.pdf?OpenElement.

48. Shaheed, 'Report of the Special Rapporteur in the Field of Cultural Rights'.

49. UNESCO, UNESCO Constitution, retrieved 14 February 2017 from http://portal.unesco.org/en/ev.php-URL_ID=15244&URL_DO=DO_TOPIC&URL_SECTION=201.html.

50. J.P. Lederach, *Preparing for Peace: Conflict Transformation across Cultures* (Syracuse: Syracuse University Press, 1995), 8–9.

51. Speech reproduced in B. Ogden, 'How Lars von Trier Sees the World', *Quarterly Review of Film and Video* 27(1) (2009), 54.

52. This point has been made forcefully by Emilios Christodoulidis and Scott Veitch; see E. Christodoulidis and S. Veitch, 'Introduction', in S. Veitch (ed.), *Law and the Politics of Reconciliation* (Aldershot: Ashgate, 2007), 4.

53. See White, *Metahistory*. In some cases, authors explicitly claim (or formally argue) that history has the form of a tragedy. The Israeli historian and former IDF officer, Mordechai Bar-On, for example, claims that 'rarely in history are conflicts simple stories of a struggle between an evil aggressor and a righteous defender. . . . Thus the escalation of violence in January and February 1948 was not only a result of the Palestinian strategy but also of the Jewish response, truly a tragic vicious circle – tragic not only because of the pain that it caused but also, as in a good Greek tragedy, because of the fateful inevitability of the events that unfolded.' M. Bar-On, 'Conflicting Narratives or Narratives of a Conflict', in Rotberg, *Israeli and Palestinian Narratives,* 153–54.

54. For an influential 'narrativist' discussion on the relation between world and word, see L. Mink, 'Narrative Form as a Cognitive Instrument', in R. Canary and H. Kozicki (eds), *The Writing of History: Literary Form and Historical Understanding* (Madison: University of Wisconsin Press, 1978), 129–49; and D. Carr, *Time, Narrative, and History* (Bloomington: Indiana University Press, 1986).

55. M. Tessler, 'Narratives and Myths about Arab Intransigence toward Israel,' in Rotberg, *Israeli and Palestinian Narratives,* 174.

56. As Yehudith Auerbach explains, 'Acknowledging the other's national narratives implies understanding and recognizing them as authentic and legitimate.' Y. Auerbach, 'The Reconciliation Pyramid: A Narrative-Based Framework for Analyzing Identity Conflict', *Political Psychology* 30(2) (2009), 305.

57. A clear example of this voluntarist idealism can be found in the work of James Liu and Tomohide Atsumi, who want to help societies obtain 'historical reconciliation' by creating a 'narrative design science': 'This is a science that acknowledges that social reality is constructed by a process of creative consent involving human beings, and as such can also be changed by them when they can see a new perspective.' J. Liu and T. Atsumi, 'Historical Conflict and Resolution between Japan and China: Developing and Applying a Narrative Theory of History and Identity', in T. Sugiman, K.J. Gergen, W. Wagner and Y. Yamada (eds), *Meaning in Action: Constructions, Narratives, and Representations* (New York: Springer, 2008), 329.

58. See R. Meister, *After Evil: A Politics of Human Rights* (New York: Columbia University Press, 2011); and idem, 'Ways of Winning', 81–111.

59. For a discussion of this more generalized application of transitional justice, see T.O. Hansen, 'The Vertical and Horizontal Expansion of Transitional Justice: Explanations and

Implications for a Contested Field', in S. Buckley-Zistel, T. Koloma Beck, C. Braun and F. Mieth (eds), *Transitional Justice Theories* (Routledge: New York, 2014), 105–24.

60. In this context, some commentators have rightly criticized the tendency to conceive of conflict as 'symmetrical', which can often be observed in theories on narrative reconciliation and in peace-discourse in general. As Anat Biletzki argues, 'Now, the bon temps of contemporary peace-discourse invigorates several factors leaning towards symmetry. . . . [and] on the whole, political audiences, as opposed to political players, are more amenable to "there are two sides to every story" than to a one-sided culprit-victim ontology. However, in spite of this general proclivity for symmetry, it is critical for the purpose of bona fide reconciliation to arrive at the cognizance that, in a particular story, the descriptive – but no less essential for that – truth might be one of asymmetry: one side may be more in the wrong than the other, one side may have suffered more profusely than the other, one side violated the rights of the other more grievously – one side was more a victim than the other.' A. Biletzki, 'Peace-less Reconciliation', in A. MacLachlan and A. Speight (eds), *Justice, Responsibility and Reconciliation in the Wake of Conflict* (Dordrecht: Springer, 2013), 39.

61. On the concept of narrative inequality see J. Blommaert, M. Bock and K. McCormick, 'Narrative Inequality in the TRC hearings: On the Hearability of Hidden Transcripts', *Journal of Language and Politics* 5(1) (2006) 1, 37–70.

62. Adwan and Bar-On, *Side by Side*, xvi.

63. H. White, *Figural Realism: Studies in the Mimesis Effect* (Baltimore: The Johns Hopkins University Press, 1999).

64. UN Special Rapporteur Farida Shaheed, for example, rejects the use of explicit visual material in textbooks 'when used to create a collective feeling of Victimization' based on 'evoking emotions instead of applying critical analysis'. Shaheed, 'Report of the Special Rapporteur in the Field of Cultural Rights', 18.

Bibliography

Adwan, S., and D. Bar-On. *Learning Each Other's Historical Narrative: Palestinians and Israelis* (Part 2). Beit Jallah: Peace Research Institute in the Middle East, 2006.

Adwan, S., D. Bar-On and E. Naveh (eds). *Side by Side: Parallel Histories of Israel-Palestine*. New York: The New Press, 2012.

Asmal, K., L. Asmal and R.S. Roberts. *Reconciliation through Truth: A Reckoning of Apartheid's Criminal Governance*. Cape Town: David Philip Publishers, 1996.

Auerbach, Y. 'The Reconciliation Pyramid: A Narrative-Based Framework for Analyzing Identity Conflict'. *Political Psychology* 30(2) (2009), 291–318.

Backer, D. 'Victims' Responses to Truth Commissions: Evidence from South Africa', in M. Ndulo (ed.), *Security, Reconciliation and Reconstruction: When the Wars End* (London: University College of London Press, 2007), 165–97.

Bar-On, D., and S. Adwan. 'The Prime Shared History Project: Peace-Building under Fire', in Y. Iram (ed.), *Educating toward a Culture of Peace* (Greenwich: Information Age Publishing, 2006), 309–23.

———. 'The Psychology of Better Dialogue between Two Separate but Interdependent Narratives', in R. Rotberg (ed.), *Israeli and Palestinian Narratives: History's Double Helix* (Bloomington: Indiana University Press, 2006), 205–24.

Bar-On, M. 'Conflicting Narratives or Narratives of a Conflict', in R. Rotberg (ed.), *Israeli and Palestinian Narratives: History's Double Helix* (Bloomington: Indiana University Press, 2006), 153–54.

Biletzki, A. 'Peace-less Reconciliation', in A. MacLachlan and A. Speight (eds), *Justice, Responsibility and Reconciliation in the Wake of Conflict* (Dordrecht: Springer, 2013) 31–46.

Blommaert, J., M. Bock and K. McCormick. 'Narrative Inequality in the TRC Hearings: On the Hearability of Hidden Transcripts'. *Journal of Language and Politics* 5(1) (2006), 37–70.

Borer T.A. (ed.). *Telling the Truths: Truth Telling and Peace Building in Post-Conflict Societies.* Notre Dame, IN: University of Notre Dame Press, 2006.

Brounéus, K. 'The Trauma of Truth Telling: Effects of Witnessing in the Rwandan Gacaca Courts on Psychological Health'. *Journal of Conflict Resolution* 54(3) (2010), 408–37.

Bundy, C. The Beast of the Past: History and the TRC', in W. James and L. Van de Vijver (eds), *After the TRC: Reflections on Truth and Reconciliation in South Africa* (Athens, OH: Ohio University Press, 2000), 9–20.

Carr D. *Time, Narrative, and History.* Bloomington: Indiana University Press, 1986.

Cattaruzza M., and S. Zala. 'Negotiated History? Bilateral Historical Commissions in Twentieth Century Europe', in H. Jones, K. Östberg and N. Randeraad (eds), *Contemporary History on Trial: Europe since 1989 and the Role of the Expert Historian* (Manchester: Manchester University Press, 2007), 123–43.

Christodoulidis, E., and S. Veitch. 'Introduction', in S. Veitch (ed.), *Law and the Politics of Reconciliation* (Aldershot: Ashgate, 2007), 1–8.

Council of Europe. *Shared Histories: For a Europe without Dividing Lines.* Strasbourg: Council of Europe Publishing, 2014.

Darnton, R. 'Poland Rewrites History'. *New York Review of Books* 28(12) (1981), 6–10.

Defrance, C., and U. Pfeil. 'Symbol or Reality? The Background, Implementation and Development of the Franco-German History Textbook', in K. Korostelina and S. Lässig (eds), *History Education and Post-Conflict Reconciliation* (New York: Routledge, 2014), 52–68.

Elmersjö, H.A. 'History beyond Borders: Peace Education, History Textbook Revision, and the Internationalization of History Teaching in the Twentieth Century'. *Historical Encounters* 1(1) (2014), 62–74.

European Cultural Convention (1954). Retrieved 6 January 2017 from http://conventions .coe.int/Treaty/en/Treaties/html/018.htm.

Gibson, J. 'Does Truth Lead to Reconciliation? Testing the Causal Assumptions of the South African Truth and Reconciliation Process'. *American Journal of Political Science* 48(2) (2004), 201–17.

Golani, M., and A. Manna. *Two Sides of the Coin: Independence and Nakba 1948. Two Narratives of the 1949 War and Its Outcome.* Dordrecht: Republic of Letter Publishing, 2011.

Grandin, G. 'The Instruction of Great Catastrophe: Truth Commissions, National History, and State Formation in Argentina, Chile, and Guatemala'. *American Historical Review* 110(1) (2005), 46–67.

Hansen, T.O. 'The Vertical and Horizontal Expansion of Transitional Justice: Explanations and Implications for a Contested Field', in S. Buckley-Zistel, T. Koloma Beck, C. Braun and F. Mieth (eds), *Transitional Justice Theories* (Routledge: New York, 2014), 105–24.

Ingrao, C. 'Introduction', in C. Ingrao and T.A. Emmert (eds), *Confronting the Yugoslav Controversies: A Scholars' Initiative* (Washington: United States Institute of Peace Press, 2009), 1–11.

———. 'Forging a Common Narrative in Former Yugoslavia: The Design, Implementation and Impact of the Scholars' Initiative,' in K. Korostelina and S. Lässig (eds), *History Education and Post-Conflict Reconciliation* (New York: Routledge, 2014), 120–39.

———. Personal page on university website. Retrieved 10 November 2014 from https:// www.cla.purdue.edu.

Institute for Historical Justice and Reconciliation' (IHJR). Webpage accessed 19 October 2014 from http://historyandreconciliation.org/.

Karn, A. 'Depolarizing the Past: The Role of Historical Commissions in Conflict Mediation and Reconciliation'. *Journal of International Affairs* 60(1) (2006), 31–50.

Kitaoka, S. 'A Look Back on the Work of the Joint Japanese-Chinese History Research Committee'. *Asia-Pacific Review* 17(1) (2010), 6–20.

Korostelina, K. 'The Tbilisi Initiative: The Story of an Unpublished Textbook', in K. Korostelina and S. Lässig (eds), *History Education and Post-Conflict Reconciliation* (New York: Routledge, 2014), 192–208.

Lederach, J.P. *Preparing for Peace: Conflict Transformation across Cultures.* Syracuse: Syracuse University Press, 1995.

Liu, J., and T. Atsumi. 'Historical Conflict and Resolution between Japan and China: Developing and Applying a Narrative Theory of History and Identity', in T. Sugiman, K.J. Gergen, W. Wagner and Y. Yamada (eds), *Meaning in Action: Constructions, Narratives, and Representations* (New York: Springer, 2008), 327–44.

Meister R., 'Ways of Winning: The Costs of Moral Victory in Transitional Regimes', in A.D. Schrift (ed.), *Modernity and the Problem of Evil* (Bloomington: Indiana University Press, 2005), 81–111.

———. *After Evil: A Politics of Human Rights.* New York: Columbia University Press, 2011.

Mink, L. 'Narrative Form as a Cognitive Instrument', in R. Canary and H. Kozicki (eds), *The Writing of History: Literary Form and Historical Understanding* (Madison: University of Wisconsin Press, 1978), 129–49.

Nevo, B., G. Salomon and I. Brem. *Worthwhile Goals for Peace Education: Bottom-up Approach.* Haifa: Center for Research on Peace Education, 2002.

Norval, A. 'Truth and Reconciliation: The Birth of the Present and the Reworking of History'. *Journal of Southern African Studies* 25(3) (1999), 499–519.

Ogden, B. 'How Lars von Trier Sees the World'. *Quarterly Review of Film and Video* 27(1) (2009), 54–68.

Pappe, I. 'The Bridging Narrative Concept', in R. Rotberg, *Israeli and Palestinian Narratives: History's Double Helix* (Bloomington: Indiana University Press, 2006), 194–204.

Partner N. 'Narrative Persistence: The Post-Postmodern Life of Narrative Theory', in F. Ankersmit, E. Domanska and H. Kellner (eds), *Re-figuring Hayden White* (Stanford: Stanford University Press, 2009), 81–104.

Peace Research Institute in the Middle East (PRIME), 'Dual-Narrative History Project'. Retrieved 10 November 2014 from http://vispo.com/PRIME/index.htm.

'Question of the Impunity of Perpetrators of Human Rights Violations (Civil and Political)'. Final report prepared by L. Joinet pursuant to Sub-Commission decision 1996/19 (26 June 1997). Retrieved 6 January 2017 from https://documents-dds-ny.un.org/doc/UNDOC/GEN/G97/129/12/PDF/G9712912.pdf?OpenElement.

Rohde, A. 'Learning Each Other's Historical Narrative: A Road Map to Peace in Israel/Palestine?' in K. Korostelina and S. Lässig (eds), *History Education and Post-Conflict Reconciliation* (New York: Routledge, 2014), 177–91.

Rotberg, R. (ed.). *Israeli and Palestinian Narratives: History's Double Helix.* Bloomington: Indiana University Press, 2006.

Salomon, G. 'A Narrative-Based View of Coexistence Education'. *Journal of Social Issues* 60(2) (2004) 273–87.

'The Scholars Initiative: Confronting the Yugoslav Controversies, 2001-2005'. Retrieved 21 November 2014 from https://www.cla.purdue.edu/si/scholarsprospectus.htm.

Shaheed, F. 'Report of the Special Rapporteur in the Field of Cultural Rights: The Writing and Teaching of History (History Textbooks)' (A/68/296) (2013), 5. Retrieved 6 January 2017 from https://documents-dds- ny.un.org/doc/UNDOC/GEN/N13/422/91/PDF/N1342291.pdf?OpenElement.

———. 'Report of the Special Rapporteur in the Field of Cultural Rights: Memorial Processes' (A/HRC/25/49). Retrieved 14 December 2014 from http://www.ohchr.org/EN/Issues/CulturalRights/Pages/AnnualReports.aspx.

Stöber, G. 'From Textbook Comparison to Common Textbooks? Changing Patterns in International Textbook Revision', in K. Korostelina and S. Lässig (eds), *History Education and Post-Conflict Reconciliation* (New York: Routledge, 2014), 26–51.

UNESCO. UNESCO Constitution. Retrieved 14 February 2017 from http://portal.unesco
    .org/en/ev.php-URL_ID=15244&URL_DO=DO_TOPIC&URL_SECTION=201
    .html.
———. 'The Slave Route.' Retrieved 20 October 2014 from http://www.unesco.org/new/
    en/culture/themes/dialogue/the-slave-route/.
Villa-Vicencio, C. 'Telling One Another Stories: Toward a Theology of Reconciliation',
    in H. Wells and G. Baum (eds), *The Reconciliation of Peoples: Challenge to the Churches*
    (Maryknoll, NY: Orbis Books, 1997), 105–21.
Wang, Z. 'Old Wounds, New Narratives: Joint History Textbook Writing and Peacebuilding
    in East Asia'. *History & Memory* 21(1) (2009), 101–26.
White, H. *Metahistory: The Historical Imagination in Nineteenth-Century Europe*. Baltimore: Johns
    Hopkins University Press, 1973.
———. *Figural Realism: Studies in the Mimesis Effect*. Baltimore: The Johns Hopkins University
    Press, 1999.
Wilson, R.A. *The Politics of Truth and Reconciliation in South Africa: Legitimizing the Post-Apartheid
    State*. Cambridge: Cambridge University Press, 2001.

CHAPTER 5

Psychoanalysis and the Indeterminacy of History

JOAN W. SCOTT

At the meeting of the Vienna Psychoanalytic Society on 27 March 1907, the presentation by a Dr Sadger was about somnambulism (sleepwalking) and its relationship to dream life. Freud made the concluding remarks, cautioning against accepting the statements of patients at face value; these always represented, he said, 'a falsified picture, compounded of fantasy and reality'. He continued:

> Fantasy fills in memory gaps in a plausible, often very clever way . . . we find this in lovers who cannot tolerate the thought that their present state is a new one and who are soon convinced that they have known each other long ago. The hysteric, too, in the etiology of whose illness seduction . . . has played no role . . . does the same thing when he transforms the autoerotism of his childhood into object love by means of fantasies corresponding to his present thinking. The historian proceeds similarly when he projects the views of his own time onto the past.[1]

Freud's preoccupation with history, the Israeli psychoanalyst Eran Rolnik tells us, came from his interest in the fallibility of human memory 'with its unconscious psychic determinants' and his desire to call into question 'history's objectifying pretensions' – pretensions that were particularly strong at that moment of the discipline's formation. 'The epistemological foundations of psychoanalysis', Rolnik tells us, 'were . . . laid in close proximity to the ideas voiced by the leading historians of his day.'[2]

For that reason it seems useful to return to some of those ideas as we contemplate questions about critique in our contemporary context. My argument is that Freud's insistence on the ultimate indeterminacy of our knowledge is the best guarantee we have of practicing critique. Freud suggested that the pursuit of knowledge was illusory – the quest for positive knowledge ('hard facts' we might call them now) was simply a disguise that concealed the primary processes – the drives – that were the true motivation for the quest. Psychoanalysis is 'suspicious' of any account that stops with the production of positive knowledge; the cure has nothing to do with the discovery of 'the facts'. This scepticism about the status of positive knowledge and the insistence that the pursuit of it is ongoing – and itself needs interpretation – enables the kind of critical work that, by constantly interrogating normative concepts, keeps future possibilities open. What does it mean to 'know history'? What does the writing of history entail beyond the construction of sequences of events? How far can we take the notion that the pursuit of knowledge itself is symptomatic of something else? Foucault characterized psychoanalysis (along with ethnology) as a 'counter-science' that flowed in the opposite direction from the empirical human sciences: 'they lead them back to their epistemological basis, and . . . they ceaselessly "unmake" that very man who is creating and re-creating his possibility in the human sciences.'[3]

Freud's comments on history recur throughout his work, whether he is talking about individual cases (the Wolfman, the Ratman), historical figures (Leonardo Da Vinci) or 'group psychology' (*Totem and Taboo*; *Moses and Monotheism*; *Civilization and Its Discontents*). A word he uses often is 'tendentious' (meaning biased, promoting a particular interest or set of beliefs) to characterize the motives of those writing history in the service of a nation; they are producing fantasized memories in much the way an individual adult does about his childhood. The analogy is a strong one: 'Closer investigation', he wrote, 'would perhaps reveal a complete analogy between the ways in which the traditions of a people and the childhood memories of the individual come to be formed.'[4] Men became concerned with their past, Freud suggests, when they 'felt themselves to be rich and powerful, and now felt a need to learn where they had come from'. So they

> gathered traditions and legends, [and] interpreted the traces of antiquity that survived in customs and usages . . . . It was inevitable that this early history should have been an expression of present beliefs and wishes rather than a true picture of the past; for many things had been dropped from the nation's memory, while others were distorted, and some remains of the past were given a wrong interpretation in order to fit in with contemporary ideas. Moreover people's motives for writing history was not objective curiosity but a desire to influence their contemporaries, to encourage and inspire them, or to hold up a mirror before them.[5]

Just as he grappled with distinguishing the truth of a patient's past from his or her unreliable recollections of it, so Freud thought it possible to discern 'the historical truth behind the legendary material' in a nation's history.[6]

In this text he suggested that traditions were analogous to an individual's unconscious: 'Tradition is a repository of facts and ideas left out by official historians.'[7] 'They owe their power to the element of historical truth which they have brought up from the repression of the forgotten and primeval past.'[8] But he also thought that historians introduced material for 'tendentious purposes': 'by recognizing the distortions produced by those purposes we shall bring to light fresh fragments of the true state of things lying behind them.'[9] This truth was not about what happened, but why. To do this, the analyst's work must be archaeological: transforming incomplete and imperfect bits of found objects into a plausible construction (or reconstruction) of the motives and meanings of past experience.

Freud distinguished between interpretation and construction, the one addressing a single element of the material under analysis, the other the creation of a fuller narrative.[10] If memory is a psychic process, informed by such things as repression, displacement, condensation, fantasy, desire, conflict, envy, aggression and ambivalence, the analyst's job is to make sense of it. Yet that sense is not pursued for itself, but only as a way of weaving together scattered elements to achieve an affective transformation in the patient. This is what Freud, speaking of the interpretation of dreams, referred to as 'secondary revision', and what one encyclopaedia defines as 'a rearrangement of the seemingly incoherent element of the dream into a form serviceable for narration. This involves logical and temporal reorganization in obedience to the principles of non-contradiction, temporal sequence, and causality which characterize the secondary processes of conscious thought'.[11] Here there is a similarity to history, but the end is different – affective transformation, not a closed narrative that stands on its own.

Freud's case histories are themselves narratives as they describe the uneven process of construction by which the analyst helps a patient rewrite his life story in order to account for troubling behaviour in the present that necessarily has its roots in the past. Freud's attempts at more conventional histories – *Totem and Taboo* and *Moses and Monotheism* are examples – are also constructions, efforts, that is, to explain contemporary phenomena (the origins of the social contract, the reputation of Jews) by critically revisiting accounts of the past, but then writing them in familiar chronological form. For the disciplined historian, there is a fascinating tension between what appears to be wild speculation (based on a variety of texts) and the familiar chronological form in which it is presented. It is all the more fascinating because Freud is fully aware of the pitfalls of his approach:

> I am very well aware that in dealing so autocratically and arbitrarily with Biblical tradition – bringing it up to confirm my view when it suits me and unhesitatingly rejecting it when it contradicts me – I am exposing myself to serious methodological criticism and weakening the convincing force of my argument.

But this is the only way in which one can treat material of which one knows definitely that its trustworthiness has been severely impaired by the distorting influence of tendentious purposes. It has to be hoped that I shall find some degree of justification later on, when I come upon the track of these secret motives. Certainty is in any case unattainable and moreover it may be said that every other writer on the subject has adopted the same procedure.[12]

Here again, we have a direct refusal of the claims of an objective science of history – it is the 'tendentious' practice that conceals the 'secret motives' that must be explored, but that exploration has no finite end. Instead, it is a recognition that the 'construction' achieved in analysis is not objective, but not untrue either. The selection, weaving and reweaving rewrites the analysand's sense of her or his history, but it does not foreclose subsequent narrations as fantasies and repressed material continue to come to light in the course of the analysis. Could we think about the process of historical revisionism in similar terms – as a process in which the desire to contest prevailing orthodoxies leads the historian to long forgotten or overlooked material that then becomes the basis for a new understanding of some aspect of the past?

Freud's insistence on the validity of his approach came from his sense that the psychic realities of human existence had been given short shrift in historians' accounts. In 1938, he noted 'the modern tendency . . . towards tracing back the events of human history to more concealed, general and impersonal factors, to the compelling influence of economic conditions, to alterations in food habits, to advances in the use of materials and tools, to migrations brought about by increases in population and climatic changes'.[13] He had no objection to these, only to the attempt to identify a single cause that eliminated any consideration of an individual's influence on events (Moses was the case in point here), since these events, he argued, were always 'overdetermined, . . . the effect of several convergent causes'.[14] The point was not to try to account for what Michel de Certeau called 'the areas where an economic or a sociological explanation forcibly leaves something aside',[15] but rather to include the irrational as a fundamental principle of human behaviour – psychic reality was a vital aspect of human experience. 'In spite of all the distortions and misunderstandings', Freud wrote of legends of early history,

> they still represent the reality of the past: they are what a people forms out of the experience of its early days and under the dominance of motives that were once powerful and still operate today; and if it were only possible, by a knowledge of the forces at work [he means the ones uncovered by psychoanalysis], to undo these distortions, there would be no difficulty in disclosing the historical truth lying behind the legendary material.[16]

The distinction between reality and truth is important here – reality is a set of manifest beliefs and the practices that follow from them; truth is the underlying psychic – we might say critical – explanation that refers to repressions, fantasies, delusions. Finding 'truth' meant looking beyond the self-justification offered by actors, not in order to impugn their motives or discredit their aims, but to uncover the desires and anxieties they contained, the collective representations they appealed to, in order to better understand how psychic processes – those of the people in the past as well as of their historians – enabled and informed what has come to count as history.[17]

The Post-Freudian Freud

I came late to psychoanalysis personally and professionally, having for a long time refused it as a useful way of thinking either about myself or about history. In retrospect, I think that is fortunate, because the Freud I discovered was what Adam Phillips calls the 'post-Freudian' Freud, the one read through the lenses of poststructuralism (Jacques Lacan, Jean Laplanche, Michel Foucault and certain feminists – Naomi Shore, Joan Copjec, Renata Salecl), post-colonialism (Frantz Fanon) and theories of race and racism (Hortense Spillers, Sylvia Wynter). This is the Freud who, according to Phillips, questions 'the very idea of the self as an object of knowledge'. 'The inevitability of infancy, the unruliness of instinctual life, the puzzling acquisition of language and its link with sexuality, the unconscious dream-work – all of these suggested to Freud a radical and formative insufficiency, something that cannot be solved by knowledge'.[18] In terms of identity, we cannot know in advance how subjects will identify. Social attribution (cultural construction in the jargon of the 1980s and '90s) is not psychic determination. Foucault tells us that the modern subject is 'always open, never finally delimited, yet constantly traversed'.[19] De Certeau puts it this way: 'The labor by which the subject *authorizes* his own existence is of a kind other than the labor for which he receives *permission* to exist. The Freudian process attempts to articulate this difference.'[20] Joan Copjec insists as well that subjects are not reducible '*to* the images social discourses construct *of* her'.[21] Within this frame, Peter Coviello reads the contributions of W.E.B. Dubois: 'All that is certain is that the black citizen will be compelled to include, among his or her other attachments in the world, a relation to the shifting imperatives of race. That relation can be described . . . but never presumed.'[22] He conceives of the relation in terms of form – the truncation of possibility by normative restrictions – and content – an affective register, consisting of 'variance and surprise'.[23] Hortense Spillers, looking to add race to psychoanalytic theorizing, suggests that 'the question . . . is not so much why and how "race" makes the difference – the police will see to it – but how it carries over its message onto an interior, how "race" as a poisonous idea insinuates itself not only across and between ethnicities, but within'.[24]

The post-Freudian Freud refuses the conflation of social construction with subjectivity. Social construction presumes an external causality for the constitution of subjects that is challenged by the operations of the unconscious in the formation of individual subjects. The post-Freudian Freud asks us not to read diagnostically (Oedipus complex, family romance, developmental stages) because these labels tend to close down interpretive possibilities. (I realize that these kinds of readings continue to be offered, but they are not the ones I am referring to.) It asks us instead to read openly, expecting to encounter the unforeseen and the unknown. This reading practice involves acute attention to language. It refuses categorical explanations and reductive causalities, opening itself instead to the vagaries of linguistic expression and to theories of psychic representation that seek to make them intelligible. Rolnik writes that 'psychoanalysis is not a reservoir of answers but a language, which touches on, yet allows itself to be surprised by, a wide range of human uncertainties and illogicalities'.[25]

Foucault noted that the Freudian approach led to considerations that exceeded the bounds of the empirical knowledge of 'Man'. It exposed 'what is there and yet is hidden . . . what exists with the mute solidity of a thing, of a text closed in upon itself, or of a blank space in a visible text'.[26] Exceeding the bounds of empirical knowledge means taking into account what Elizabeth Wilson calls the 'unruly unconscious',[27] and recognizing that human histories and history-writing itself have something in common with Freud's description of 'a day-dream or a phantasy', in which 'past, present and future are strung together, as it were, on the thread of the wish that runs through them'.[28] The wish (an unconscious expression) at once links past, present and future *and* undermines any permanent linkage. This is not to say that anything goes in historical accounts, only that our relationship to the realities of history is more complex than the one that locates the historian's truth solely in the excavation of documents from archives, in quantitative measures of such events as births, deaths, marriages, prices, strikes and wars, or in the literal acceptance of testimony offered in courts of law, memoirs or oral history interviews. The evidence of experience is neither transparent nor self-evident; it is only grist for the historians' analytic mill.

I think it is important to add, in this moment of 'alternative facts', that neither psychoanalysis nor the history influenced by it denies 'reality' in the manner of Donald Trump or other authoritarian types. The point is to introduce another register of interpretation, an attempt to understand the psychic underpinnings of the stories we tell, of the ways we account for events and actions – individual and collective. This is what Freud was after when he pondered the story of Moses and the founding myths of nations. What is at stake, he asked, in the need to locate an origin or to define a set of national character traits? This kind of question does not deny the existence of Moses or of nation-states; rather, it asks, How do unconscious processes influence politics? How do they influence the work of historians? The critical role of psychoanalysis here is to attempt to account for the unconscious motives that play into and define what counts as an event or a fact, and that colour the debates – on all sides – about their meaning.

Incommensurable Differences

Having said this, I do not want to suggest that psychoanalysis is the only way for historians to approach their task, though I think it adds a necessary dimension precisely by underlining the aspect of the ultimate uncertainty or indeterminacy of all knowledge. There are significant, even incommensurable, differences between the disciplines of history and psychoanalysis. Freud may have taken history-writing as an object for analytic attention, and he certainly constructed narratives in a way familiar to historians, but as epistemological projects and as disciplines they differ in important ways.

Like psychoanalysis, the discipline of history acknowledges that facts are in some sense produced through interpretation, but each understands this production to take place differently. For historians, events are the starting point of the analysis – the taken for granted occurrences whose effects come afterwards.[29] (Here I am referring to disciplinary orthodoxies, not to the Foucauldian notion that discursive conditions produce events that become detached from their conditions of production as objects in themselves.) For psychoanalysts, it is the other way around: events are deduced from their effects. Analysts attend to what Freud called *Nachträglichkeit* (translated as 'deferred action') to indicate the way in which events acquire significance through revision, 'rearrangement in accordance with fresh circumstances . . . a re-transcription'.[30] As he wrestled with the timing of the primal scene in the Wolf Man case, Freud insisted on 'the part played by phantasies in symptom-formation and also the "retrospective phantasying" of later impressions into childhood and their sexualization after the event'.[31] While he concluded that the obsessional neurosis of his patient must have originated when he witnessed his parents' coitus, there was no way finally to establish the fact that the event had actually occurred. Freud acknowledged the difficulty of attributing the dream of a four-year-old boy, recalled by a grown man undergoing analysis some twenty years later, to a trauma experienced by a one-and-a-half-year-old child. (Indeed the trauma happens only retrospectively when the boy – witnessing copulating animals – makes the connection to what he thought he saw earlier.) But finally Freud dismissed the effort at precision as beside the point: 'It is also a matter of indifference in this connection whether we choose to regard it as a primal *scene* or a primal *phan-*

tasy.'[32] The actual witnessing of an event, in other words, is not the issue; it is the role it plays in unconscious manifestations (symptoms) that matters. As de Certeau puts it, 'Analysis establishes history by virtue of a relation among successive manifestations'.[33]

If historians assume that the linear narratives they create capture the past's relationship to the present (and, in some cases, the present's to the past), psychoanalysts operate in more than one temporal register. There is the time of the analysis and the times remembered in analysis, and these do not add up to a single chronology. Brady Brower puts it this way: 'Within the practical time of the analysis, the analysand's speech designated a second temporality, one that made it possible for the analyst's speech to be attributed a role with little or no correspondence to his actual personal characteristics or his formal capacities as an analyst.'[34] Unlike historians who make an object (an other) of the denizens of the past (and who rarely consider their own reasons for studying those objects), analysts refuse objectification, seeking instead to bring analysands to recognition of the unconscious agency – the condition and limits – of their own subjectivity. It is not, as some have noted, that for Freud, the past always haunts the present, but that the objective times of past and present are confused, often indistinguishable. The point is that time is a complex creation, a constructed dimension of subjectivity, not, as for historians, a chronological given. Freudian theory is sceptical of the evolutionary chronology that shapes professional historians' presentations, instead attending to the role repression or nostalgia play in the construction of memory and of the historian's version of events, as well as to the interruptions and discontinuities that characterize the necessarily uneven and often chaotic interactions of past and present in the psyche.

And there is no end to the individual's story. Although an analysis itself may eventually terminate, the patient is not cured, only better aware of how to deal with her or his symptoms. This is different from the arbitrary closure that historians provide at the end of their accounts, whether by drawing boundaries of periodization between one age and another, or tracing the lives and deaths of institutions, groups and individuals subsumed into set categories of identity. In our accounts, for the most part, it is the operations of finite changes (their causes and effects) that demand our attention.

Although Freud likened human memory to an archive in 1898, he soon preferred the concept of archaeology. And there is good reason for this, as pointed out compellingly by Carolyn Steedman in *Dust*, her response to Derrida's *Archive Fever*. Archives, she notes, are formal repositories, ordered by 'principles of unification and classification'. The human memory, in contrast, is a 'fathomless and timeless place in which nothing goes away', whereas the archive, she writes, 'is made from selected and consciously chosen documentation from the past and also from the mad fragmentations that no one intended to preserve and that just ended up there'.[35] This means that the space of the archive is not the fetishized container that, for many historians in these days of Big Data, Big History and the so-called empirical (re)turn, has come to be seen as the indisputable, because transparent, source of complete historical knowledge. It is instead, in Steedman's words, full of 'stories caught half way through: the middle of things, discontinuities'.[36] The archive is a space, she says, 'of dreams, of imaginative play', where historians pursue lost objects that are ultimately impossible to retrieve in their original completeness. Yet it is the quest for completeness (to say nothing of the sheer pleasure of the journey) that drives us from archive to archive, text to text, and it is the manner of writing our stories – the conventions of narrative itself – that assures a sense of completeness or at least of closure. There is no recognition (as there would be in the analytic setting I am thinking of) that the closure is necessarily imaginary, imposed on the materials, unifying them to defy their multiplicity. This is a different imperative from the one that drives the psychoanalyst.

Unlike the analyst, who confronts his patient and works with him or her through the transference, there is no transference for historians in the archive.[37] There is instead a one-sided relationship to the dead, who are made (in the French historian Jules Michelet's depiction of it) 'to walk and talk again'.[38] Wrote Michelet, 'I have given to many of the disregarded dead the assistance that I myself shall need. I have exhumed them for a second life.'[39] De Certeau reflects on the relationship of history to death this way: 'Historiography tends to prove that the site of its production can encompass the past: it is an odd procedure that posits death, a breakage everywhere re-iterated in discourse, and that yet denies loss by appropriating to the present the privilege of recapitulating the past as a form of knowledge. A labor of death and a labor against death.'[40]

On the question of life and death, time and causality, subject and object, there is thus an incompatibility between the aims of psychoanalysis and of the discipline of history. De Certeau captures the disparity: 'Now I must ask: what disturbing uncanniness does Freudian writing trace within the historian's territory, where it enters dancing? Reciprocally, in what fashion will my question, born of an archival and scriptural labor that cultivates this territory, and seduced by the fiction of psychoanalytical history, be enlightened/distorted through Freud's analysis?'[41] For de Certeau, the seductive dance of Freudian analysis necessarily distorts even as it sheds new light on the territory of the historian. He designates writing as 'fiction' in the sense both of fabrication and deception. The Freudian 'dance' is counterposed to the historians' 'labor'; 'dance' refers to the multiple and mobile forms taken by imaginative representation and also to a certain artful pleasure, while 'labor' stresses the imposition of order on (the disciplining of) the materiality of archives and their transcription. Historical writing, he says, is the unconscious or unacknowledged way of working through the historian's relationship to death, at once erasing it by resurrecting the past and avowing it through its very erasure. For de Certeau, the crucial term is 'uncanniness' – psychoanalysis brings back something once familiar, but now estranged, through the operations of distance and repression.

It is the clash, not the compatibility, of the two different concepts of history that proves productive for de Certeau: 'The interdisciplinarity we look toward would attempt to apprehend epistemological constellations as they reciprocally provide themselves with a new delimitation of their objects and a new status for their procedures.'[42] The clash is effectively disruptive in both directions, although de Certeau's interest (and mine as well) is in bringing psychoanalytic disruption to the attention of historians.

Gender

The immediate question which drew me to psychoanalysis had to do with my work on gender. Dissatisfied with arguments about cultural construction, economic interest and patriarchy (though all of these have relevance and utility), I turned increasingly to what seemed to me *the* source for thinking about sex and sexuality – psychoanalytic theory. It was in the theorizing of sexual difference, and, beyond that, in philosophical discussions of the formation of subjects, that I found the perspective I was seeking. In that theorizing – Freud's and the Lacanian rereading of Freud – the difference of sex is ultimately inexplicable. It is the riddle that defies fixed meaning, the understanding that always seems to escape control, the dilemma that gives rise to myth and fantasy. It is the place where questions of the relationship of mind and body are confounded. Psychoanalytic theory refuses a separation between the biological and the social or cultural, attending instead to what Alenka Zupančič describes as

> the zone where the two realms overlap; i.e., where the biological or somatic is already mental or cultural and where, at the same time, culture springs from the very impasses of the somatic functions which it tries to resolve (yet, in doing so, creates new ones). In other words . . . the overlapping in question is not simply an overlapping of two well-established entities ('body' and 'mind'), but an intersection which is generative of both sides that overlap it.[43]

Sex and sexual difference are generated by this intersection. The mind/body and culture/nature oppositions do not work here. Anatomy is not a fact apart, but rather a fantasy about the body's meaning that follows from gender assignment (naming, gender designation – the identification as male or female at birth) and from a child's efforts to account for what he or she sees or does not see (imagined as castration).[44] Jean Laplanche (invoking history to think psychoanalysis) refers to 'the contingent, perceptual and illusory character of anatomical sexual difference', which cannot ground the gender assignment that precedes it.[45] Zupančič points out that 'the central point of Freud's discovery was precisely that there is no "natural" or pre-established place of human sexuality . . . the sexual is not a substance to be properly described and circumscribed, it is the very impossibility of its own circumscription or delimitation . . . . Sexual is not a separate domain of human activity or life, and this is why it can inhabit all the domains of human life.'[46] But precisely because it is impossible to describe or limit, great effort has been expended to fix its meaning, locating anatomy as an explanation for gender. (This, I take to be the effort of the so-called 'new materialism' which invokes 'the body' as the ground on which sex is built.) Entire social and cultural edifices are built on the shaky foundations of so-called immutable gender difference. Whether taken as God's word or Nature's dictate, gender – the historically and culturally variable attempt to insist on the duality of sex difference – becomes the basis for imagining social, political and economic order.

By thinking gender in these terms, I found I could gain insight not only into the articulation, implementation, regulation and transgression of what used to be called 'sex roles', but also into the ways difference (at least in modern times) organizes perceptions of societies, polities and economies. This, of course, meant assuming the fragility of these perceptions, and it required reading for specific, contextual articulations of what male/female differences were taken to mean.

That gender plays a crucial definitional role in the organization of societies and politics is evident these days in the anguished warnings from opponents of feminist and queer theories, who argue that 'gender theory' is an assault against the very foundations of civilized life. To take only two examples: during the debates that led to the creation of the International Criminal Court in 1999, one commentator noted that if gender were allowed to refer to anything beyond biologically defined male and female, the court would be in the position of 'drastically restructuring societies throughout the world'.[47] This same concern about the radical potential of the concept was expressed by the opponents of a French curriculum that aimed at gender equity in 2011 and of France's law on gay marriage in 2013. The 'theory of gender', they argued, 'by denying sexual difference, [would] overturn the organization of our society and call into question its very foundations'.[48]

It is not only that gender is a primary way of conceiving of differentiation, extending beyond sex to race, class and nation; it is also that the illusory nature of anatomical sex difference introduces ambivalence, anxiety, indeterminacy and instability into these organizing conceptual systems. Knowing that this is the case opens the way to thinking about the dynamic operations of these systems, reading for their points of tension and contradiction, for the ways devised to deny or displace norms and regulations and thus for the sources of their transformation.

I do not think of my work as exclusively psychoanalytic (it is not psychohistory), but nor is psychoanalysis only supplementary, accounting for reason's leftovers or deviations, those pathological outbursts that otherwise do not fit within conventional frames. Rather, psychoanalysis has become an integral aspect of my thinking about the past. (And, my friend the psychoanalyst, seeking to historicize gender for his clinical practice, adds, 'and your historian's perspective is a fundamental aspect to our rethinking of psychoanalysis'.)[49] It is probably most useful at this point to offer some examples of what I mean by this. They come from my current work on secularism, a book that is a synthetic history, based on reading and rereading lots of work – feminist, postcolonial, queer theory, theories about race and racism – on the foundational place of gender in the emergence of modern nation-states.

The first example has to do with the politics of the nuclear family from the eighteenth century on, particularly the idea that the only legitimate aim of sexual activity was reproduction, confined to a married, heterosexual couple. What Lee Edelman, invoking Freud and Lacan, calls 'reproductive futurism' helps me account for this far-reaching phenomenon. Edelman's is a manifesto for a queer politics; my interest in his work has to do with understanding historical developments. It is his emphasis on reproduction as a denial of the death drive that inspires my thinking.[50] To put it all too briefly, the advent of the discourse of secularism, what Max Weber called 'disenchantment' – the substitution of rational calculation for religious belief – brought with it questions about the meaning of life. In the discourses of secularists, there was no longer a guarantee of immortality, of some kind of spiritual life after death, nor was it possible to imagine death as continuous with life. This led, Weber observed, to a sense not only of the 'meaninglessness of death', but also to 'the senselessness of life itself'. He writes, 'the stronger, the more systematic the thinking about the "meaning" of the universe becomes, the more the external organization of the world is rationalized, and the more the conscious experience of the world's irrational content is sublimated.'[51] Sublimation is used here in the classic Freudian sense: the turning of unappeasable anxiety to socially constructive ventures. A.K. Kordela describes it as the 'administration and management of the subject's relation to mortality and immortality, as compensation for the loss of eternity'.[52] In this discourse, biological reproduction becomes not only the sole legitimate aim of sexual intercourse, but the guarantee of immortality – securing life's meaning by deferring its realization to succeeding generations. This is what Edelman means by 'reproductive futurism': 'children secure our existence through the fantasy that we survive in them'. Edelman notes that it is not so much real children as an iconic Child that embodies this promise, 'the promise of a natural transcendence of the limits of nature itself'.[53] From this secular insistence on the importance of reproduction follows what Jacques Donzelot has called 'the policing of families' – the intervention of state power in the supposedly private life of individuals.[54] 'The old power of death that symbolized sovereign power', Foucault wrote, 'was now carefully supplanted by the administration of bodies and the calculated management of life.'[55] The 'unruly unconscious' refuses to disappear. But the question of what counted as a man or woman could never be entirely settled; it persisted in challenging and undermining those calculated management schemes. Reading for the rearticulations of gender in these terms and, of course, in the context of political, economic and social developments from the eighteenth century on provides critical insight into that politics and history.

The second example has to do with political institutions and citizenship and takes off from Claude Lefort's observation about the 'indeterminacy' of democracy. In the discourse of disenchantment, the loss of preeminent religious authority meant the loss of a transcendent affirmation for political power. Possession of the phallus, the symbol of the ruler's power, was no longer the prerogative of God's representative on earth. And, as the reign of kings (and the occasional queen) gave way to representative systems of government (parliaments, constitutional monarchies, republics, democracies), the physical body of the ruler as the incarnation of sovereignty was replaced by a set of disembodied abstractions: state, nation, citizen, representative, individual. Lefort puts it this way: 'the locus of power becomes an empty place . . . it is such that no individual and no group can be consubstantial with it – and it cannot be represented.'[56] The impossibility of representation, he continues, leads to a permanent state of uncertainty: 'The important point is that democracy is instituted and sustained by the dissolution of the markers of certainty. It inaugurates a history in which people experience a fundamental indeterminacy as to the basis of power, law and knowledge and as to the relations between *self* and *other* at every level of social life.'[57] Indeterminacy is a feature of democracy, not a denial of its history or institutions. It can help account not only for the long-standing exclusion of women and minorities from access to political office, but also for the populist appeal of figures like Trump and Berlusconi.

Freud theorized in *Totem and Taboo* that social contracts emerged when the original band of brothers, fed up with their father's monopoly of women, killed and ate him. The equal distribution of power among them, however, remained a challenge.[58] Although there have been many attempts to equate the phallus with the penis and so political power with masculinity, the fit has not been as persuasive as when a single ruler wielded all the power. Indeed, the penis might be seen as a poor substitute for the large, central and singular authority of the king. In any event, making the literal case for the penis as phallus has required continuous effort, the invention and reinvention of explanations. And it has not solved the matter of competition among the brothers. Can one of them ultimately take the father's place and so be exempt from or above the law? If so, which one? What are the signs of what Lacan called 'phallic exceptionalism'?[59] The search for answers to these questions plays out in the writing of constitutions, in the structure of political parties, in competition for office, in debates about the access of women to politics, in politicians' sexual liaisons and in varieties of political conflict, some of which have shaken the very foundations of nation-states.

To the extent that those foundations rest, at least in the western imaginary, on notions of naturalized, immutable sex differences, they will remain indeterminate (and that is probably all to the good). It is not (as I once argued) gender that itself constitutes a useful category for historical analysis, but gender understood as the impossible resolution to what psychoanalysis tells us is the enigma of the difference of sex. Far from imprisoning our history in closed diagnostic categories, this approach opens us to new readings of the past, and it also reminds us that those readings are never entirely definitive, never the last word. For Lefort, the indeterminacy of democracy was its hallmark and its guarantee. Perhaps we can say that the indeterminacy of interpretation insisted upon by psychoanalysis offers a similar guarantee for the practice of history.

Joan W. Scott is professor emerita in the School of Social Science at the Institute for Advanced Study in Princeton, New Jersey. Scott is the author of the classic essay 'Gender: A Useful Category of Historical Analysis', and her most recent books are *The Politics of the Veil* (2007), *The Fantasy of Feminist History* (2011) and *Sex and Secularism* (2017). An adjunct professor of history at the Graduate Center of the City University of New York, she is also an editor of *History of the Present: A Journal of Critical History*.

Notes

I am grateful to Ben Kafka, Brian Connolly, Thamy Ayouch and Elizabeth Weed for their critical comments.

1. H. Nunberg and E. Federn (eds), *Minutes of the Vienna Psychoanalytic Society,* 4 vols (New York: International Universities Press, 1962–75), vol. 1, 156.

2. E. Rolnik, 'Between Memory and Desire: From History to Psychoanalysis and Back', *Psychoanalysis and History* 3(2) (2001), 130. Rolnik's work led me to the *Minutes* cited in endnote 1.

3. M. Foucault, *The Order of Things: An Archaeology of the Human Sciences,* trans. unknown (New York: Vintage Press, 1994), 379.

4. S. Freud, *The Psychopathology of Everyday Life*, vol. 6 of *The Standard Edition of the Complete Psychological Works of Sigmund Freud* (*SE*), ed. and trans. J. Strachey (London: The Hogarth Press, 1995), 148. Childhood memories, Freud maintained, 'correspond, as far as their origins and reliability are concerned, to the history of a nation's earliest days, which was compiled later and for tendentious reasons' (84).

5. Freud, *The Psychopathology of Everyday Life*, 83.

6. Freud, *The Psychopathology of Everyday Life*, 84.

7. S. Freud, *Moses and Monotheism*, vol. 23 of *SE*, 69.

8. Freud, *Moses and Monotheism*, 269.

9. Freud, *Moses and Monotheism*, 42.

10. Freud, *Moses and Monotheism*, 261.

11. 'Secondary Revision', retrieved from https://www.encyclopedia.com/psychology/dictionaries-thesauruses-pictures-and-press-releases/secondary-revision (date of retrieval unknown).

12. Freud, *Moses and Monotheism*, 27. Elsewhere in this same text he writes, 'Once again I am prepared to find myself blamed for having presented my reconstruction of the early history of the people of Israel with too great and unjustified certainty. I shall not feel very severely hit by this criticism, since it finds an echo in my own judgement. I know myself that my structure has its weak spots, but it has its strong points too. On the whole my predominant impression is that it is worth while to pursue the work in the direction it has taken' (41).

13. Freud, *Moses and Monotheism*, 107.

14. Freud, *Moses and Monotheism*, 107.

15. M. de Certeau, *The Writing of History*, trans. T. Conley (New York: Columbia University Press, 1988), 289.

16. S. Freud, *Leonardo da Vinci and a Memory of his Childhood*, vol. 11 of *SE*, 84.

17. There is no collective unconscious for Freud, and I do not mean to imply that here. Rather, it is the case that individual unconscious processes can involve identification between members of a group or with a particular leader, producing collective action in certain instances. Historically specific representations provide a common repertoire or vocabulary for this kind of collective action. See Freud, *Group Psychology and the Analysis of the Ego*, vol. 18 of *SE*, 67–143.

18. A. Phillips, *Terrors and Experts* (London: Faber and Faber, 1995). Cited in P. Coviello, 'Intimacy and Affliction: DuBois, Race, and Psychoanalysis', *MLQ: Modern Language Quarterly* 64(1) (March 2003), 24.

19. Foucault, *The Order of Things*, 322.

20. De Certeau, *The Writing of History*, 303.

21. J. Copjec, 'Cutting up', in T. Brennan (ed.), *Between Feminism and Psychoanalysis* (New York: Routledge 1989), 241–2.

22. Coviello, 'Intimacy and Affliction', 15.

23. Coviello, 'Intimacy and Affliction', 31.

24. H.J. Spillers, 'All the Things You Could Be by Now, If Sigmund Freud's Wife Was Your Mother: Psychoanalysis and Race', *boundary 2* 23(3) (1996), 88.

25. Rolnik, 'Between Memory and Desire', 148.

26. Foucault, *The Order of Things*, 394.

27. E. Wilson, 'Another Neurological Scene', *History of the Present* 1(2) (2011), 156.

28. S. Freud, 'Creative Writers and Day-Dreaming', in *Jensen's 'Gravida' and Other Works*, vol. 9 of *SE*, 147–48.

29. This is how Philip Rieff put it: 'If for Marx the past is pregnant with the future, with the proletariat as the midwife of history, for Freud the future is pregnant with the past, with the psychoanalyst as the abortionist of history.' P. Rieff, 'The Meaning of History and Religion in Freud's Thought', *Journal of Religion* 31(2) (April 1951), 114–31, reprinted in

Bruce Mazlish (ed.). *Psychoanalysis and History* (New York: Grosset and Dunlap, 1971), 23–44. Citation is on 28.

30. Cited in J. Laplanche and J.-B. Pontalis, *The Language of Psychoanalysis*, trans. D. Nicholson-Smith (New York: Norton, 1973), 112.

31. S. Freud, *The History of an Infantile Neurosis*, vol. 17 of *SE*, 103.

32. Freud, *The History of an Infantile Neurosis*, 120.

33. De Certeau, *The Writing of History*, 303.

34. M.B. Brower, 'Science, Seduction and the Lure of Reality in Third Republic France', *History of the Present* 1(2) (2011), 172.

35. C. Steedman, *Dust: The Archive and Cultural History* (New Brunswick, NJ: Rutgers University Press, 2002), 68.

36. Steedman, *Dust*, 45.

37. This is a disagreement with the idea of transference offered by D. LaCapra in 'Is Everyone a *Mentalité* Case? Transference and the "Culture Concept"', in *History and Criticism* (Ithaca, NY: Cornell University Press, 1985), 72–73.

38. Cited in Steedman, *Dust*, 150.

39. Cited in Steedman, *Dust*, 71.

40. De Certeau, *The Writing of History*, 5.

41. De Certeau, *The Writing of History*, 309.

42. De Certeau, *The Writing of History*, 291.

43. A. Zupančič, *Why Psychoanalysis: Three Interventions* (Aarhus: Aarhus University Press, 2008), 7.

44. Samuel Weber's 1973 reading of Freud's essay on the uncanny points out that the phallus is not an object, but instead symbolizes the structure of castration itself. 'Not only do the eyes present the subject with the shocking "evidence" of a negative perception – the absence of a maternal phallus – but they also have to bear the brunt of a new state of affairs' – the subject 'will never again be able to believe its eyes, since what they have seen is neither simply visible nor wholly invisible. . . . What is involved here is a restructuring of experience, including the relation of perception, in which the narcissistic categories of identity and presence are riven by a difference they can no longer subdue or command'. S. Weber, 'The Sideshow, or: Remarks on a Canny Moment', *MLN* 88(6) *Comparative Literature* (December 1973), 1133.

45. J. Laplanche, 'Gender, Sex and the Sexual', in *Freud and the Sexual* (International Psychoanalytic Books, 2011), 159–202.

46. Zupančič, *Why Psychoanalysis*, 19.

47. Rome Statute of the International Criminal Court, 17 July 1998.

48. 'La Théoricienne du gender honoré par l'université Bordeaux 3', a protest circulated by the Association pour la Fondation de Service politique, a Catholic organization, protesting the award to Butler. Retrieved from www.libertepolitique.com (date of retrieval unknown).

49. Private email communication with Thamy Ayouch. See T. Ayouch, 'La déportation pour motif d'homosexualité: mémoire et histoire', in *Déportations en héritage, Revue française de Phénoménologie et de Psychanalyse* (Paris: L'Harmattan, 2015), 89–116.

50. L. Edelman, *No Future: Queer Theory and the Death Drive* (Durham, NC: Duke University Press, 2004).

51. M. Weber, 'Religious Rejections of the World and Their Directions', in H.H. Gerth and C. Wright Mills (eds), *From Max Weber: Essays in Sociology* (New York: Routledge, 1998), 356–7.

52. A.K. Kordela, '(Psychoanalytic) Biopolitics and Bioracism', *Umbr(a): A Journal of the Unconscious* (2011), 19.

53. Edelman, *No Future*, 12.

54. J. Donzelot, *La Police des Familles* (Paris: Les Editions de Minuit, 1977).

55. M. Foucault, *The History of Sexuality*, vol. 1, *An Introduction*, trans. R. Hurley (New York: Vintage Books, 1990), 139–40.

56. C. Lefort, *Democracy and Political Theory*, trans. David Macey (London: Polity Press, 1991), 17.

57. Lefort, *Democracy and Political Theory*, 19.

58. S. Freud, *Totem and Taboo*, vol. 13 of *SE*, 1–161.

59. J. Lacan, 'The Signification of the Phallus', in *Écrits*, trans. A. Sheridan (New York: WW Norton, 1977), 281–91. See also B. Fink, *A Clinical Introduction to Lacanian Psychoanalysis: Theory and Technique* (Cambridge, MA: Harvard University Press, 1997).

Bibliography

Ayouch, T. 'La déportation pour motif d'homosexualité: mémoire et histoire', in Daniel Beaune (ed.), *Revue française de phénoménologie et de psychanalyse: Déportations en héritage* (Paris : L'Harmattan, 2015), 89–116.

Brower, M.B. 'Science, Seduction and the Lure of Reality in Third Republic France'. *History of the Present* 1(2) (2011), 170–93.

Copjec, J. 'Cutting up', in Teresa Brennan (ed.), *Between Feminism and Psychoanalysis* (New York: Routledge, 1989), 227–46.

Coviello, P. 'Intimacy and Affliction: DuBois, Race, and Psychoanalysis'. *MLQ: Modern Language Quarterly* 64(1) (2003), 1–32.

de Certeau, M. *The Writing of History*, trans. T. Conley. New York: Columbia University Press, 1988.

Donzelot, J. *La Police des Familles*. Paris: Les Editions de Minuit, 1977.

Edelman, L. *No Future: Queer Theory and the Death Drive*. Durham: Duke University Press, 2004.

Fanon, F. *A Dying Colonialism*, trans. H. Chevalier. New York: Grove Press, 1965.

Fink, B. *A Clinical Introduction to Lacanian Psychoanalysis: Theory and Technique*. Cambridge, MA: Harvard University Press, 1997.

Foucault, M. *The History of Sexuality*. Vol. 1, *An Introduction*, trans. R. Hurley. New York: Vintage Books, 1990.

———. *The Order of Things: An Archaeology of the Human Sciences*, trans. unknown. New York: Vintage Press, 1994.

Freud, S. 'Creative Writers and Day-Dreaming', in *Jensen's 'Gravida' and Other Works*, vol. 9 of *The Standard Edition of the Complete Psychological Works of Sigmund Freud (SE)*, ed. and trans. J. Strachey. London: The Hogarth Press, 1995.

———. *Group Psychology and the Analysis of the Ego*. Vol. 18 of *SE*.

———. *The History of an Infantile Neurosis*. Vol. 17 of *SE*.

———. *Leonardo da Vinci and a Memory of His Childhood*. Vol. 11 of *SE*.

———. *Moses and Monotheism*. Vol. 23 of *SE*.

———. *The Psychopathology of Everyday Life*. Vol. 6 of *SE*.

———. *Totem and Taboo*. Vol. 13 of *SE*.

Gerth, H.H., and C. Wright Mills (eds). *From Max Weber: Essays in Sociology*. New York: Routledge, 1998.

Kordela, A.K. '(Psychoanalytic) Biopolitics and Bioracism'. *Umbr(a): A Journal of the Unconscious* (2011), 11–24.

Lacan, J. 'The Signification of the Phallus', in *Écrits*, trans. A. Sheridan (New York: Norton, 1977), 281–91.

LaCapra, D. 'Is Everyone a *Mentalité* Case? Transference and the "Culture Concept"', in *History and Criticism* (Ithaca: Cornell University Press, 1985), 71–94.

Laplanche, J. 'Gender, Sex and the Sexual', in *Freud and the Sexual* (n.p.: International Psychoanalytic Books, 2011), 159–202.

Laplanche, J., and J.-B. Pontalis. *The Language of Psychoanalysis,* trans. D. Nicholson-Smith. New York: Norton, 1973.

Lefort, C. *Democracy and Political Theory,* trans. D. Macey. London: Polity Press, 1991.

Mazlish, B. (ed.). *Psychoanalysis and History.* New York: Grosset and Dunlap, 1971.

Nunberg, H., and E. Federn (eds). *Minutes of the Vienna Psychoanalytic Society.* 4 vols. New York: International Universities Press, 1962–75.

Phillips, A. *Terrors and Experts.* London: Faber and Faber, 1995.

Rieff, P. 'The Meaning of History and Religion in Freud's Thought'. *Journal of Religion* 31(2) (1951), 114–31.

Rolnik, E. 'Between Memory and Desire: From History to Psychoanalysis and Back', *Psychoanalysis and History* 3(2) (2001), 129–51.

Salecl, R. *The Spoils of Freedom: Psychoanalysis and Feminism after the Fall of Socialism.* New York: Routledge, 2002.

Schor, N. *Reading in Detail: Aesthetics and the Feminine.* New York: Routledge, 2007.

Spillers, H.J. 'All the Things You Could Be by Now, if Sigmund Freud's Wife Was Your Mother: Psychoanalysis and Race'. *boundary 2* 23(3) (1996), 75–141.

Steedman, C. *Dust: The Archive and Cultural History.* New Brunswick: Rutgers University Press, 2002.

Weber, M. 'Religious Rejections of the World and Their Directions', in H.H. Gerth and C. Wright Mills (eds), *From Max Weber: Essays in Sociology* (New York: Routledge, 1998), 323–61.

Weber, S. 'The Sideshow, or: Remarks on a Canny Moment', *MLN* 88(6) *Comparative Literature* (December 1973), 1102–33.

Wilson, E. 'Another Neurological Scene'. *History of the Present* 1(2) (2011), 149–69.

Wynter, S. 'Unsettling the Coloniality of Being/Power/Truth/Freedom: Towards the Human, After Man, Its Overrepresentation – An Argument', *CR: The New Centennial Review,* 3(3) (2003), 257–337.

Zupančič, A. *Why Psychoanalysis: Three Interventions.* Aarhus: Aarhus University Press, 2008.

CHAPTER 6

Does Time Have a Gender?

Queer Temporality, Anachronism and the Desire for the Past

KRISTINA FJELKESTAM

Does time have a gender? Or, rather, does time have *a* gender, in the singular? Historically, in Western culture, time has been signified as male. Ancient Greek for 'time' is 'chronos', which furthermore implies the measuring of time, chronology. 'Cronos' is also the famous titan of Greek mythology who ate all his children so that no one else would be able to claim world dominion. Thus we have the common metaphor of human ageing and death as 'time devouring its children' – and perhaps also the grotesque Swedish saying that 'grandchildren are the dessert of life'. However, Cronos's son Zeus managed to make Cronos disgorge him and his siblings, after which they imprisoned their father in the underworld. There he stayed, but remained an inspiration to all forthcoming rulers of chronology: male historians.

The historical consciousness of Western modernity, as it was shaped by the European Enlightenment and its amalgamation of the nation-state, secularism, scientific rationality and the idea of progress, would subsequently posit the historical past of the West as comprising *all* pasts. Hence, it became considered as the *only* past, all in the spirit of Enlightenment universalism. The representation of this singular past consists of certain chosen events piled up sequentially, turning the present into both the crowning glory and a kind of Rome to which all roads lead. But of course the historical consciousness of the West, traditionally denoted as masculine, is only one of many possible conceptions of the past.[1]

Notes for this section begin on page 122.

So what about women and time? Well, the ancient muse of historiography – Clio – had to settle for being only an inspiration to the male historians, and thus commemoration turned into a strictly masculine affair. This exclusively male kind of history writing – especially its supposed objectivity – has of course spurred critical debates. Recent debates emanate from the polyphonic reality entering academia in the postwar era, giving way to more recent feminist, postcolonial and queer ideas on temporality. Here the 'history of conquerors', which drew up lists of kings and war battles, was soon to be replaced by 'history from below', or from the side, including the histories of women, children and ethnic and sexual minorities.

As (hi)stories always have a narrative, and narratives always have a story, the question that consistently must be asked is *what* story is being told – and *how* it is narrated. Who speaks to whom, and why? In the following, I will develop an argument concerning the latter – that is, the 'why' of history writing, its ethos, understood here as a driving force – which, I suggest, is an often politically charged inclination 'to know' the past, also in the sensually affective and erotically charged sense of 'knowing'. In my conclusion I will propose a three-dimensional model of what I call *the desire for the past,* which might (or might not) prove to be a productive analytical tool for further explorations in this matter. But I begin the essay by tracing the desire for the past with a selective discussion of theories of gendered temporalities. Then I move on to more recent issues concerning queer temporality studies and its accompanying norm-critical focus on anachronism and affect before I arrive at my concluding remarks.

Time and Gender

Second-wave feminist thinking on temporality critiques Western modernity's historical consciousness as founded on the notion of constant linear progression. This is the case in, for instance, Julia Kristeva's classic essay 'Women's Time' from 1981, which brings out the historical association of women with a cyclical conception of time (usually due to their reproductive capacities).[2] Kristeva argues that as first-wave feminism strove to place women in linear time – that is, to give women their rightful place in the political and historical chronology of the West – second-wave feminism instead preferred placing women outside of the linear time axis, to transcend it, thus linking the repetitive character of the cyclical conception of time to an eternal perspective.

Teresa de Lauretis is another now classic example, and she adds the aspect of desire. In 'Desire in Narrative' from 1984, she discusses narrative time structure through the lens of her critique of structuralist narratology.[3] All of these schematics à la Lévi-Strauss (structures of kinship), Propp (element functions) and Greimas (the actantial model) draw up a course of events based on an active male agent who sets the story in motion and moves it forward. Here, the female element only figures as a hindrance to be over-come or engulfed on the way to the final destination of signification. A story is driven by desire, but it is solely a heterosexually masculine kind of desire that is articulated, referred to and addressed. De Lauretis considers *boundary* and *passage* as the basic distinction in structuralist narratology, and as such she claims that it is modelled on an ideological assumption of sexual difference. Only the male agent gets to pass the boundary: 'In doing so the hero, the mythical subject, is constructed as human being and as male, he is the active principle of culture, the establisher of distinction, the creator of differences. Female is what is not susceptible to transformation, to life or death; she (it) is an element of plot-space, a topos, a resistance, matrix and matter.'[4] Transcending boundaries implies being 'the active principle', de-noted as masculine, and as such the male hero is identified as the only true human being. And to make things worse, says Teresa de Lauretis, narrativity as such is sadistic; paraphrasing Laura Mulvey, she says, 'Sadism demands a story, depends on making something happen, forcing a change in another person, a battle of will and strength, victory/defeat, all occurring in a linear time with a beginning and an end'.[5] This constant linear progression driven forward by masculine heterosexual desire is thus akin to an act of violence. As an alternative, however, de Lauretis advocates the cyclical conception of time as a milder and merrier, more 'feminine' kind of temporality, with a resemblance to, for instance, the menstrual cycle.

It is, of course, reductive to talk about temporality in terms of 'male' linearity and 'female' cyclicality as these second-wave feminists do, especially when the two gendered conceptions of time are opposed to each other in a hierarchical relationship. Also nonfeminists used this kind of gender-hierar-chical argument, though, as in Marshall Berman's well-known 1982 inter-pretation of Goethe's *Faust* in terms of male progressivity, positively pointing towards the future, with Faust's Gretchen acting as a foil to futurity by signi-fying female iterability and being pejoratively associated with the past.[6]

However, hierarchical arguments continue to crop up. Now, for in-stance, everything that is not linear and chronological is often considered as somehow 'better'. Indeed, the idea of constant progression and capitalism's demand of constant growth have clearly been a bad thing for both humans and the environment, but historiography reaches a dead end when it is called upon to estimate the relative value of different time conceptions. What in-stead appears interesting with scholars like de Lauretis et al. is their pertinent questioning and defamiliarization of habitual representations of temporality in both fact and fiction. They also initiated new concepts, such as desire, in relation to historiographic issues – something to which I shall return in a moment.

Queer Temporality

Historiography, not least its theoretical aspects, has enjoyed a revival in the humanities in recent years. In these current debates, historicizing manoeuvres use the present as a critical point of reference, which must be kept distinct from using the present as a normative standard (presentism) as well as from the teleological notion of the present as a fulfilment of the past. Instead, time is considered as a concept that not only involves measurement and a synchronizing impulse, but also rhythm, sequence, tempo and intensity.[7] For instance, 'the event' is theorized in terms of excessive being – that is, something hitherto unknown and unnamed that creates a fracture in the onward march of chronology.[8] Other alternative temporalities oppose experienced versus material time, diachronic versus synchronic time, etc. in their questioning of linearity, but they somehow always risk reverting to binary thinking – as in the above-mentioned linear/cyclical and time-bound/timeless oppositions. What, then, are the more productive avenues for exploring multifaceted temporalities, at least in gendered terms? Some suggestive answers are to be found within the field of queer temporality studies.[9]

What makes queer criticism particularly pertinent to this discussion is that history writing must always respond to the embodiedness of temporal experience: 'Historicism is queer when it grasps that temporality itself raises the question of embodiment and subjectivity', as Carolyn Dinshaw puts it.[10] Thus an important aspect of temporality studies is the critique of 'chrononormativity', a term coined by Elizabeth Freeman as signifying chronological norms of a heterosexual life curve consisting of 'a technique by which institutional forces come to seem like somatic facts'.[11] Childhood and puberty are to be followed by adulthood's matrimony and child rearing – all in the right order – into old age, where you will be served with grandchildren as the chronological icing on the cake, as the dessert of life. The concept of chrononormativity discloses the naturalization of this pattern, and how self-evident it has become for individuals, society and politics geared towards maximizing gains in production and reproduction.

'Chronology' is, according to the dictionary, an order 'naturally' arranged.[12] But linearity is, of course, not 'natural', as it only constitutes a particular design of perception. The interpretation of biological ageing is similarly a social construction – for instance, scholars have noticed that the only age valued by Western capitalism is the productive mid-life, while children are regarded as a bunch of 'not-yets' and the elderly a gaggle of 'has-beens'.[13]

Another pertinent issue concerns how time in general is valued – whose time is considered valuable and whose is considered worthless? Why has 'slowness' suddenly become valorized over against the previously privileged speed and acceleration of Western modernity, and how is this tied to power structures of class, gender, ethnicity and sexuality? When asking these kinds of questions, it becomes clear that the renaissance of historiography has an ethical and political dimension. In this context – as one example among many – Sarah Sharma's definition of temporality as differential power relations played out in time becomes highly relevant.[14]

Queer temporality studies are at the core of these matters. Elizabeth Freeman puts a central concept – chrononormativity – into words in her book *Time Binds* (2010), and other attempts of formulating something similar consist, for instance, of Judith Halberstam's concept of 'life schedules' denominated in *In a Queer Time and Place* (2005), and Sara Ahmed's discussion of 'the straight line' in *Queer Phenomenology* (2006). What Halberstam calls life schedules contain our perceptions of how life is supposed to be led. Heteronormativity is pivotal since childbearing composes the zenith of the life curve, creating meaning and hope of a future for both individuals and society. The representation of the universal Child can even be viewed as a cultural and social staging of a reproductive futurism that excludes all other alternatives, as Lee Edelman claims in *No Future* (2004). Habitually and re-iteratively, life schedules are set up along a 'straight line' – that is, the path of heterosexuality, which can lead in only one direction. This beaten track decides our direction of travel, and Sara Ahmed's phenomenological study shows how the straight line both shapes and is shaped by our actual bodies. In conclusion: the cultural and social Western values pinpointed by concepts such as chrononormativity, life schedules and the straight line are all about human succession, maturity and development, and in breaking them one will appear as immature, unfashionable and out of joint with time.

Anachronism

Thus the concept of 'anachronism' can be considered as another pivotal discussion point in queer temporality studies, within the analytic realm of chrononormativity. To be uncoeval means amongst other things to be anachronistic – asynchronic, 'unsynced', somehow out of place. The concept of anachronism is, as such, a modern invention, first conceived in the eighteenth century.[15] During the Western premodern era concepts such as 'syncretic chronology', a kind of timelessness, were used instead.[16] A medieval painting, for instance, could self-evidently represent soldiers wearing fourteenth-century armours when standing beside the tomb of Jesus. This modus operandi created a temporal unity between then and now, in which Jesus became 'not of a distant, foreign past, but of an eternal present'.[17] Thus the past was made into something continuously present, just like the past was considered the source of knowledge to which you turned for the truth of old authority.

In the historical consciousness of modernity, the past was instead turned into a space of ignorance and error. Today, the worst vice of anachronism is to apply present thinking and contemporary concepts on historical phenomena – for instance, to talk about 'homosexuality' when discussing premodernity. However, one will necessarily have to commit a measure of violence on the past in order to conceive of it in the present. After all, when facilitating a rendering of the past, 'the necessary anachronism' is needed – at least according to Hegel in his posthumously published lectures on aesthetics. To be sure, temporality will demand certain circumlocution and 'translation' – time needs its metaphors, as Lynn Hunt points out.[18]

In the classical terms of historical materialism, this also involves *actualizing* history – that is, as for example Walter Benjamin claimed, repeatedly putting history in dialogue with present conceptions of it in order to achieve political transformation.[19] Hence, New Historicists have noted that actualization as such is a mode of anachronism, since the interpretative strategies used do not derive from the epochs on which they are used. Catherine Belsey wrote something to this effect in 1985, which has lingered in my mind:

> To read the past, to read a text from the past, is thus always to make an interpretation which is in a sense an anachronism. Time travel is a fantasy. We cannot reproduce the conditions – the economy, the diseases, the manners, the language and the corresponding subjectivity – of another century. To do so would be, in any case, to eliminate the difference which makes the fantasy pleasurable: it would be to erase the recollection of the present, to cease to be, precisely, a traveller. Reading the past depends on this difference. The real anachronism, then, is of another kind. Here history as time travel gives way to history as costume drama, the reconstruction of the past as the present in fancy dress. The project is to explain away the surface strangeness of another century in order to release its profound continuity with the present. The past is read as – and for – evidence that change is always only superficial, that human nature, what it is to be a person, a man or a woman, a wife or a husband, is palpably unchanging. This history militates against radical commitment by denying the possibility of change.[20]

Modern anachronism, understood as an awareness of difference, thus has its productive aspects as well. It can enable contemporary political commitment, and does not have to be only a negative, fault-finding invective. The real mistake, according to Belsey, is instead to try to reconstruct the past on the premise of similarity, in which the time gap between then and now attempts to be bridged. If one does not recognize difference – which implies putting topics of current interest in an ongoing dialogue with the past – one will risk merely smoothing things over. The negative anachronism of Belsey's thus

consists of a belief in a 'resemblance' between then and now. The more positive approach towards anachronism based on difference instead multiplies
temporality. One must, in other words, alienate the past rather than identify
with it, and that is why the questions we ask history cannot be anything but
anachronistic. But that is also why our questions can become interesting,
important even, to our own time. In this sense, to be 'out of sync' allows for
an emancipatory potential.

However, temporal power discourse can make use of this kind of binary
difference strategy too – for instance, when what is to be defined as Other
is viewed as primitive and out of date, placed in what Anne McClintock
names 'anachronistic space': 'According to this trope, colonized people –
like women and the working class in the metropolis – do not inhabit history
proper but exist in a permanently anterior time within the geographic space
of the modern empire as anachronistic humans, atavistic, irrational, bereft of
human agency – the living embodiment of the archaic "primitive."'[21] To
autocratically place the Other in a heterogeneous temporality is close to an
act of violence, culminating in a loss of significance: 'History cannot represent, except through a process of translation and consequent loss of status and
signification for the translated, the heterotemporality of that world', writes
the postcolonial theorist Dipesh Chakrabarty.[22] But to stress the fact that
estrangement not only implies spatial markers but also temporal ones – such
as anachronisms – is in my view still a necessary statement.

Insofar as anachronisms are concerned, they are an essential but complex
metaphor of temporality. In addition to the aspects already discussed, I also
want to suggest that anachronism might be anthropomorphized, not unlike
the individualization of historical epochs as, for example, 'spirit' and 'consciousness', *Zeitgeist* and *mentalité,* in order to distinguish them both from
each other and from the present.[23] Carolyn Dinshaw, for instance, asks how
it might feel affectively to be an anachronism in her discussion of the English
medieval mystic Margery Kempe (who cried as if Christ had just died when
she caught sight of a pietà), and Alison Bechdel materializes an anachronism
when she ironically has one of the characters in her graphic novel *Fun Home*
from 2006 claim that an encountered butch lesbian is a relic from the twentieth century.[24] When exploiting the potentiality of multiple temporalities,
both time and sexuality are thus interestingly problematized through the
materialization of anthropomorphic anachronism.

Desiring the Past

I will now turn to affect in relation to temporality, and specifically to the
affect of desire in a historiographical sense of 'desiring the past'. As norm-

criticism constitutes the core of queer temporality studies, which I have exemplified above with the concept of chrononormativity and suggesting one
of its main analytic instances as anachronism, an important implication is the
fact that norms of temporality are carved out on actual bodies and accordingly create affects that are bodily determined.

'Desire' is here supposed to function as a driving force that incorpo-
rates a longing for a past that no longer is – or even ever was. Desiring the
past can thus involve striving for acknowledgement within the framework
of the symbolic order, for instance as in constructing homosexual identity
retroactively or in enhancing certain kinds of masculinity.[25] Striving for acknowledgement is compelled by 'an overwhelming desire to *feel historical*',
according to Christopher Nealon – that is, the desire to be included into
collective histories.[26] This kind of desire is all about vindication and, by
extension, political transformation through the writing of history. A 'queer
desire for history', as Carolyn Dinshaw puts it, therefore make affective con-
nections to the past possible.[27]

I would like to claim that desire thus makes up for one of the most
central concepts of gendered historiography. An interesting aspect of the
complex of affects that shape the desire for the past is what I consider to be
a renaissance of the affirmation of culturally defined emotions in relation to
historiography in general (in the wake of the affective and ontological turns).
Indeed, the foundation of history as a modern discipline initially involved
subjective feelings for the past, but soon the institutionalization of the discipline demanded a putative repression of sentiment in order to promote
scientific objectivity. Feelings were eradicated when history writing became
a scholarly profession in the nineteenth century.

But the sentimental antiquarian of the eighteenth century had not been
shying away from expressing his explicit desire for the past. This desire was
close to erotic, according to Mike Goode. Goode gives an example from
Edmund Burke, who in *Reflections of the Revolution in France* from 1790, in an
often quoted scene, represents the royal couple being captured at Versailles by
Parisians during the French revolution:

> From this sleep the queen was first startled by the voice of the sentinel at her
> door, who cried out to her to save herself by flight – that this was the last proof
> of fidelity he could give – that they were upon him, and he was dead. Instantly
> he was cut down. A band of cruel ruffians and assassins, reeking of his blood,
> rushed into the chamber of the queen, and pierced with a hundred strokes of
> bayonets and poniards the bed, from whence this persecuted woman had but
> just time to fly *almost naked,* and, through ways unknown to the murderers, had
> escaped to seek refuge at the feet of a king and husband, not secure of his own
> life for a moment.[28]

Burke's desire for the past consists of a longing for the lost days of *l'ancien ré-
gime* dressed in an obvious sexual attraction towards Marie Antoinette. In the

quote above, it is expressed in the form of an erotic fantasy in which Marie Antoinette 'almost naked' tries to escape her pursuers. Mike Goode claims that Burke's sentimental historicism here 'devolves from sexual feeling', implying an 'erotics of historicism'.[29] As such, it aims towards a sensuous staging of the past similar to the contemporaneous antiquarians whose desire for archaeological findings earned them the sexually impinged characterization of *retrophiles*. Thus, desire is not to be reduced to signifying sexual relations between persons, but rather considered as collective social formations in a wider sense.

In psychoanalytic theories we are all basically defined as desiring beings, and our desires continuously engender new ones and thus make satisfaction unattainable. This constant deferral of fulfilment is compelled by metonymic movements, which can take the rhetorical form of temporal figures — anachronism, for instance, as discussed above. Thus historical writings can turn into something akin to erotic fantasy, to paraphrase Joan Scott.[30]

However, as for example Gilles Deleuze and Félix Guattari pointed out 1972 in their *Anti-Oedipus* critique of Freud, desire is not only about lack and dissatisfaction but can also be a constructive force aiming to achieve political goals and being an active part of social transformation.[31] Neither is desire a transhistorical concept, considered along the lines of the metaphysical tradition of lack stretching from Plato to Lacan in which human desire is defined in ahistorical terms such as 'origin' (cf. Plato's androgyne) or as 'cause' (cf. Lacan's differentiation between subject and desired object).[32] Historical manifestations of human desire are instead complex interrelations of psychic structures, social norms and aesthetic representations, and are in this sense preferably viewed as discursive processes that can assume a variety of social and cultural expressions. The question, rather, concerns what desire *does* instead of what it *is*.[33] Defining desire as a social and cultural force thus makes it possible to consider it a performative act.[34] In this sense, it can be exploitable for ideological ends, not only 'good' but also 'bad' ones. So-called affective historiography is thus in constant need of scrutiny, both concerning epistemology and ethics, since it has a potential not only for emancipatory goals but for distorting historical knowledge and preventing critical insights.[35] However, with these dangers in mind, I will conclude my essay by suggesting a three-dimensional model of desire, possibly useful as an analytical tool when discussing different expressions of the desire for the past.

Conclusion

'I began with the desire to speak with the dead' is the often quoted opening to Stephen Greenblatt's *Shakespearean Negotiations* from 1988. This secret desire, which scholars have preferred to downplay, can, after all, receive some satisfaction through fiction, according to Greenblatt. He is right in considering fiction (as well as history writing) an active communicator, especially when these texts are treated as answers instead of questions. Questions are instead to be put to them by scholars, which inevitably make their present-day queries to the past anachronistic. But it is also the reason why questions can become interesting and important, just like the 'answers' of the documents already are. The productive tension between now–then–later is what keeps the dialogue going.

It seems to me as if considerable scholarly energy at present is spent on problematizing narrated *histories* rather than (as did postmodernism) the *narratives* of history. This tendency is ethical in kind, and can be explained as a turning of scientific and artistic attention from history as fiction to fiction as history. Postmodern narratives illuminated both the literariness of history writing and the impossibility of writing History in the singular with a capital H, which involved liberation from static forms and empowering narrativity. However, the narrative zest of postmodernity is now transformed into a slightly more resolute effort to depict new kinds of histories – mostly still in fictional form, judging by the current boom in historical fiction.[36]

In an attempt to interpret these diverse cultural manifestations of the desire for the past, I suggest putting a three-dimensional model to work. My essay has been exploring theoretical underpinnings for this model, but there is not enough space to put it to the test empirically. However, the sensual and affective investments in the desire for the past can be considered as a wish 'to know' history in a close to erotically charged sense since, besides acquiring knowledge, to 'know' also implies sexual possession.[37] The entanglement of historical narrative and desire can thus be conceived of as a mode of knowing, as manifested in the dual ambition to attain both knowledge and a sensuously affective connection to the past, a popular tendency that is apparent in various historical reenactments and TV shows such as BBC's *The Supersizers* (in Sweden *The History Eaters*) where the presenters immerse themselves in a chosen historical period. These dimensions are of a cognitive and of an affective kind, respectively. However, the desire to 'feel historical' as Christopher Nealon puts it in an earlier quotation, also includes a striving for social recognition. Desiring inclusion in collective histories of both fiction and fact is of a political kind, which composes the third dimension.

My tripartite model of desire indicates, I believe, a central driving force in historical writing. It combines the inclination 'to know' the past in a cognitive but also sensually affective sense of 'knowing', with a political twist. This concept of desire is based on the difference between then and now (and not on any ideological perceptions of sexual difference), and as such it allows for anachronistic interpretation as a highly conscious collapsing of temporalities (which is not to be mistaken for the collapsing of any differences between past and present).

Stories are driven by desire, as Teresa de Lauretis rightly pointed out. I claim that this is the case also when referring to historical writings, but not in the shape of her 'masculine' and 'heterosexual' kind of desire that sadistically demands a linear story with a forced beginning and end. Instead, anachronism, understood as awareness of difference, offers more productive possibilities. To be 'out of sync' multiplies both temporality and desire, as well as enabling emancipatory potential and political commitment.

In sum: here we are, then, in the past's sensuous presence. However, temporality is like all other social and cultural phenomena steeped in power relations – apart from gender, also those of sexuality, ethnicity, class .... The list goes on. So my initial question about whether time has a gender or not can undoubtedly be answered in the affirmative. But rather than being gendered in the singular, time is gendered in multifaceted and complex ways and in a sense in which the desire for the past is open-ended.

Kristina Fjelkestam is professor in gender studies at Stockholm University. Her main research interests include feminist cultural theory and historiography, and she has published three monographs in Swedish concerning these subjects, as well as several articles in national and international academic journals. She is currently working on a book concerning the way our desire of the past forms and is formed by cultural expressions such as historical novels, films and reenactment.

Notes

1. See D. Chakrabarty, *Provincializing Europe: Postcolonial Thought and Historical Difference* (Princeton: Princeton University Press, 2000). For a further survey of contemporary historiography, see A. Tucker (ed.), *A Companion to the Philosophy of History and Historiography* (London: Blackwell, 2010).

2. J. Kristeva, 'Women's Time', in T. Moi (ed.), *The Kristeva Reader* (Blackwell, Oxford, 1986).

3. T. de Lauretis, 'Desire in Narrative', in *Alice Doesn't: Feminism, Semiotics, Cinema* (London: Macmillan, 1984).

4. De Lauretis, 'Desire in Narrative', 119.

5. De Lauretis, 'Desire in Narrative', 103; de Lauretis here paraphrases Laura Mulvey's classic text 'Visual Pleasure and Narrative Cinema'.

6. M. Berman, *All That Is Solid Melts into Air: The Experience of Modernity* (New York: Simon & Schuster, 1982).

7. R. Felski, *Doing Time: Feminist Theory and Postmodern Culture* (New York: New York University Press, 2000), 17.

8. See H. White, 'The Historical Event', *Differences* 19(2) (2008).

9. I am aware of the problems involved in drawing up a kind of history in which scien-

tific 'answers' are supposed to replace each other in a course of steady progression. To construct the past in such a dismissive manner is both reductive and excluding, so instead I choose to consider the so-called temporal turn in terms of deepening and complication of certain aspects in earlier historiographical research. But according to, for instance, Ben Davies and Jana Funke (eds) in *Sex, Gender and Time in Fiction and Culture* (Basingstoke: Palgrave Macmillan, 2011), 2, the temporal turn is 'the latest' of theoretical turns; and Sarah Sharma sees the temporal turn as a congenial consequence of the spatial turn in her book *In the Meantime: Temporality and Cultural Politics* (Durham: Duke University Press, 2014), 10.

10. C. Dinshaw, 'Temporalities', in P. Strohm (ed.), *Middle English* (Oxford: Oxford University Press, 2007), 109.

11. E. Freeman, *Time Binds: Queer Temporalities, Queer Histories* (Durham: Duke University Press, 2010), 3.

12. 'Tideräkning', in *Nationalencyklopedin*, vol. 18 (Höganäs: Bra Böcker, 1995).

13. See A.-L. Närvänen, 'Age, Ageing and Life Course', in B.-M. Öberg et al. (eds), *Changing Worlds and the Ageing Subject: Dimensions in the Study of Ageing and Later Life* (Aldershot: Ashgate, 2004).

14. Sharma, *In the Meantime*, 4.

15. M. de Grazia, 'Anachronism', in B. Cummings and J. Simpson (eds), *Cultural Reformations: Medieval and Renaissance in Literary History* (Oxford University Press: Oxford, 2010); P. Burke, 'The Sense of Anachronism from Petrarch to Poussin', in C. Humphrey and W.M. Ormrod (eds), *Time in the Medieval World* (York: York Medieval Press, 2001).

16. A. Kemp, *The Estrangement of the Past: A Study in the Origins of Modern Historical Consciousness* (Oxford: Oxford University Press, 1991), 47.

17. Kemp, *The Estrangement of the Past*, 50.

18. L. Hunt, *Measuring Time, Making History* (Budapest: Central European University Press, 2008), 3.

19. W. Benjamin, 'Eduard Fuchs, der Sammler und der Historiker', in *Gesammelte Schriften* II:2 (Frankfurt am Main: Suhrkamp 1977), 468.

20. C. Belsey, *The Subject of Tragedy: Identity and Difference in Renaissance Drama* (London: Methuen, 1985), 2.

21. A. McClintock' *Imperial Leather: Race, Gender and Sexuality in the Colonial Contest* (New York: Routledge, 1995), 30; see also 40–42.

22. Chakrabarty, *Provincializing Europe*, 95.

23. De Grazia, 'Anachronism', 13.

24. Dinshaw, 'Temporalities', 107; A. Bechdel, *Fun Home: A Family Tragicomic* (London: Jonathan Cape, 2006), 108.

25. See H. Love, *Feeling Backward: Loss and the Politics of Queer History* (Cambridge, MA: Harvard University Press, 2007); M. Goode, *Sentimental Masculinity and the Rise of History 1790–1890* (Cambridge: Cambridge University Press, 2009).

26. C. Nealon, *Foundlings: Lesbian and Gay Historical Emotion before Stonewall* (Durham: Duke University Press, 2001), 8.

27. C. Dinshaw et al., 'Theorizing Queer Temporalities: A Roundtable Discussion', in *GLQ* 13(2–3) (2007), 178.

28. E. Burke, *Reflections on the Revolution in France* (New Haven: Yale University Press, 2003) 60 (my emphasis).

29. M. Goode, *Sentimental Masculinity and the Rise of History 1790–1890*, 41 and 45.

30. See J.W. Scott, *The Fantasy of Feminist History* (Duke: Duke University Press, 2011).

31. See chapter 5 on desire in C. Colebrook, *Understanding Deleuze* (Crows Nest: Allen & Unwin, 2002).

32. A tradition neatly presented and criticized in J. Butler, 'Desire', in F. Lentricchia and T. McLaughlin (eds), *Critical Terms for Literary Study*, 2nd ed. (Chicago: Chicago University Press, 1995).

33. See K. Gorton, *Theorising Desire: From Freud to Feminism to Film* (London: Palgrave Macmillan, 2008).
34. See S.S. Lanser, *The Sexuality of History: Modernity and the Sapphic, 1565–1830* (Chicago: University of Chicago Press, 2014).
35. A. Koivunen, 'Affective Historiography: Archival Aesthetics and the Temporalities of Televisual Nation-Building', *International Journal of Communication* 10 (2016), 5275.
36. J. de Groot comments on the recent boom in his book *The Historical Novel* (London: Routledge, 2010), 98.
37. See S.S. Friedman, 'Making History: Reflections on Feminism, Narrative, and Desire', in *Mappings: Feminism and the Cultural Geographies of Encounter* (Princeton: Princeton University Press, 1998), 218.

Bibliography

Ahmed, S. *Queer Phenomenology: Orientations, Objects, Others.* Durham: Duke University Press, 2006.

Bechdel, A. *Fun Home: A Family Tragicomic.* London: Jonathan Cape, 2006.

Belsey, C. *The Subject of Tragedy: Identity and Difference in Renaissance Drama.* London: Methuen, 1983.

Benjamin, W. 'Eduard Fuchs, der Sammler und der Historiker', in *Gesammelte Schriften* II:2 (Frankfurt am Main: Suhrkamp, 1977), 465–505.

Berman, M. *All That Is Solid Melts into Air: The Experience of Modernity.* New York: Simon & Schuster, 1982.

Burke, E. *Reflections on the Revolution in France.* New Haven: Yale University Press, 2003.

Burke, P. 'The Sense of Anachronism from Petrarch to Poussin', in C. Humphrey and W.M. Ormrod (eds), *Time in the Medieval World* (York: York Medieval Press, 2001), 157–73.

Butler, J. 'Desire', in F. Lentricchia and T. McLaughlin (eds), *Critical Terms for Literary Study,* 2nd ed. (Chicago: Chicago University Press, 1995), 369–87.

Chakrabarty, D. *Provincializing Europe: Postcolonial Thought and Historical Difference.* Princeton: Princeton University Press, 2000.

Colebrook, C. *Understanding Deleuze.* Crows Nest: Allen & Unwin, 2002.

Davies, B., and J. Funke (eds). *Sex, Gender and Time in Fiction and Culture.* Basingstoke: Palgrave Macmillan, 2011.

de Grazia, M. 'Anachronism', in B. Cummings and J. Simpson (eds), *Cultural Reformations: Medieval and Renaissance in Literary History* (Oxford: Oxford University Press, 2010), 13–33.

de Groot, J. *The Historical Novel.* London: Routledge, 2010.

de Lauretis, Teresa. *Alice Doesn't: Feminism, Semiotics, Cinema.* London: Macmillan, 1984.

Dinshaw, C. 'Temporalities', in P. Strohm (ed.), *Middle English* (Oxford: Oxford University Press, 2007), 107–23.

Dinshaw, C. et al. 'Theorizing Queer Temporalities: A Roundtable Discussion'. *GLQ* 13(2–3) (2007), 177–95.

Edelman, L. *No Future: Queer Theory and the Death Drive.* Durham: Duke University Press, 2004.

Freeman, E. *Time Binds: Queer Temporalities, Queer Histories.* Durham: Duke University Press, 2010.

Friedman, S.S. 'Making History: Reflections on Feminism, Narrative, and Desire', in *Mappings: Feminism and the Cultural Geographies of Encounter* (Princeton: Princeton University Press, 1998), 199–228.

Goode, M. *Sentimental Masculinity and the Rise of History 1790–1890.* Cambridge: Cambridge University Press, 2009.

Gorton, K. *Theorising Desire: From Freud to Feminism to Film.* London: Palgrave Macmillan, 2008.

Greenblatt, S. *Shakespearean Negotiations: The Circulation of Social Energy in Renaissance England.* Berkeley: University of California Press, 1988.

Halberstam, J. *In a Queer Time and Place: Transgender Bodies, Subcultural Lives.* New York: New York University Press, 2005.

Hunt, L. *Measuring Time, Making History.* Budapest: Central European University Press, 2008.

Kemp, A. *The Estrangement of the Past: A Study in the Origins of Modern Historical Consciousness.* Oxford: Oxford University Press, 1991.

Kristeva, J. 'Women's Time', in T. Moi (ed.), *The Kristeva Reader* (Oxford: Blackwell, 1986), 187–213.

Koivunen, A. 'Affective Historiography: Archival Aesthetics and the Temporalities of Televisual Nation-Building'. *International Journal of Communication* 10 (2016), 5270–83.

Lanser, S.S. *The Sexuality of History: Modernity and the Sapphic, 1565–1830.* Chicago: The University of Chicago Press, 2014.

Love, H. *Feeling Backward: Loss and the Politics of Queer History.* Cambridge, MA: Harvard University Press, 2007.

McClintock, A. *Imperial Leather: Race, Gender and Sexuality in the Colonial Contest.* New York: Routledge, 1995.

Nealon, C. *Foundlings: Lesbian and Gay Historical Emotion before Stonewall.* Durham: Duke University Press, 2001.

Närvänen, A.-L. 'Age, Ageing and Life Course', in B.-M. Öberg et al. (eds), *Changing Worlds and the Ageing Subject: Dimensions in the Study of Ageing and Later Life* (Aldershot: Ashgate, 2004), 65–81.

Scott, J.W. *The Fantasy of Feminist History.* Durham: Duke University Press, 2011.

Sharma, S. *In the Meantime: Temporality and Cultural Politics.* Durham: Duke University Press, 2014.

'Tideräkning', in *Nationalencyklopedin*, vol. 18. Höganäs: Bra Böcker, 1998.

Tucker, A. (ed.). *A Companion to the Philosophy of History and Historiography.* London: Blackwell, 2010.

White, H. 'The Historical Event'. *Differences* 19(2) (2008), 9–34.

CHAPTER 7

'The One Who Should Die Is the One Who Shall Live'

Prophetic Temporalities in Contemporary Colonial Brazil

PATRICIA LORENZONI

Introduction

On the night between 19 and 20 April 1997, a man was burned to death in central Brasília. I have written on this murder before. It haunts me, and I keep coming back to it. This murder seems to point to the limits of what is possible to make sense of in academic writing. The following is therefore part of an effort to come to terms with these limits, which are also the limits of the ethos of history. Such a 'coming to terms' is at the same time an occasion to reflect on the possibilities of expanding or reconfiguring those very limits. I do this by exploring nonacademic practices of narrating history, in particular that of the Catholic indigenist mission in Brazil.

My concern is with historical authenticity in Michel-Rolph Trouillot's sense. While empirical accuracy is necessarily a part of the historian's practice, authenticity for Trouillot does not reside here. Authenticity, he states, lies in an honesty vis-à-vis that present in which the past is represented.[1] For the past lives on in the present – in unequal opportunities, in violence targeting specific kinds of bodies rather than others. Trouillot's concern is with narratives of transatlantic slavery. Mine is with the colonization of indigenous Brazil.

The assassination of Galdino Jesus dos Santos Pataxó from Caramuru-Catarina Paraguassu in Bahia, northeastern Brazil, brought to the fore not just a colonial past. It also laid bare a colonial present, mildly disturbing to some, acutely painful for others. Galdino's death provoked indignation in national media, triggering coping techniques and a process of public mourning. Two memorials have since then been erected next to the scene of the crime, and the park adjacent to the crime scene has been renamed.

In this essay, I will contrast two ways of understanding the murder of Galdino Pataxó, both articulated from colonial positions. I say colonial, for as Sara Ahmed points out, even when criticizing coloniality, those of us who are the great-grandchildren of conquistadores and settlers must recognize that we are still walking on stolen ground.[2] While the Catholic indigenist mission in Brazil has articulated itself as allied in indigenous struggles, it must still deal with the role of the church in a 500-years-long history of colonization.

The Crime: Time and Place

Galdino Pataxó was murdered on the night of the Dia do Índio (day of the Indian), 19 April. Instituted in the 1940s by President Getúlio Vargas in honour of all those who had been lumped together under the label 'Indians', the Dia do Índio is today an occasion for grassroots movements and activism. All over Brazil, indigenous people mobilize locally and send representatives to Brasília. It so happened that Galdino's burial took place on the Dia do Descobrimento (day of discovery), 22 April. This interval between the murder and the burial came to frame the public understanding of the events.

The scene of the murder was Brasília, a product of the radical utopian modernism of the 1950s, imagined by its architects as an island of justice in a country torn apart by social injustices.[3] However, the city is also the material expression of settler ideology, embodying the call to push the frontier forward and populate the backlands.[4]

Galdino was killed at a bus stop near Setor Hoteleiro Sul, the southern hotel sector.[5] Five youngsters were driving home from a party. Passing the bus stop they spotted a sleeping man and decided to 'joke' with him. Having stopped at a nearby gas station to buy ethanol, they returned to the sleeping man, poured the liquid over him and set him on fire, after which they quickly left.

Witnesses put out the fire and called an ambulance. Twenty hours later Galdino Pataxó died in the hospital. Witnesses had also noted the registration number of the car and the five perpetrators were soon arrested. They all belonged to the city's upper middle class; one was the son of a federal judge.

In court, one of the perpetrators would explain that they had taken the sleeping man for a *mendigo,* a street beggar. Homeless people are frequently exposed to brutal and sometimes fatal violence in Brazil. Media seldom report on these crimes, and the victims are rarely mourned in public. Galdino was not a street beggar, however; he was an *índio,*[6] and that seemed to change everything.

Galdino was in Brasília to participate in meetings and rallies. He came as a representative for Pataxó-Hã-Hã-Hãe, a people with a history of forced displacements, assimilation projects and invasion of land.[7] He came because 19 April is the one day of the year when índios at least nominally are listened to by the powers that be. Nine years prior to Galdino's death, his brother João Cravim had been murdered by *pistoleiros* hired by local landlords. Índios and poor rural workers are killed in the countryside in this way all the time.[8] As with violence against the urban homeless, media seldom report these crimes, and the victims are rarely mourned in public.

So why did Brazil mourn Galdino Pataxó?

To answer this question, we must understand what is at stake in this misidentification: *We believed he was a street beggar.* Being índio, Galdino belonged, just like the mendigos of the city, to a category already marked for violence. We could say he was the right victim in the wrong place. Or he was the wrong victim in the right place. What happened in the early morning hours of 20 April 1997 provoked a public outcry: an índio was killed in the city.

The Catholic Church and the Articulation of a New Indigenist Mission

On the very day of Galdino's death, the Catholic organization Cimi (Conselho indigenista missionário) published an open letter. The murder, Cimi stated, shows that both general Custer's old maxim and its modern Brazilian version remains in force: *A good Indian is a dead Indian / A good street beggar is a dead street beggar.* For Brazil's political and economic elite there is neither place for mendigos nor índios.[9]

Since the early 1970s, the Catholic mission in Brazil has had a central role in the articulation of nonindigenous solidarity with indigenous peoples. This implies continuous reflection on the historical complicity of the church in colonial conquest. In 1973, during the regime of general Médici, a document was published titled *Y-Juca-Pirama,* signed by twelve Catholic bishops and missionaries.[10] The title comes from an expression in Tupi, and translates as 'the one who should die'. But it is also a reference to one of the classic works of romantic indigenism,[11] Antônio Gonçalves Dias's epic poem 'I-Juca-Pirama' from 1851. While this poem depicts precolonial war cults, the manifesto denounces a project of modernization that leaves the índio with no alternative but death.

Y-Juca-Pirama was written in the context of the Second Vatican Council 1962–1965 and the Conference of Latin American Bishops in Medellin in 1968. Priests as well as lay people voiced a strong urge to bring the church closer to the realities of the people. Latin American Liberation Theology was an expression of this orientation towards praxis, which priests such as Jon Sobrino and Leonardo Boff spoke of as *orthopraxy* rather than *orthodoxy*.[12] In Brazil, the influence of ideas of social praxeology was notable on the highest church level, and many bishops adopted a prophetic posture that challenged the military regime. This included denouncing existing power structures and oppression, as well as articulating a hope of liberation emanating from the most marginalized segments of Brazilian society. For as archbishop Dom Hélder Câmara put it, the protest of the poor is the voice of God.[13]

Cimi was created in 1972 by the National Bishops Council (CNBB). Through its direct relation to CNBB, the organization was relatively – although far from completely – protected during the military regime. Some of Cimi's founding members were involved in the authorship of *Y-Juca-Pirama,* but abstained from signing it for strategic reasons.[14]

The manifesto denounces a line of politics that in the name of development sacrifices the índio. The title alludes to a widely held assumption that the índio is incompatible with modernity. Belonging to the past, s/he is always already marked for death. By emphasizing indigenous resistance, however, the text undermines this assumption and creates a tension between the allusions in the title and the content of the text. By refusing to die, the índio of the text comes to embody a universal hope of *another* future than the one promised by grand modernisation projects.

I will return to this prophetic hope, but let me first say something about the narratives it contests.

The Poetics of Genocide

Gonçalves Dias's poem 'I-Juca-Pirama' describes a brief moment in a war between two peoples. The narrated events predate the conquest, but at the same time seem to foresee it. A young Tupi warrior is taken prisoner by Timbira warriors. Their intention is to sacrifice him so as to anthropophagously subsume his courage into their own bodies. He is killed for his courage, but will live on in the bodies of the Timbiras.[15]

The poem conforms to what Antônio Paulo Graça has named a 'poetics of genocide'. Several nineteenth-century Brazilian writers strove to articulate a national narrative for the newly independent nation. They put the índio at centre stage in order to distinguish themselves against the former Portuguese rulers. The índio was transformed into a symbol of the noble origin of the nation, destined to perish yet remaining as a bloodline in the Brazilian people. Romantic nineteenth-century indigenism typically places the plot before the conquest or at its very beginning.[16] In Gonçalves Dias's poem, the devouring of the noble Tupi anticipates a larger devouring: the arrival of colonial society and its absorption of the índio.

The poetics of genocide, as Graça points out, works as a device to divert attention from ongoing violence. At the very moment when romantic indigenism celebrated an índio assumed to be already extinct, an intensified colonization targeted indigenous communities in the backlands, communities that simply refused to discreetly vanish into the shadows of the past. Writers such as Gonçalves Dias and José de Alencar were also part of a wider cultural and intellectual current that included associations such as the Instituto Histórico e Geográfico Brasileiro (IHGB) founded in 1838. IHGB mapped the newly born nation-state in time as well as in space. A main concern among its early members was to create a narrative of national origin compatible with a colonial past that was anything but past. In John Monteiro's words, 'Lacking the spectacular ruins of ancient civilizations – a problem discussed in some of their early meetings – and facing open conflict with existing native societies, the elite generation that grew up with the Emperor Dom Pedro II himself began to develop a national mythography that placed the noble, valiant and (especially) extinct coastal Tupi at centre stage.'[17] The figure of the noble Tupi had already been established by European works such as Robert Southey's *History of Brazil* (1810–1819) and Ferdinand Denis's *Brésil* (1837). This idealized coastal índio contrasted sharply to contemporaneous indigenous populations who were regarded rather as obstacles to national formation. The índio struggling for autonomy and against colonization in the present became a negation of the nationally defined noble savage of the past.[18]

As Graça points out, the poetics of genocide does not disappear with the decline of romanticism. Across styles and genres, the índio keeps appearing in Brazilian literature as the one destined to disappear with the coming of colonial modernity. As Stefan Helgesson has pointed out in relation to the 'native' in a South African context, settler colonial narratives create a category of people who can only fully signify within the narrative of modernity through death, and who thus live an impossible life marked by the contradiction between meaning and existence.[19] Colonial society might mourn, as in Renato Rosaldo's notion of 'imperialist nostalgia'. However, it cannot change the course of things.[20]

Monteiro notes that most historians, when addressing indigenous history in Brazil, have subscribed to the same story of how colonialism brought an end to the índio.[21] If the índio is absorbed into colonial society, it is only as part of this society that they will eventually liberate themselves from colonization, in the sense of independence from Portuguese rule. Resistance against colonialism will therefore be associated with aspirations towards national liberation.[22] Since the independent nation is thus defined as anticolonial, and indigenous populations are excluded from the political by being banned to the past, contemporary indigenous claims in Brazil are frequently explained as being orchestrated by foreign interests. Indigenous struggles will thereby be understood as expressions of neocolonialism.[23]

On the national level, the contradiction between meaning and existence is translated into a contradiction between being índio and being Brazilian. Until very recently, this contradiction was manifested both in legislation and in official demographics. The Brazilian indigenist bureau, Funai (Fundação Nacional do Índio), long refused to recognize as indigenous those who had moved from indigenous communities and taken up life in cities and other places.[24] It was not until the 1991 census that *indígena* became a category equal to other population groups. Prior to 1991, data on the indigenous populations were based on Funai's reports of inhabitants in indigenous communities. Official demographics thus erased the índio at the moment they left the village.[25] The change in 1991 took place shortly after índios, through the democratic constitution of 1988, for the first time attained full and equal rights as citizens without having to give up claims on indigeneity.[26]

We now begin to understand the misidentification of Galdino Jesus dos Santos Pataxó. In spite of the historical records showing differently, in spite of indigenous labour having built cities such as São Paulo and Manaus, in spite of an increasing number of 'extinct' people making themselves known again: five hundred years into the invasion, an índio in the city is still regarded as a contradiction.[27]

Galdino and the Temporality of Conquest

Let us dwell for a moment on the misidentification: *We believed he was a street beggar.* In reporting this statement as an 'explanation', media coverage contributed to the normalization of violence against the urban poor. Galdino's body became visible in its misplacement, as an índio in the city. It is not unreasonable to assume that if Galdino had lived up to the expectation of being a mendigo, the murder would have gone relatively unnoticed, as did the murder of his brother nine years earlier.[28] Who cares for all these mendigos being killed in the city? Or all these índios being killed in the backlands?

On the night between 19 and 20 April, the movements of both victim and perpetrators followed specific patterns. Galdino was an official representative of his people, but he did not stay in one of the 'representative' hotel sectors; instead he was housed in a pension who had an agreement with Funai. When he arrived at the pension after a long day of meetings, the hostess refused to let him in, blaming the late hour. Galdino found himself in the same situation as many homeless and sought shelter in a bus stop.

While Galdino was an anonymous body in the city, the assailants moved around as identifiable individuals in a private car. The car made the crime possible; it transported them to the gas station and helped them to escape quickly from the scene. But the car also eventually made possible their identification and arrest.

As already touched upon, the timing of the crime was charged with symbolical meaning. Galdino was killed in the interval of three days and three nights between Dia do Índio and Dia do Descobrimento. A street beggar is burned to death, but proves to be an Indian. For the first time, he becomes visible to the hegemonic classes.

Let us think of this temporal interval as a space in which the present collapses into the past. When Pedro Álvares Cabral's fleet reached the coast of Bahia on 22 April 1500, he called the land Ilha da Vera Cruz, the island of the true cross. In April 2000, three years after the murder of Galdino, Brazil celebrated its fifth centennial. A cross was erected in Santa Cruz de Cabrália in remembrance of the first Holy Mass on Brazilian soil. A few days prior to the anniversary itself, the cross was symbolically reclaimed by indigenous people from all over Brazil who danced *toré* around it. Order was brutally restored on the day of the anniversary: a march uniting indigenous people, *quilombolas*[29] and landless rural workers was broken up by riot police and tear gas.[30] A few days after, Cardinal Angelo Sodano officiated in Santa Cruz, on the day five hundred years after the first Holy Mass in the Portuguese colony.

If Cimi's narrative of an ongoing invasion represents one end in the complex relation of the church to colonial history in Pindorama, the sermon of cardinal Sodano represents the other:

> With joyful souls we today remember that 26 April 1500, when in Santa Cruz de Cabrália the first Holy Mass was celebrated. It was the first time that the Gospel of Christ was proclaimed to this people, illuminating its daily life. For the first time, the Body and Blood of Christ got to sanctify the men of this blessed land, purifying and sanctifying their existence. . . . Who [sic] has done more to help civilizing the indigenous populations than the missionary work?[31]

Every 22 April, time is turned out of joint. On the one hand, the *discovery* of Brazil is celebrated, as if Brazil had always been there, but unknown. On the other hand, Brazil is *born* through this discovery. How can that which is born through the very act of discovery be discovered? In this out-of-jointness, modern Brazil is projected backwards in time, upon a domain in the uttermost peripheries of Portuguese colonial rule. The nation-state of Brazil becomes the only possible and logical continuation of Cabral's Ilha da Vera Cruz. Through this teleological interpretation of history, victims in the past are given meaning in the march towards a predetermined future. The same teleology continues to legitimize large-scale modernization projects in the Amazon during the late twentieth century. For this mechanism of redemption to work, however, violence must be kept at a temporal and/or spatial distance, as belonging to the 'not yet civilized' world. When violence appears in the middle of the modern city, its meaning is at once disrupted.

Conflicting claims are laid on indigenous figures of the past. In nationalist narratives of the heroic death of the índio, we can see how the violence of conquest is articulated as a 'reassuring fratricide', in Benedict Anderson's sense: a family dispute of sorts, supposedly behind us now.[32] One of the most outspoken voices against indigenous rights in today's political landscape, Congressman Aldo Rebelo mentions in one of his indigenist essays how he proudly possesses a figurine of Guaraní leader Sepé Tiarajú, famous for having uttered the words 'this land already has masters'.[33] Sepé Tiarajú fought in the eighteenth-century Guaraní wars, which led to the expulsion of the Jesuit order from Portuguese and Spanish America. Cimi also claims Sepé Tiarajú as part of a common history of anticolonial resistance. Guaraní warriors and Jesuits fought side by side against the Portuguese. While for Cimi, however, there is a direct continuity between this history and indigenous struggles in the present, Rebelo inscribes Sepé Tiarajú's heroic death in the nation's (anticolonial) body. This same body is then threatened with disintegration when the anachronistically surviving índio articulates today what Sepé Tiarajú did in the eighteenth century. For, if there is one thing that must be kept silent in the nationalist narrative, it is that the 'liberation' of Brazil with its independence in 1822 was for the índio nothing but a continuation of a history of conquest that has yet not seen its end.

The insistence on a continuous conquest is central to Cimi's understanding of the history of Pindorama. When celebrating its fortieth anniversary in 2012, Cimi dedicated its commemorative publication to two newly murdered Guaraní Kaiowá leaders – Nisio Gomes and Zezinho – and with them to 'all those indigenous martyrs who have fallen in defence of their people, their land and their lives during these 512 years of invasion'.[34] By talking about invasion in the present tense, the text closes the gap between historical meaning and contemporary violence.

It was precisely this gap that lay at stake in the public understanding of the murder of Galdino Pataxó.

Generic Victims and Historical Martyrs

On 22 April 1997, the editorial in one of Brazil's largest newspapers, *O Globo*, stated that Galdino's fate should not be understood in the context of historical violence suffered by indigenous peoples. After all, Galdino had not been murdered for being an índio; it was, so it seemed, a mistake.[35] Galdino's physical exposure that night was thus isolated from the history that had reduced his people to a rural proletariat and brought him to the capital. Detached and decontextualized, he became in the news 'the índio', a generic figure whose purpose in Brasília was to 'celebrate' the day of the Indian. By contrast, the perpetrators were depicted as individuals, albeit enigmatic ones: these five boys of good families should have known better. It could have been your son, or mine. How could this have happened? As Ana Paula Freire shows, the news reports' identification with the perpetrators came to overshadow the victim.[36]

O Globo addresses a readership mainly to be found in the upper middle and upper classes. It is thus hardly surprising that the paper invites its readers to identify with the culprits rather than the victim. What is more significant is the underlying question: *How could this happen?* This conceals what one does not want to know that one knows: that it could happen because it happens all the time. This we know: it happens when city businessmen contract police working on the side to keep the streets 'clean'. It happens when landlords contract *pistoleiros* to teach a lesson to anybody who opposes land invasion. It happens in the daily violence that confirms the reigning order of privilege.

What the five perpetrators did was to abolish the intermediate stage of violence. More than that, they committed the ultimate transgression: they killed an índio in a city that is the very emblem of Brazilian modernity. Like the historical *desbravadores* (tamers) who pushed the colonial frontiers further into the backlands by turning humans into slaves and wilderness into settlements, they expelled the remaining uncivilized element from the heart of the city.[37] For a brief moment light was shed on what one should never have to be reminded of having forgotten: that conquest not only did happen, but that it continues to happen, day after day.

On the day following Galdino's burial, *O Globo* noted that this year's day of discovery had turned into a day of tears for Galdino's family. A curious statement, indeed. For the Pataxó-Hã-Hã-Hãe, could not every 22 April be expected to be a day of tears, of remembering invasion and dispossession? After the crime, and with participation of indigenous and indigenist organisations, a sign was placed at the bus stop, a small memorial in the park. The park itself was named Praça do Compromisso, a name alluding to both debt and commitment. A second memorial, designed by Siron Franco in the shape of an iron plate with the cut-out silhouette of a man surrounded by flames, was later added.[38] Colloquially, the place has come to be known as Praça do Índio, the Indian's square. Today it gives an abandoned impression. No information is given to visitors who are unfamiliar with the events in April of 1997, and Franco's memorial is worn down and rusty.[39]

The perpetrators' careers through jail and prison were followed closely by media and triggered new debates on impunity and upper-class privilege in the penal system. The victim and his family, however, soon lost the attention of the media. Freire concludes: The one who was murdered in these media narratives was not Pataxó-Hã-Hã-Hãe activist Galdino Jesus dos Santos. The victim was not even an índio. He was simply unplaceable.[40]

We can thus read the massive attention given to the murder also as a plea that we (whoever is included in this 'we') shall remember the 'índio' so that we may once again forget about the 'índio'.

Cimi, however, in newsletters as well as in the magazine *Porantim,* also covered the murder and its aftermath. Here, the individual Galdino comes across as a member of a community of martyrs in the struggle against colonization.[41] In letters, pamphlets and articles, Galdino is given an identity and a context: name, history, a family who speaks. By naming him as a martyr, Cimi links his struggle to a spiritual order, through direct praxis negating the reigning order.[42] Galdino, in the writings of Cimi, thus opens a space where the spiritual and the political coincide.

Opening the Future Once Again

Even when he was alive, Galdino travelled under the sign of death, to use Alicia Schmidt Camacho's expression.[43] Being índio, he belonged to a category perceived as an anachronism in the present. Academic history has its own complicity in reproducing this sign of death. As Monteiro puts it, most historians dealing with indigenous history have long imagined that the best they could do was to add yet another chapter to a chronicle of extinctions.[44] However, when Pedro Álvares Cabral set foot on the soil of Pindorama and took the right to give it a new name, the future that is now past was still radically undetermined. The projection of an inevitable historical outcome hides the complexity of any given historical moment. If we are to take Trouillot's call for authenticity seriously, this complexity of the past could and should be linked to decolonial struggles in the present.

It is no coincidence that several of the historical works going against the tendency criticized by Monteiro are written by researchers trained also in anthropology. The link between practices of narrating the past and contemporary decolonial struggles becomes exceptionally clear in Nadia Farage's study of the colonization of the Rio Branco area in the northern Amazon,

As Muralhas dos Sertões: Os povos indígenas no rio Branco e a colonização (1991). Through archival documents of Portuguese presence in the eighteenth century, Farage shows that the indigenous populations had a key role not only in legitimizing colonial projects, but also in actively shaping them – in alternate negotiations, conflicts and alliances. For the Portuguese, the indigenous were a living frontier, *muralhas dos sertões,* through which they moved their positions forward and against rivalling Dutch interests.[45]

As Farage was working on this material, the peoples she encountered in the archives – Macuxi, Wapixana, Taurepang – were involved in bitter conflicts with new settlers claiming the land to be unpopulated. Not only did Farage provide historical evidence of indigenous presence, the evidence also placed indigenous people at the very heart of colonial projects, thus enabling indigenous activists to claim the right to land not just in their capacity as 'indigenous' but also in their capacity as 'colonizers'. Thus, the place of the índio in the origin of the nation was reaffirmed at the same time as breaking with the mythology of extinction.[46]

Farage's study is an example of how historical knowledge production may open up possibilities in a conflicted present. Yet, an unresolved tension remains between the critique of coloniality and its reaffirmation. Indigenist legislation subsumes indigenous people and their relationship to the land in a territorial system of borders as well as a notion of rights connected to a history of *use,* disregarding local geographies and cosmologies. These local histories might involve notions of nature in direct conflict with Brazilian legislation and the agency of nonhuman inhabitants.[47] Questions of (human) origins and historical presence become crucial for *who* has the right to dwell *where.* Through archival evidence, the historian can offer crucial tools for people to defend their right to a space within a legal–political order. Still, the only place for the índio is as a 'protected special case', and any possibility of a radically different future remains closed.

Let us return, then, to the prophetic posture guiding Cimi's narrative. Rather than criticizing hegemonic historical narratives, Cimi produces a radical alternative, prophetic in the way it uncovers and denounces the wrongs of this world. This narrative also places, as we will see, the Passion of Christ at the centre of historical understanding.

Y-Juca-Pirama begins as an allusion to the poetics of genocide that has given aestheticized meaning to the death of indigenous people. The text then goes on to denounce violence and emphasize indigenous resistance. In a radical turn on the very last pages, the critique of colonial violence shifts into a prophetic promise of a coming life. In a world of materialistic capitalism, the índio is not only the victim, but also the one who through their own life can bring new life to a Gospel fettered to the dead letter: 'Only through a process of incarnation in the bosom of indigenous people, in which one *assumes their culture, their ways of life and ways of thinking,* will one convincingly demonstrate the transcendence of the Gospel which is affirmed in theory but denied in practice through the demands of a rigid legalism.'[48] In the last lines then, *Y-Juca-Pirama* arrives at a direct analogy between the fate of the índio and the suffering, death and resurrection of Christ: 'Now is the moment to proclaim, in hope, that the one who should die is the one who shall live.'[49] In this proclamation of the victory of life over death, the manifesto negates that imperialist nostalgia with which it initially sought resonance.

By placing the passion of Christ at the centre of historical understanding, the mission rearticulates a Christian universalism on behalf of the poor and marginalized (but not a universalism *by* the poor). However, as Brazilian theologian Ivone Gebara argues, the very emphasis on the figure of Jesus Christ risks silencing other experiences of suffering and other paths towards salvation. Gebara's work is part of a critique from within liberation theology, pointing to the risks in reproducing an idolatrous relationship to the figure of Jesus as single path to the 'Christly' dimension of the world. In particular, Gebara is concerned with the exclusion of female experiences and experiences connected to nature from the dimension of the salvific.[50]

This critique is also aimed at the confusion of the Christly with the person of Jesus. Returning to Cimi's narrative of Galdino's death, in April 2001, four years after the murder of Galdino Pataxó, Cimi's magazine *Porantim* published an article with the title 'The Resurrection of Galdino':

> But the long wait for the court verdicts does not prevent the Hã-Hã-Hãe people from experiencing Easter, for they feel confidence in resurrection. Therefore, Galdino lives, just like many other leaders of his people who have died in the struggle. Their tormentors have never been able to destroy their main weapon in the struggle, the memory of resistance. This has made them stand firm against these 500 years of dominance initiated by the European project of colonization.[51]

If imperialist nostalgia copes with the historical pain (of others) by turning their suffering into an aestheticized object, the prophetic historical narrative activates the same pain in the service of life, and it does so by prescribing that even the one acting from an inescapably colonial position – in this case the missionary – must *incarnate* the life of the other. The nostalgia over the one who perished is replaced with the radical coevalness of the Passion, implying that another world always has been possible and continues to be so. In this coevalness the missionary's own self is at stake; in a sense they become coeval with their own conqueror ancestors, and are forced to confront the histories of violence that made missionary activity on the soil of Pindorama possible in the first place. When Bishop Emeritus Dom Pedro Casaldáliga introduces Cimi's five hundred anniversary publication, *Outros 500,* he accordingly signs it without his bishop title (Dom), but with the addition to his name: *Tatameto arrependido de conquistador,* 'repenting great-grandchild of conquerors'.[52]

Coda

Can the repenting great-grandchild be an authentic ally? The question implicit in Dom Pedro's signature is also my question. And where is the line – if it exists – between academic integrity and activism?

Admitting historical complicity is in itself no guarantee for an authentic relation to the struggle of colonized people for liveable lives. As pointed out by both Michel-Rolph Trouillot in referring to transatlantic slavery, and Sara Ahmed in referring to displacements of indigenous Australians, feeling bad over crimes of the past can just as well function as a way to relieve the white subject from responsibility vis-à-vis how this past lives on in the present. Solidarity, Ahmed states, is only possible if it involves active support for indigenous sovereignty.[53]

The posture of Dom Pedro can therefore not be separated from the orthopraxis he lives. A close relation between theory and practice is indeed nothing strange within theology in general, even if it can be defined in a number of different ways. But how does this relate to an academic knowledge-practice where we, as academic scholars, have been taught that what is known must also be communicable. What can we do with that which resists communicability?

The murder of Galdino Pataxó keeps haunting me, for while I am trying to understand the wound it lays bare academically, it points to the impossibilities involved in grasping as well as communicating such an understanding from within the premises of academic knowledge. While the public mourning of Galdino seems perfectly legitimate as an object of study, from within the cracks of this history a silent pain keeps screaming out from beyond that which I can put into words. In a frequently quoted formulation, Fredric Jameson states that 'history is what hurts'.[54] If we accept this statement in the very acute meaning it takes in relation to indigenous pasts and present in Brazil, what then is the relation between pain and practices of writing history? My formal training as an academic scholar did not prepare me for the complicated relationship between past and current pain. Nor did it prepare me for dealing with the fact of being, as Dom Pedro puts it, a repenting great-grandchild to conquerors, and as such concretely favoured by centuries of pain inflicted on others.

Claiming, from an academic position, to be able to make sense of the suffering of others can in itself be regarded as a reproduction of power structures that regulate how history can be written and by whom. Ahmed notices how the word 'solidarity' often evokes sentiment; solidarity is described as 'fellow feeling', closely related to empathy. She suggests that we instead turn to the etymology of the word, in 'solid', and concludes that perhaps solidarity 'only works when sentiments solidify into actions'.[55]

While agreeing with Ahmed on the relation between sentiment and action – or between theory and practice – I wish to add another suggestion. Perhaps solidarity sometimes also requires giving up any explicit or implicit claim on the possibility of 'making sense' of the painful histories of others, that is, making them communicable within a specific set of knowledge premises. As Gebara notes, even the radical coevalness of the passion carries with it its blind spots in the universalizing of local, androcentric and anthropocentric histories.

Indeed, this murder keeps haunting me, for what it points to is the urgent form Trouillot's question on authenticity takes in relation to the Brazilian colonial present. There is traditionally little room for silence in academic writing. But if keeping one's humble silence is sometimes the only honest stance in the face of the pain of others, how do we make room for this silence to *speak* in the writing of history? How can I, as a scholar, write a text that is recognizable as an academic text, and that yet not only can acknowledge its limits, but also make actual room for its own silences?

Patricia Lorenzoni holds a PhD in history of ideas from the University of Gothenburg and is a research fellow at the Centre for Multidisciplinary Research on Racism (Cemfor) at Uppsala University. She is the author of *Att färdas under dödens tecken: Frazer, imperiet och den försvinnande vilden* (Travelling under the sign of death: Frazer, empire and the vanishing savage, 2008) and *Mama Dolly: Bilder av moderskap från jungfru Maria till Alien* (Mama dolly: Images of motherhood from Virgin Mary to Alien, 2012). Currently she is working on a book on the category of the *índio* in Brazilian thinking of nation and territory.

Notes

1. M.-R. Trouillot, *Silencing the Past: Power and the Production of History* (Boston: Beacon Press 1995), 148.

2. S. Ahmed, 'The Politics of Bad Feeling', *Australian Critical Race and Whiteness Studies Association Journal* 1 (2005), 78–79.

3. J. Holston, *The Modernist City: An Anthropological Critique of Brasilia* (Chicago: University of Chicago Press, 1989).

4. On the frontier and the concept of nation in Brazil, see J. de S. Martins, *Fronteira: A degradação do Outro nos confins do humano* (São Paulo: Editora Contexto, 2009).

5. On the murder and its aftermath, see A.P. Freire, 'Notícias de um crime no mundo civilizado: As mortes de Galdino Pataxó' (Master diss., Universidade Federal Fluminense, 2004).

6. I do not translate índio unless it is directly related to a specific colonialist imagination. In Brazil, índio is used both in formal policy contexts and as a self-designation, which differs from uses of the corresponding term in English.

7. Instituto Socioambiental, 'Povos Indígenas no Brasil: Pataxó-hã-hã-hãe'. Retrieved 25 September 2015 from http://pib.socioambiental.org/pt/povo/pataxo-ha-ha-hae.

8. Freire, 'Notícias de um crime', 90.

9. Freire, 'Notícias de um crime', 77.

10. M. Biennès et al. 'Y-Juca-Pirama. O índio: aquele que deve morrer', in S. Feitosa, E. Heck and R. Santana (eds), *Povos Indígenas: Aqueles que devem viver* (Brasília: Cimi, 2012).

11. 'Indigenism' is a set of ideas and assumptions about the relation between indigenous people and colonial society. See A.C. de S. Lima, *Um grande cerco e paz: Poder tutelar, indianidade e formação do Estado no Brasil* (Petrópolis: Vozes, 1995); and Alcida Ramos, *Indigenism: Ethnic Politics in Brazil* (Madison: University of Winsconsin Press, 1998).

12. See, for example, L. Boff, *Iglesia, carisma y poder: Ensayos de eclesiología militante* (Santander: Sal Terrae 1982).

13. H. Câmara, *O deserto é fértil* (Rio de Janeiro: Civilização Brasileira, 1976), 23–24.

14. E. Schwade, 'Sobre Y-Juca-Pirama: O índio aquele que deve morrer', in S. Feitosa, E. Heck and R. Santana (eds), *Povos Indígenas: Aqueles que devem viver. Manifesto contra os decretos de extermínio* (Brasília: Cimi, 2012), 158.

15. G. Dias, 'Y-Juca-Pyrama', in *Cantos: Colecção de poesias* (Leipzig: F.A. Brockhaus, 1857), 460.

16. A.P. Graça, *Uma poética do genocídio* (Rio de Janeiro: Topbooks, 1998), 26–27.

17. J. Monteiro, 'The Heathen Castes of Sixteenth-Century Portuguese America: Unity, Diversity and the Invention of the Brazilian Indians', *Hispanic American Historical Review* 80(4) (2000), 710.

18. Monteiro, 'Heathen Castes', 711–13.

19. See S. Helgesson, 'Radical Time in Postcolonial Narrative', chapter 8 in this volume.

20. R. Rosaldo, *Culture and Truth: The Remaking of Social Analysis* (Boston: Beacon Press, 1989), 69–70.

21. Monteiro, 'Heathen Castes', 717.

22. On Brazilian self-image as anticolonial, see O. Souza, *Fantasia de Brasil: As identificações na busca da identidade nacional* (São Paulo: Editora Escuta, 1994), 29–30.

23. For an argument of this kind from the political elite, see A. Rebelo, *Raposa-Serra do Sol: O índio e a questão nacional* (Brasília: Theasaurus, 2010).

24. F. Saillant and L. Forline, 'Memória fugitiva, identidade flexível: caboclos na Amazônia', in A. Leibing and S. Benninghoff-Lühl (eds), *Devorando o tempo: Brasil, o país sem memória* (São Paulo: Mandarim, 2001), 150.

25. N. de O.M. Pereira et al., 'Demography, Territory, and Identity of Indigenous Peoples in Brazil: The Xavante Indians and the 2000 Brazilian National Census', *Human Organization* 68 (2) (2009), 167–68.

26. On indigenous citizenship, see Ramos, *Indigenism*, chapter 3.

27. J. Monteiro, *Negros da terra: Índios e bandeirantes nas origens de São Paulo* (São Paulo: Companhia das Letras, 2005); J.G. Melo, 'Identidades fluidas: Ser e perceber-se como Baré (Aruak) na Manaus contemporânea' (Ph.D. diss., Universidade de Brasília, 2009); J.P. Oliveira (ed.), *A viagem de volta: Etnicidade, política e reelaboração cultural no Nordeste indígena* (Rio de Janeiro: Contra Capa, 1999).

28. Freire, 'Notícias de um crime', 90, 103. Also, Ramos, *Indigenism*, 289–91.

29. *Quilombo* is the Brazilian term for maroon society, created by people escaping slavery from the sixteenth to the nineteenth centuries. *Quilombolas* were granted the right to the land they inhabit by the Federal Constitution of 1988.

30. Cimi, *Outros 500: Construindo uma nova história* (São Paulo: Editora Salesiana, 2001), 14–17.

31. A. Sodano, 'Homilia do Cardeal Angelo Sodano, Secretário de Estado de Sua Santidade e Legado Pontifício, na Comemoração dos 500 Anos da Primeira Santa Missa no Brasil' (sermon), 26 April 2000. Retrieved 2 April 2013 from www.vatican.va/roman_curia/secretariat_state/documents/rc_seg-st_doc_20000426_sodano-brazil_po.html (Eng. trans. by the author).

32. B. Anderson, *Imagined Communities: Reflections on the Origin and Spread of Nationalism* (London: Verso, 1991), 199–201.

33. Rebelo, *Raposa-Serra do Sol*, 29.

34. S. Feitosa, E. Heck and R. Santana (eds) *Povos indígenas: Aqueles que devem viver* (Brasília: Cimi, 2012), 3.

35. Freire, 'Notícias de um crime', 123.

36. Freire 'Notícias de um crime', 95–97.

37. Thanks to Cristhian Teófilo da Silva for drawing my attention to this.

38. Freire, 'Notícias de um crime', 137.

39. The description is from a visit in 2014. Shortly afterwards, the city replaced the missing sign at the original memorial, defining the spot as 'ponto de cura', a place of healing.

40. Freire, 'Notícias de um crime', 154.

41. Freire, 'Notícias de um crime', 140.

42. On political martyrdom in Latin America, see also A. Peralta, 'Väpnat motstånd i Latinamerika 1950–2000', in M. Lilja and S. Vinthagen (eds), *Motstånd* (Malmö: Liber, 2009), 153–70.

43. A.S. Camacho, 'Body Counts on the Mexico-U.S. Border: Feminicidio, Reification, and the Theft of Mexicana Subjectivity', *Chicana/Latina Studies* 4(1) (2004), 22–60.

44. Monteiro, 'Heathen Castes', 718.

45. N. Farage, *As muralhas dos sertões: Os povos indígenas no rio Branco e a colonização* (São Paulo: Paz e Terra 1991).

46. For an example, see Conselho Indígena de Roraima, 'Carta das comunidades indígenas da Raposa Serra do Sol', 28 April 2008. Retrieved 10 July 2009 from www.cir.org.br/manifesto-da-rss.doc.

47. For an example of tensions between the legal premises for indigenous land rights and local ways of relating to the land, see P. Santilli, *Pemongon Patá: Território Macuxi, rotas de conflito* (São Paulo: Editora Unesp, 2000), 131.

48. M. Biennès et al., 'Y-Juca-Pirama. O índio: Aquele que deve morrer', 177 (emphasis and trans. by the author).

49. 'Y-Juca-Pirama', 177.

50. In contrast to this idolatrous relation, Gebara talks of an 'open centrality' of the figure of Jesus, always in relation to a collectivity and turning the community 'Christly'. Ivone Gebara '¿Quién es el "Jesús liberador" que buscamos?', in J.J. Tamayo Acosta (ed.), *10 palavras clave sobre Jesús de Nazaret* (Navarra: Verbo Divino, 1999), 165–70.

51. Quoted in Freire, 'Notícias de um crime', 141–42 (trans. by the author).

52. Cimi, *Outros 500*.

53. Ahmed, 'The Politics of Bad Feeling', 109; Trouillot, *Silencing the Past*, 148.

54. F. Jameson, *The Political Unconscious: Narrative as a Socially Symbolic Act*, (London: Routledge, 2002), 88.

55. Ahmed, 'The Politics of Bad Feeling', 81.

Bibliography

Ahmed, S. 'The Politics of Bad Feeling'. *Australian Critical Race and Whiteness Studies Association Journal* 1 (2005), 72–85.

Anderson, B. *Imagined Communities: Reflections on the Origin and Spread of Nationalism*. London: Verso 1991.

Biennès, M., H. Campos, E.C. de Avellar, P. Casaldáliga, T. Balduino, A.J. Sartori, G.G. Leitão, A. Iasi, D.M. Leite, A. Canuto, L. Brustolin, T, Lisboa. 'Y-Juca-Pirama. O índio: aquele que deve morrer', in E. Heck, R. Santana and S. Feitosa (eds), *Povos Indígenas: Aqueles que devem viver* (Brasília: Cimi, 2012), 161–80.

Boff, L. *Iglesia, carisma y poder: Ensayos de eclesiología militante*. Santander: Sal Terrae 1982.

Camacho, A.S. 'Body Counts on the Mexico–U.S. Border: Feminicidio, Reification, and the Theft of Mexicana Subjectivity'. *Chicana/Latina Studies* 4(1) (2004), 22–60.

Câmara, H. *O deserto é fértil*. Rio de Janeiro: Civilização Brasileira, 1976.

Cimi. *Outros 500: Construindo uma nova história*. São Paulo: Editora Salesiana, 2001.

Conselho Indígena de Roraima. 'Carta das comunidades indígenas da Raposa Serra do Sol', 28 April 2008. Retrieved 10 July 2009 from www.cir.org.br/manifesto-da-rss.doc.

Farage, N.F. *As muralhas dos sertões: Os povos indígenas no rio Branco e a colonização*. São Paulo: Paz e Terra, 1991.

Feitosa, S., E. Heck and R. Santana (eds). *Povos indígenas: Aqueles que devem viver*. Brasília: Cimi, 2012.

Freire, A.P. 'Notícias de um crime no mundo civilizado: As mortes de Galdino Pataxó'. Master diss., Universidade Federal Fluminense, 2004.

Gebara, I. '¿Quién es el "Jesús liberador" que buscamos?', in J.J. Tamayo Acosta (ed.), *10 palavras clave sobre Jesús de Nazaret* (Navarra: Verbo Divino 1999), 149–88.

Goçalves Dias, A. 'I-Juca-Pyrama', in *Cantos: Colecção de poezias* (Leipzig: F.A. Brockhaus, 1857), 442–61.

Graça, A.P. *Uma poética do genocídio*. Rio de Janeiro: Topbooks, 1998.

Holston, J. *The Modernist City: An Anthropological Critique of Brasilia*. Chicago: University of Chicago Press, 1989.

Jameson, F. *The Political Unconscious: Narrative as a Socially Symbolic Act*. London: Routledge, 2002.

Lima, A.C. de S. *Um grande cerco e paz: Poder tutelar, indianidade e formação do Estado no Brasil*. Petrópolis: Vozes, 1995.

Martins, J. de S. *Fronteira: A degradação do Outro nos confins do humano*. São Paulo: Editora Contexto, 2009.

Melo, J.G. 'Identidades fluidas: Ser e perceber-se como Baré (Aruak) na Manaus contemporânea'. Ph.D. diss., Universidade de Brasília, 2009.

Monteiro, J. 'The Heathen Castes of Sixteenth-Century Portuguese America: Unity, Diversity and the Invention of the Brazilian Indians'. *Hispanic American Historical Review* 80 (4) (2000), 697–719.

———. *Negros da terra: Índios e banderiantes nas origens de São Paulo*. São Paulo: Companhia das Letras, 2005.

Oliveira, J.P. (ed.). *A viagem de volta: Etnicidade, política e reelaboração cultural no Nordeste indígena*. Rio de Janeiro: Contra Capa, 1999.

Peralta, A. 'Väpnat motstånd i Latinamerika 1950–2000', in M. Lilja and S. Vinthagen (eds), *Motstånd* (Malmö: Liber 2009), 153–70.

Pereira, N. de O.M., R.V. Santos, J.R. Welch, L.G. Souza, C.E.A. Coimbra Jr. 'Demography, Territory, and Identity of Indigenous Peoples in Brazil: The Xavante Indians and the 2000 Brazilian National Census'. *Human Organization* 68 (2) (2009), 166–80.

'Povos Indígenas no Brasil: Pataxó-hã-hã-hãe', Instituto Socioambiental. Retrieved 25 September 2015 from http://pib.socioambiental.org/pt/povo/pataxo-ha-ha-hae.

Ramos, A. *Indigenism: Ethnic Politics in Brazil*. Madison: University of Wisconsin Press, 1998.

Rebelo, A. *Raposa-Serra do Sol: O índio e a questão nacional*. Brasília: Theasaurus, 2010.

Rosaldo, R. *Culture and Truth: The Remaking of Social Analysis*. Boston: Beacon Press, 1989.

Saillant, F., and L. Forline. 'Memória fugitiva, identidade flexível: caboclos na Amazônia', in A. Leibing and S. Benninghoff-Lühl (eds), *Devorando o tempo: Brasil, o país sem memória* (São Paulo: Mandarim, 2001), 143–56.

Santilli, P. *Pemongon Patá: Território Macuxi, rotas de conflito*. São Paulo: Editora Unesp 2000.

Schwade, E. 'Sobre Y-Juca-Pirama: O índio aquele que deve morrer', in S. Feitosa, E. Heck and R. Santana (eds), *Povos Indígenas: Aqueles que devem viver. Manifesto contra os decretos de extermínio* (Brasília: Cimi 2012), 157–60.

Sodano, A. 'Homilia do Cardeal Angelo Sodano, Secretário de Estado de Sua Santidade e Legado Pontifício, na Comemoração dos 500 Anos da Primeira Santa Missa no Brasil' (sermon), 26 April 2000. Retrieved 2 April 2013 from www.vatican.va/roman_curia/secretariat_state/documents/rc_seg-st_doc_20000426_sodano-brazil_po.html.

Souza, O. *Fantasia de Brasil: As identificações na busca da identidade nacional*. São Paulo: Editora Escuta 1994.

Trouillot, M.-R. *Silencing the Past: Power and the Production of History*. Boston: Beacon Press, 1995.

CHAPTER 8

Radical Time in (Post)Colonial Narratives

STEFAN HELGESSON

Introduction

Reinhart Koselleck's coinage of the 'space of experience' and the 'horizon of expectation' provides a powerful conceptual tool for approaching history immanently. It is only with reference to lived experience that the terms become meaningful, and as such they pinpoint a temporal dialectic that will always be unique in any specific instance yet is generalizable, even (paradoxically) transcendental, in terms of its logic.[1] For Koselleck, it was in the *Sattelzeit* (saddle-time) from 1750 to 1850 that it became evident – in Europe – that the horizon of expectation differed increasingly from the space of experience. Not only did the difference increase – the increase itself accelerated, leading to a rapidly diminishing correspondence between experience and expectation: 'it became a rule that all previous experience might not count against the possible otherness of the future'.[2] Articulated as an abstract principle, this variable difference between experience and expectation captures precisely the quality of historicity and the acceleration of time.

The standard understanding of this acceleration is that it nurtured, for an extended period, a tremendously pervasive secular ideology of progress. In other words, as Koselleck argues in a discussion of Kant, it was not just the case that the worldly future would be radically different, but also substantially *better*.[3] This expectation – a defining element of the modern ethos of history – has never been uniform, however, and has always been accompanied, in European intellectual traditions, by its (male) doubters: Johann Gottfried Herder, Fyodor Dostoevsky, Friedrich Nietzsche, Walter Benjamin, Michel Foucault. What interests me here is not this specific countertradition, but rather narrative responses to accelerated time emerging from colonial and postcolonial spaces. The guiding assumption in this chapter is that the European high-imperial moment around 1900 (being also a moment of capitalist globalization) was characterized by uniquely brutal contradictions between spaces of experience and horizons of expectation in the plural. In sharp abbreviation: the expectation of progress among segments of mainly European and/or white creole populations had its counterpart in the horizon of *extinction* for colonized and racialized others – either literally, through death, or figurally, through disenfranchisement and cultural assimilation.

The larger question underlying my discussion is this: how can narrative form contend with a hegemonic horizon of expectation? In my restricted corpus of Brazilian and South African texts – all from circa 1900 – this becomes a particularly acute problem. Produced as they were within globally dispersed moments of aggressive, racially coded, accelerated change, they are themselves *of* history. My argument is, however, that their narrative ordering of time – particularly in the form of prophecy – exploits and exposes the contradictions of the temporal regime of colonial modernity (particularly its narrativization of genocide and extinction) and allows a 'radical time' of decoloniality to be intimated. If history has an ethos in the sense of 'character', it is marked by rifts and tensions between different, radically plural spaces and horizons. It is this split nature of historical experience that the narratives in question, in their partial way, allow us to explore.

As indeed an entire library of postcolonial scholarship shows, the contradictions of time and history in the colonial era are remarkably difficult to countenance and theorize.[4] The minor contribution of the present chapter to this vast discussion is to look at the dialectic of loss and hope in the narrativization of time. What I aim to investigate in my limited corpus is (1) *how* the narrativization of time is achieved, particularly through prophecy, and (2) in what ways this narrativization challenges the hegemonic temporal regime of colonial modernity. At stake in these narratives, as I soon shall explain, is nothing less than the need to combine meaning with existence.

Progress and Extinction

In the mid-1890s, the Brazilian army is waging a war against a small, insurgent community in the remote hinterland. The leader of the insurgents is known as Antonio Conselheiro. Regarded by his followers as a prophet,

Conselheiro rails against the recently instituted republican order in Brazil
(which had supplanted the monarchy in 1889), denouncing it as the work
of the devil. The community bravely resists the onslaught of the republican
army, but ultimately to no avail: this infamous war ends with the extermination of the entire ramshackle town of Canudos in the deep interior of Minas
Gerais.

The story will be familiar to readers of Mario Vargas Llosa's novel *La
guerra del fin del mundo,* or *The War of the End of the World* (1981). It is also
reworked in Glauber Rocha's classic Brazilian film *Deus e o diabo na terra
do sol* (1964), or 'God and the devil in the land of the sun'. Both of these
reworkings are based, however, on *Os sertões* (*Backlands: The Canudos Campaign*), published in 1902. In this dense account of a bizarre and horrifying
civil war, the city-dweller and military engineer Euclides da Cunha (1866–
1909) struggles to make sense of what happened (and of what he himself
witnessed in the last days of the campaign). Steeped in Comtean positivism
and nineteenth-century racial thinking, he clings to the idea that the disaster
was historically inevitable. The inhabitants of the backlands were 'three centuries' behind modern Brazil and therefore destined to perish: 'Civilization
will advance across the backlands, driven by that implacable "motive force
of history" that Gumplowicz, much wiser than Hobbes, foretold in a flash
of genius: the inevitable crushing of the weak races by the strong.'[5] *Os sertões*
can thus be read as the story of the crushing of the rebellious Canudos community by the impersonal workings of progress. A unique historical event
was in this way literally *made* meaningful through the superimposition of an
aggressive, developmental philosophy of history. However, the contradictory
nature of Cunha's account demonstrates that the authority of that philosophy
is less than absolute. The temporal regime of progress and racial extinction is
in fact challenged by the narrative itself. It is the nature of this challenge – and
the way in which it allows us to read coloniality not as a uniformly imposed
condition but as a site of 'temporal struggle' – that interests me in this essay.

Concurrently with Cunha, across the Atlantic, we find a South African author who is writing and rewriting the chapters of a novel that she
never will finish. This is Olive Schreiner (1855–1920), whose *From Man
to Man* was published posthumously in 1926. In one of the chapters, the
main protagonist Rebekah spends an evening in her cramped study in Cape
Town, adjacent to her children's bedroom, reflecting on the justifications
for genocide. 'Is it not practically our duty and for the benefit of humanity',
Rebekah asks herself, 'that we should forcibly suppress, cut off and destroy
the less developed individuals and races, leaving only the highly developed
to survive?'[6] (195). Rebekah then elaborates her own thorough refutation
of this social Darwinist mindset, even as she struggles to find an alternative

to the temporal paradigm of progress and development. The juxtaposition of middle-class domesticity and genocidal thinking in this chapter is jarring, to say the least, yet fully consistent with the predicaments of Rebekah and her author alike: what Schreiner stages in her fiction of Rebekah – mother, wife, white colonial subject and fiercely independent thinker – are the absurd and lethal contradictions of patriarchy and racism in the British version of colonial modernity.

In yet another meanwhile, in what is today Lesotho and in the aftermath of the Bambatha rebellion, the last anticolonial uprising in South Africa prior to the Union of 1910, Thomas Mofolo (1875–1948) is working on what will become one of the canonical masterpieces of African literature: *Chaka*. This is a historical fiction, written in Sesotho, about the early nineteenth-century Zulu king Shaka and his reign. At the end of the novel, the king is assassinated by his brothers. As he is dying, Chaka (the character) utters this prophecy: 'You are killing me in the hope that you will be kings when I am dead, whereas you are wrong, that is not the way it will be because *umlungu*, the white man, is coming, and it is he who will rule you, and you will be his servants.'[7] The novel ends on a melancholic note, envisioning history as loss: 'when they [the Zulus] remember their kingdom which has fallen, tears well up in their eyes, and they say: "They ferment, they curdle! Even great pools dry away!"'[8]

We have here three fundamentally different narratives produced by writers whose social positions are all but incomparable: a former male military engineer in Brazil; a self-taught female intellectual in the Cape Colony; a male Sotho convert taught by French missionaries. Yet, despite these differences, each narrative conceptualizes history in terms of extreme unevenness and racialized conflict within a universal timeline – in Mofolo's case by implicating even Chaka as an agent in the unfolding of this time. If, as Helge Jordheim phrases it, the modern regime of historicity is shaped by 'practices of synchronization', it appears that our three narrators independently register the fatal consequences of such practices.[9] In this way, they all bear witness to the brutalization of time, and to time as brutalization. This brutalization, in turn, demonstrates that the synchronization of modernity can only ever be notional, an ideological fantasy that will always fall short of full actualization. This point has been made elegantly by Peter Osborne:

> As a geohistorical category, the modern can never be actual . . . without 'reserve'. And this reserve must necessarily be, in part, spatially conceived . . . [O]n the one hand, [the colonial reserve] is that which is held back, delimited, segregated, enclosed; but on the other hand, it is also that which contains the future within itself: the postcolonial. It is in the postcolonial that the colonial modern actualises its futurity, that is, its temporal status as 'reserve'.[10]

The impact of this logic is evident in Cunha and Schreiner; in Mofolo's *Chaka* it is less foregrounded, written as it is so unequivocally from the receiving end of the temporal regime of colonial modernity. In all three cases, however, the narratives not only exhibit profound ambivalence towards this temporal regime, but draw on other temporal modes that split off from or fold into dominant time, registering thereby resistant, sometimes transformative, elements. Indeed, as I elaborate on such resistant elements under the rubric of 'radical time', I am also arguing that an attention to the narrative entanglement of multiple durées – to use Achille Mbembe's influential term – carries a critical potential.[11] Arguably, in comparison with historiographical discourse, literature (along with its interpretive traditions) has a wider range of tools at hand for exploring and externalizing the rifts and tensions of historical experience. This is not so surprising, given the liberty of literary writing to examine precisely subjective, immanent dimensions of time.

Meaning versus Existence

As Paul Ricoeur once argued, it is not least by way of 'the epistemology of the narrative function' that 'the phenomenology of time experience' can be accessed: 'if time-experience is *mute,* narrating is *eloquent*'.[12] Anchoring his discussion in an Augustinian conception of time as constituted by memory, attention and expectation, Ricoeur supplements this with Heidegger's hierarchical distinction between 'levels of radicality' in time experience, of which 'the most radical one is temporality properly so-called'.[13] By this Heidegger meant a mode of time that privileges 'the primacy of the future in the dialectic between the three temporal intentionalities and above all by the finite structure of time arising from the recognition of the centrality of death, or, more exactly, of *being-toward-death*.'[14] What makes such a modality of time 'radical', it seems, is its directedness both towards the (or rather a) future and the cancellation of that future through death. The structure of such time is tragic, hence irrefutably serious. It is here that my corpus not only provides confirmation of Ricoeur's claim on behalf of the 'eloquence' of narrative with regard to time, but also challenges us to combine existential and world-historical aspects of time in our reading: personal destiny in these three narratives is never just personal; rather, death itself is thematized as collective and historical. The 'radical time' in focus here is radical precisely by dint of this fraught duality, which exposes the human cost of the accelerated time we know as modernity. Importantly, however, we need to recognize that invocations of the future inevitably bear upon the present, just as the space of experience and horizon of expectation always do. As Koselleck expresses it, 'Experience is present past, whose events have been incorporated and can be remembered. Within experience a rational reworking is included, together with unconscious modes of conduct which do not have to be present in awareness.' By the same token, expectation 'is the future made present; it directs itself to the not-yet, to the nonexperienced, to that which is to be revealed. Hope and fear, wishes and desires, cares and rational analysis, receptive display and curiosity: all enter into expectation and constitute it.'[15]

Historical consciousness is not the *same* as narrative temporality. But literary narrative has the capacity to mediate historical experience as well as disrupt, question or resist hegemonic accounts of history. What my examples can teach us is how egregious an error it would be to see Koselleck's terms as neutral categories, as though experience and expectation were simply *shared* rather than agonistically and antagonistically constituted. It is this split nature of historical experience that the narratives in question, in their partial way, allow us to explore.

An added twist to this way of approaching narrative and history is provided by Roland Barthes's striking observation, in his famous essay on the reality effect, of the incompatibility between meaning and existence in modern literature: 'The pure and simple "representation" of the "real", the naked relation of "what is" (or has been) thus appears as a resistance to meaning; this resistance confirms the mythic opposition of the *true-to-life* (the lifelike) and the *intelligible* . . . as if by some statutory exclusion, what is alive cannot signify – and vice versa.'[16] One should note that in the translation, 'true-to-life' substitutes for 'vécu', and 'the lifelike' for 'vivant'. There is, in other words, a certain distancing at work in the English version, whereas the French words much more directly denote what we might alternatively call 'the lived' and 'the living', reinforcing thereby Barthes's point. As he wrote this in his high-structuralist moment, it must be remembered that Barthes viewed the opposition as ideological. Indeed, the *apparent* escape of being from meaning is precisely what produced the ideological force of realism. If the narratively insignificant barometer, in the famous example from Flaubert's short story 'Un coeur simple', simply denoted the 'real', then this was nothing less than a measure of its success in creating an ideological ruse on behalf of bourgeois normality. Barthes's argument, in other words, invoked the 'real' not as a substantive category but as an index of false consciousness and bad faith.

This critical conception of realism is well-rehearsed and informs large swathes of postcolonial critique, at least as it took shape in the 1990s.[17] My motivation for returning to it is somewhat different, however. What happens if we think of being (understood as the real) and meaning (understood as the hegemonic temporal regime) in terms of a more dynamic relationship, in which both are implicated in one another, disturbing each other even as they act as foils for each other? This is essentially Fredric Jameson's approach in *Antinomies of Realism,* where he speaks of a widening rift between 'récit', or narrative, and 'scene' in nineteenth-century realism, a rift which ultimately leads to the breakdown of narrative and the valorization of scene in modernism.

Jameson's argument is complex, but the point I want to highlight is the temporal nature of the opposition he identifies. If récit represents traditional, established and hence ideological ways of ordering events 'that have entered history once and for all' in chronological succession, scene opens itself towards an atemporal 'present of consciousness' (what Ricoeur called 'attention') – and thereby to the nonrepresentable experience of unanticipated historical change that récit no longer can contain.[18] The difference from Barthes should be obvious: if the nonsignifying element in realism was merely ideological, for Jameson it presents an enabling disruption of ideology that needs, in its own right, to be understood historically.

My suggestion here is the following: if the space of experience and the horizon of expectation together constitute the potential sequence of narrative, then the present, the modality of attention, will be left in a precarious state. What we can find in narratives engaging colonial and postcolonial conditions are texts riven and traversed by a high degree of incommensurability between spaces of experience and horizons of expectation, and where 'scene' does not really offer respite from the temporal regime of modernity.[19] As narratives of temporal crisis that challenge the separation of meaning from existence, it seems that they have few available alternatives.

To phrase my point as sharply as possible: it is what is 'alive' that gets lost between the space of experience and the horizon of expectation. In all three examples, we see how it is only through death (symbolic or real) that Schreiner's imagined 'less developed individuals and races' (but also her character Rebekah's constrained living space), the Canudos rebels and the fallen kingdom of the Zulus can fully signify within the hegemonic narrative of colonial modernity. The incompatibility of meaning and existence signals in this way an economy of (historical) meaning and death within colonial modernity.

Prophecy

This stark and unbearable reading, consonant with Spivak's subaltern that cannot speak, is, however, rendered moot by the narratives themselves.[20] As already key features of Mofolo's novel alert us, written as it is in an African language and with narrative agency granted exclusively to Africans, there is more to their treatment of historical time than merely a reproduction of colonial temporality. Instead, the incompatibility of meaning and existence haunts them on a formal level, through the *splitting* and *expansion* of narrative time. This is achieved in many ways; for the purposes of this chapter, I wish to highlight one particular narrative device that offers an alternative to Jameson's 'scene', namely prophecy.

The word 'prophecy' bears a dual meaning, both temporal and critical. It is a message from elsewhere, deriving its authority from a divine or otherworldly origin, uttered critically in a given social context. Indeed, in the monotheistic religions, emphasis has been placed on the critical dimension: it is a matter of making God's will clear, a task that may or may not involve speaking of the future. In these traditions, William Hasker explains, the prophet witnesses to the people 'concerning God's purposes and requirements', seeking in this way 'to recall them to obedience'.[21] It is, in other words, the *present* which is the crucible of such prophecy. Even so, a particularly effective way to criticize the present state of things is through reference to the future, *to that which is not yet the case*. In the examples invoked here, prophecy makes use of the future as a life-affirming temporal resource; it speaks in the name of the living who are obliterated by present meaning, even when predicting a dark future. The resulting 'competing visions of a world remade', in Jennifer Wenzel's turn of phrase, present a challenge to Peter Osborne's implied claim that futurity is the temporal reserve only of colonial modernity.[22] Here, futurity is rather harnessed as precisely the radical time that in Benjaminian fashion ruptures the unbearable present. I would even claim that it is not the assumed knowability of the future that is most important in these examples. On the contrary, by allowing for radical alternatives to the present and to its colonial ideologies of linear progress, it is in fact the human *unknowability* of the future that is exploited as a source of social and political authority.

In my three narratives, we will find a number of prophetic moments that trouble the narrative of progress. In *Os sertões,* as I have discussed elsewhere, it enters the story most dramatically when Cunha recounts the prophecies of Antonio Conselheiro:

> In 1896 a thousand herds will run from the coast to the backlands; then the backlands will become the coast and the coast will become the backlands. . . .
> In 1899 the waters will turn to blood and the planet will appear in the east at sunrise and the bough will find itself on the earth and the earth will find itself in the heavens.
> In 1900 the light will go out of the sky. There shall be a great rain of stars and that will mark the end of the world.[23]

While still adhering to the modern calendar, Conselheiro's apocalyptic prophecies effectively split time in Cunha's story, presenting not only a time parallel but also other to modernity, a messianic time in which his followers could believe, given its proximity to their own space of experience; the

'great rain of stars' marking the end of the world – the end of their alternative
social order – did indeed fall upon the rebels of Canudos in the form of the
Republican army's onslaught. When Cunha writes them down, these are
already prophecies past, a future past and a memorialization of a horizon of
expectation that, unnervingly, was both accurate and misguided.

Similar ambiguities in the horizon of expectation crop up in *Chaka,*
where prophecy is rife and achieves a de facto doubling of narrative time by
consistently foreshadowing that which will later occur in the novel. There
are, however, diverse modalities of prophecy at work in the novel that produce different effects. Let us look briefly at two examples.

The first is Chaka's well-known encounter with the King of the Deep
Pool. After greeting Chaka in 'a heavy, stentorious voice', the serpent starts
speaking in 'a very soft voice':

> This land is yours, child of my compatriot,
> You shall rule over nations and their kings
> You shall rule over peoples of diverse traditions
> You shall even rule over the winds and the sea storms
> And the pools of large rivers that run deep;
> And all things shall obey you with unquestioning obedience,
> And all shall kneel at your feet![24]

Earlier commentators have noted how this serpent is grounded both in African and Christian cosmologies.[25] What has less often been noted is the formal
distinctiveness of its prophecy. Being one of the main instances of oral poetic
form in the novel, it is set apart from the bulk of the narration, generically
but also in terms of voice – it is the only time in the novel when the nonhuman realm is granted a voice. At the same time, the prophecy is highly self-
referential, tracing as it does Chaka's subsequent trajectory in the narrative.

Contrary to Conselheiro, this prophecy seems to issue from a social
order in which the horizon of expectation remains contained by the space
of experience. Despite foretelling a dramatic turn in Chaka's life, it does
not imply that his ascendancy will threaten the social order: Chaka will be a
greater ruler than others, but this is a difference in degree, not in kind. The
King of the Deep Pool is not saying, in other words, that Chaka will threaten
the world as we know it, only that he will be a master of this world.

But compare this with another dramatic high point in the novel: Chaka's encounter with Isanusi. Isanusi is described as a diviner who 'receives
revelations through his head', but his relationship with the future is different
from the serpent's.[26] At every stage in his treatment of Chaka, he says two
things at once: that he can fulfil Chaka's desires, and that this fulfilment is
dependent on Chaka's own agency. These desires are moreover presented

as ambivalent, quite unlike the serpent's epic valorization of power. Isanusi describes his most powerful medicine in the following terms: 'It is extremely evil, but it is also extremely good. Choose!'[27] The emphasis on choice is in keeping with the Christian doctrine of free will, which complicates the narrative's overarching notion of destiny. Isanusi's prophetic agency does not deal with the inevitable, but with the probable. Even more importantly, the outcome of the future is presented as dynamic. The serpent's prediction is now revealed as having been conditional: 'if you do not spill blood, he will not be pleased with you'. Similarly, the effectiveness of Isanusi's medicine is dependent on Chaka's actions: 'if you do not spill much blood, it will turn against you and kill you instead'. Like a latter day Machiavelli, Isanusi repeats that Chaka 'must be a cultivator of kingship'.[28]

With Isanusi, then, we have prophecy with a difference. Uncertainty is introduced into the temporal equation, blurring the horizon of expectation and preparing the reader to expect the unexpected. In formal terms, this is brilliantly executed. Mofolo strikes a precise balance between anticipation and surprise, with the killing of his beloved Noliwa as the culminating turning point and final confirmation that Chaka, in a Faustian wager, willingly sacrifices his soul in exchange for power. This is also what allows for the generic shift from an individual drama – from romance, to use Simon Gikandi's words – to a cosmic, apocalyptic one.[29] Freed from the bounds of reason, Chaka cultivates sheer destructiveness:

> Ahead of Chaka's armies the land was beautiful, and was adorned with villages and ploughed fields and numerous herds of cattle; but upon their tracks were charred wastes without villages, without ploughed fields, without anything whatsoever, except occasionally some wild animals. . . . The land became wild and unfriendly and threatening; the smell of death was upon the earth and in the air. . . . Where villages once stood was utter desolation, the ghostly sight of which made one's hair stand on end.[30]

The narrator continues by claiming that 'on account of hunger, people began to eat each other', placing the blame for this, too, on Chaka, who is now called 'originator-of-all-things-evil'.[31] It is explained that Chaka 'destroyed the nations in a manner *never known before*' (emphasis mine), leaving 'only charred ruins all around'.[32] This is the representation of an unprecedented experience. Chaka's actions are qualitatively new and even have an anthropogenic significance. In this respect, he doubles narrative time by becoming an allegory of history as such – that is, of the widening gap between experience and expectation. It is this gap that characterizes modernity, as we know, but the striking nature of Chaka as allegory is its denial of a benign futurity.

Mofolo's novel presents in this way an exceptionally complex engagement with the entangled durées of colonial modernity. Isanusi's mode of prophecy, which dominates the narrative, *opens* the horizon of expectation on behalf of the ambiguous protagonist Chaka by asserting his capacity to choose between alternative paths of action. The unfolding of narrative events, however, is in keeping with the negative experience of colonial imposition that marked Mofolo's own present.

It is, finally, in allegorical form that we encounter Olive Schreiner's secular mode of prophecy in *From Man to Man*. Schreiner often engaged in allegorical writing (as in her best-selling *Dreams*, 1890) and tended to include allegories in otherwise realist narratives. In the chapter where Rebekah grapples with the genocidal logic of social Darwinism, we find that she concludes her argument by penning down a prophetic allegory. The allegory speaks of 'the Spirit of the Ages', who chances upon a woman's figure on a plain, 'bare and beautiful from the waist upwards, but clothed below in a coarse garment'.[33] Puzzled by the sad look on the woman's face, and her lack of mobility, the Spirit discovers that 'about her feet were iron fetters, upon the limbs were marks of unhealed stripes, old gangrenous wounds festered there, and the flesh was shrunken from the bones and the feet deep sunken in the sand'.[34] This painfully unsynchronized female body, we will not be surprised to discover, is called Humanity, the point of the allegory being that only *she* will be able to liberate herself. Written around the turn of the last century, this is a remarkably early figuration of 'combined and uneven development' and the 'wretched of the earth' as being produced in and by the logic of a globalizing modernity.[35]

What is striking about this chapter in *From Man to Man* is its combination of earnestness and inconclusiveness. Even the allegory, presented as a flash of inspiration and a crystallization of Rebekah's seemingly endless inner debate over genocide, inequality and progress, is relativized as soon as we return to the narrative mode of metonymic realism: 'She closed the exercise book and put it in the drawer. Perhaps some day the little allegory would enlarge itself and she would write it in fit words to make others see the picture. Probably she would never touch it again because it takes time to write things for other people. But the little picture she would never forget, because the pictures one sees are actual and one never forgets them.'[36] This contrast between narrative modes is nonetheless significant in and of itself. Rebekah's inner dialogue, although 'realistic', lacks anchorage. Large chunks of it consist of rhetorical questions whose force is derived from an appeal to ethical principles:

> You say that, with your guns shooting so many shots a minute, you can destroy any race of men armed only with spears; but how does that prove your superiority, except as the superiority of the crocodile is proved when it eats a human baby, because it has long teeth and baby has none? You say that the fact you can command the labour of so many of your fellow men and gratify your desires proves that you are higher than they; it proves that your belly is large and your

power of filling it great; but what, in these matters, are even you compared to the old saurians with their vast claws and paws and rough tongues, who could have licked you off the face of the earth in a moment? . . . But you may say: If the perfecting of humanity is not to be accomplished by this destruction of one part by the other, how then is it to be accomplished?

Is it not possible only in two ways? Is there any hope of our in any way raising and hastening the rate of human advance if we cannot do it by the killing and suppressing of individuals?

Surely there are ways. . . . Has not the time come when the slow perfecting of humanity can find no aid from the destruction of the weak by the stronger, but by the continual bending down of the stronger to the weaker to share with them their ideals and aid them in the struggle with their qualities?[37]

I quote this at some length for several reasons. The first is to underline how explicit Schreiner's character is about the genocidal logic of a particular imperial ideology of progress. The second is to show how adamantly she clings to the notion of progress as such – not least in the sense of evolutionary progress. The value of change and improvement is, from her vantage point as a cheated wife and mother with frustrated intellectual ambitions, not negotiable. The third is to demonstrate how her voice lacks authority. In this narrative situation, it is not directed outwards but back at herself, an inner voice echoing in her secluded 'room of her own'. The ethical appeal carries some force of its own, but Rebekah's rhetorical ethos – her speaking position – is weak. Within the grey constraints of realism, there simply is no transcendence on offer for Rebekah in her subordinate gendered position as a white colonial woman.

This, then, is one way to account for the stylistically awkward introduction of allegory as a partial resolution of her intellectual and political predicament. I agree with Jade Ong's claim that the 'clarity' Schreiner found in allegory can be thought of 'as the ability to express radical politics at the level of content and form'.[38] By completely altering the scales both of narrative temporality and of subjectivity, the allegory momentarily shifts the terms of debate. For the Spirit of the Ages, 'moments are millenniums', 'minutes are aeons' and 'hours are a human eternity'; the female figure is not an individual but the collective, universal subject of 'Humanity'.[39] This generates a sense of defamiliarization whereby the need for a global and historical imaginary other than the one produced by high imperialism becomes apparent. Contrary to Bruce Robbins's recent argument about how deep-time perspectives risk attenuating political critique, Schreiner employs deep time (with reference both to the past and the future) precisely as an indictment of the present.[40]

What is noticeable in all three examples is how the affirmation of the living (or the recently dead) through prophecy entails not only splitting and expansion, but also a *qualitative* transformation of time. Rebekah's allegory, which she hastily scribbles as a momentary conclusion to her long and tortuous argument, establishes a deep, nonhuman time that is also a nontime, comparable to the messianic time that Cunha acknowledges as a socially meaningful temporality by quoting Conselheiro's prophecies. Likewise, the closing words of *Chaka* – 'Even great pools dry away!' – present yet another mode of prophecy, consonant with the allegorization of Chaka as a figure of history itself. 'Even great pools dry away' (note again the anthropogenic overtones) issues collectively from 'the Zulus' and has a dual temporal significance: it claims, on the one hand, to manifest the mournful space of experience of Mofolo's contemporaries, the Zulus. On the other hand, placed at the very textual limit of the narrative and verging thereby on the extra-textual abyss of the future, it reads as a prophetic statement on the ultimate passing of the powers that be, bracketing Mofolo's colonial present as an episode in the slow march of time and enabling another horizon of expectation than that presented by colonial modernity. Contrary to Osborne's claim that 'it is in the postcolonial that the colonial modern actualises its futurity', it reduces the colonial modern to an episode. This is radical time as a politics of extreme futurity and muted hope.

Stefan Helgesson is professor of English at Stockholm University. His work has dealt with southern African literature in English and Portuguese, Brazilian literature, postcolonial theory, translation theory and theories of world literature. He is the author of *Writing in Crisis: Ethics and History in Gordimer, Ndebele and Coetzee* (2004) and *Transnationalism in Southern African Literature* (2009), has edited volume four of *Literary History: Towards a Global Perspective* (2006) and is coeditor (with Pieter Vermeulen) of *Institutions of World Literature: Writing, Translation, Markets* (2015). He is currently leading the Swedish research initiative 'Cosmopolitan and Vernacular Dynamics in World Literatures'.

Notes

1. J. Zammito, 'Koselleck's Philosophy of Historical Time(s) and the Practice of History', *History and Theory* 43 (2004), 126–9.

2. R. Koselleck, '"Space of Experience" and "Horizon of Expectation": Two Historical Categories', in *Futures Past: On the Semantics of Historical Time,* trans. K. Tribe (Cambridge, MA: MIT Press, 1985), 280.

3. Koselleck, '"Space of Experience"', 280.

4. Just to mention a few of the more notable contributions to this debate (in alphabetical order): D. Attwell, *Rewriting Modernity: Studies in Black South African Literary History* (Pieter-maritzburg: UKZN Press, 2005); P. Bannerjee, *Politics of Time: 'Primitives' and History-Writing in a Colonial Society* (New Delhi: Oxford University Press, 2006); H.K. Bhabha, *The Location of Culture* (London: Routledge, 1994); D. Chakrabarty, *Provincializing Europe: Postcolonial Thought*

and Historical Difference (Princeton: Princeton University Press, 2000); J. Fabian, *Time and the Other: How Anthropology Makes Its Object* (New York: Columbia University Press, 1983); H. Harootunian, 'Some Thoughts on Comparability and the Space-Time Problem', *Boundary 2* 32(2) (2005), 25–52; N. Lazarus, *The Postcolonial Unconscious* (Cambridge: Cambridge University Press, 2011); A. Mbembe, *On the Postcolony* (Berkeley: University of California Press, 2001); G.C. Spivak, *A Critique of Postcolonial Reason: Toward a History of the Vanishing Present* (Cambridge, MA: Harvard University Press, 1999); J. Wenzel, *Bulletproof: Afterlives of Anticolonial Prophecy in South Africa and Beyond* (Chicago: University of Chicago Press, 2009). See also S. Helgesson, 'Radicalizing Temporal Difference: Anthropology, Postcolonial Theory, and Literary Time', *History and Theory* 53 (2014), 545–62, where I develop a longer theoretical discussion of these matters.

5. E. da Cunha, *Backlands: The Canudos Campaign,* trans. Elizabeth Lowe (New York: Penguin, 2010), 2.

6. O. Schreiner, *From Man to Man, or Perhaps Only* (Cape Town: UCT Press, 2015), 158.

7. T. Mofolo, *Chaka,* trans. D.P. Kunene (Oxford: Heinemann, 1981), 167.

8. Mofolo, *Chaka,* 168.

9. H. Jordheim, 'Introduction: Multiple Times and the Work of Synchronization', *History and Theory* 53 (2014), 505.

10. P. Osborne, 'Global Modernity and the Contemporary: Two Categories of the Philosophy of Historical Time', in C. Lorenz and B. Bevernage (eds), *Breaking Up Time* (Göttingen: Vandenhoeck and Ruprecht, 2013), 75.

11. Mbembe, *On the Postcolony.*

12. P. Ricoeur, 'The Human Experience of Time and Narrative', *Research in Phenomenology* 9 (1979), 17, 21.

13. Ricoeur, 'Time and Narrative', 19.

14. Ricoeur, 'Time and Narrative', 19–20.

15. Koselleck, '"Space of Experience"', 272.

16. R. Barthes, 'The Reality Effect', in Barthes, *The Rustle of Language,* trans. R. Howard (Oxford: Blackwell, 1986), 146. 'La "représentation" pur et simple du "réel", la relation nue de "ce qui est" (ou a été) apparaît ainsi comme une résistance au sens; cette résistance confirme la grande opposition mythique du vécu (du vivant) et de l'intelligible . . . comme si, par une exclusion du droit, ce qui vit ne pouvait signifier – et réciproquement.' R. Barthes, 'L'effet du réel', in Barthes, *Oeuvres complètes,* vol. 2 (Paris: Seuil, 1994), 485.

17. See, for example, L. Bethlehem, '"A Primary Need as Strong as Hunger": The Rhetoric of Urgency in South African Literary Culture under Apartheid', *Poetics Today* 22(2) (2001), 365–89; Bhabha, *The Location of Culture*; S. Gikandi, *Reading Chinua Achebe: Language and Ideology in Fiction* (London: James Currey, 1991).

18. F. Jameson, *The Antinomies of Realism* (London: Verso, 2013), 18, 25.

19. Patricia Murphy, in a discussion of Schreiner's first novel, *The Story of an African Farm* (1883), does claim that she establishes an 'eternal present' in the otherwise sequential mode of narration. In my view, however, this eternal present could just as readily be understood in terms of stasis. P. Murphy, 'Timely Interruptions: Unsettling Gender through Temporality in *The Story of an African Farm*', *Style* 32(1) (1998), 80–101.

20. G.C. Spivak, 'Can the Subaltern Speak?', in Cary Nelson and Lawrence Grossberg (eds), *Marxism and the Interpretation of Culture* (Urbana: University of Illinois Press, 1988), 271–313.

21. W. Hasker, *God, Time, and Knowledge* (Ithaca: Cornell University Press, 1989), 194.

22. Wenzel, *Bulletproof,* 41.

23. Cunha, *Backlands,* 142. See also Helgesson, 'Radicalizing'.

24. Mofolo, *Chaka,* 25.

25. C.F. Hallencreutz, 'Tradition and Theology in Mofolo's *Chaka*', *Journal of Religion in Africa* 19(1) (1989), 71–85; Attwell, *Modernity,* 67–70.

26. Mofolo, *Chaka*, 25–26.
27. Mofolo, *Chaka*, 43.
28. Mofolo, *Chaka*, 45–46.
29. S. Gikandi, 'Realism, Romance, and the Problem of African Literary History', *Modern Language Quarterly* 73(3) (2012), 323–6.
30. Mofolo, *Chaka*, 136–37.
31. Mofolo, *Chaka*, 137.
32. Mofolo, *Chaka*, 141.
33. Schreiner, *From Man to Man*, 185.
34. Schreiner, *From Man to Man*, 186.
35. WReC (Warwick Research Collective), *Combined and Uneven Development: Towards a New Theory of World-Literature* (Liverpool: Liverpool University Press, 2015); F. Fanon, *Les damnés de la terre* (Paris: Maspéro, 1961).
36. Schreiner, *From Man to Man*, 187.
37. Schreiner, *From Man to Man*, 183–4.
38. J.M. Ong, 'Dream Time and Anti-imperialism in the Writings of Olive Schreiner', *Journal of Postcolonial Writing* 50(6) (2014), 705.
39. Schreiner, *From Man to Man*, 185.
40. B. Robbins, 'Prolegomena to a Cosmopolitanism in Deep Time', *Interventions* 18(2) (2016), 172–86.

Bibliography

Attwell, D. *Rewriting Modernity: Studies in Black South African Literary History*. Pietermaritzburg: UKZN Press, 2005.
Bannerjee, P. *Politics of Time: 'Primitives' and History-Writing in a Colonial Society*. New Delhi: Oxford University Press, 2006.
Barthes, R. 'The Reality Effect', in *The Rustle of Language*, trans. Richard Howard (Oxford: Blackwell, 1986), 141–48.
———. 'L'effet du réel', in *Oeuvres complètes*, vol. 2 (Paris: Seuil, 1994), 479–84.
Bethlehem, L. '"A Primary Need as Strong as Hunger": The Rhetoric of Urgency in South African Literary Culture under Apartheid', *Poetics Today* 22(2) (2001), 365–89.
Bhabha, H.K. *The Location of Culture*. London: Routledge, 1994.
Chakrabarty, D. *Provincializing Europe: Postcolonial Thought and Historical Difference*. Princeton: Princeton University Press, 2000.
Cunha, E. da. *Backlands: The Canudos Campaign*, trans. Elizabeth Lowe. New York: Penguin, 2010.
Fabian, J. *Time and the Other: How Anthropology Makes Its Object*. New York: Columbia University Press, 1983.
Fanon, F. *Les damnés de la terre*. Paris: Maspéro, 1961.
Gikandi, S. *Reading Chinua Achebe: Language and Ideology in Fiction*. London: James Currey, 1991.
———. 'Realism, Romance, and the Problem of African Literary History', *Modern Language Quarterly* 73(3) (2012), 309–28.
Hasker, W. *God, Time, and Knowledge*. Ithaca: Cornell University Press, 1989.
Helgesson, S. 'Radicalizing Temporal Difference: Anthropology, Postcolonial Theory, and Literary Time', *History and Theory* 53 (2014), 545–62.
Hallencreutz, C.F. 'Tradition and Theology in Mofolo's *Chaka*', *Journal of Religion in Africa* 19(1) (1989), 71–85.

Harootunian, H. 'Some Thoughts on Comparability and the Space-Time Problem', *Boundary 2* 32(2) (2005), 25–52.

Jameson, F. *The Antinomies of Realism*. London: Verso, 2013.

Jordheim, H. 'Introduction: Multiple Times and the Work of Synchronization', *History and Theory* 53 (2014), 498–515.

Koselleck, R. '"Space of Experience" and "Horizon of Expectation": Two Historical Categories', in *Futures Past: On the Semantics of Historical Time*, trans. K. Tribe (Cambridge, MA: MIT Press, 1985), 267–88.

Lazarus, N. *The Postcolonial Unconscious*. Cambridge: Cambridge University Press, 2011.

Mbembe, A. *On the Postcolony*. Berkeley: University of California Press, 2001.

Mofolo, T. *Chaka*, trans. D.P. Kunene. Oxford: Heinemann, 1981.

Murphy, P. 'Timely Interruptions: Unsettling Gender through Temporality in *The Story of an African Farm*', *Style* 32(1) (1998), 80–101.

Ong, J.M. 'Dream Time and Anti-imperialism in the Writings of Olive Schreiner', *Journal of Postcolonial Writing* 50(6) (2014), 704–16.

Osborne, P. 'Global Modernity and the Contemporary: Two Categories of the Philosophy of Historical Time', in C. Lorenz and B. Bevernage (eds), *Breaking Up Time* (Göttingen: Vandenhoeck and Ruprecht, 2013), 69–84.

Ricoeur, P. 'The Human Experience of Time and Narrative', *Research in Phenomenology* 9 (1979), 17–34.

Robbins, B. 'Prolegomena to a Cosmopolitanism in Deep Time', *Interventions* 18(2) (2016), 172–86.

Schreiner, O. *From Man to Man, or Perhaps Only*. Cape Town: UCT Press, 2015.

Spivak, G.C. 'Can the Subaltern Speak?', in Cary Nelson and Lawrence Grossberg (eds), *Marxism and the Interpretation of Culture* (Urbana: University of Illinois Press, 1988), 271–313.

———. *A Critique of Postcolonial Reason: Toward a History of the Vanishing Present*. Cambridge, MA: Harvard University Press, 1999.

Wenzel, J. *Bulletproof: Afterlives of Anticolonial Prophecy in South Africa and Beyond*. Chicago: University of Chicago Press, 2009.

WReC (Warwick Research Collective). *Combined and Uneven Development: Towards a New Theory of World-Literature*. Liverpool: Liverpool University Press, 2015.

Zammito, J. 'Koselleck's Philosophy of Historical Time(s) and the Practice of History', *History and Theory* 43 (2004), 124–35.

CHAPTER 9

Engaged History

MARCIA SÁ CAVALCANTE SCHUBACK

And meet the time as it seeks us.
—Shakespeare, *Cymbeline*

The need to engage with the meaning of history has become a central question in our contemporary moment. Since the end of World War II, and in
the wake of decolonization, a vast amount of research has been done on the
relation between historical knowledge and memory, trauma, community
and the shaping of visions of the future.[1] One of the main threads of this
critical undertaking is the conviction that the very idea of History with a
capital 'H' is a Western and Eurocentric idea. As such, it was imposed on
other cultures and resulted not only in violent histories of destruction, but
also in self-destruction. If some historians see and even defend a competition
of sorts between the Shoah – the catastrophe of European history destroying
itself through the extermination of its others – and the colonial past – the
catastrophe of History destroying other histories when reducing all otherness
to itself – the concept of History has proved to be proved by history itself.[2]
To use a phrase by Albert Camus, the twentieth century bears witness to
how 'History has murdered History'.[3]

The tendency of this vast intellectual endeavour is, on the one hand, to
concede to the concept of shared memory the role that the concept of History previously had. This is done, on the one hand, by replacing a universal
idea of history with a pluralistic vision, and, on the other, by relocating the
meaning of history from the past to the present. If History with a capital

'H' has been shaped in an antiquarian mode, as Nietzsche liked to describe it,[4] that is as passéist, or as futurist and progressivist, shared memory is currently shaped in a presentist manner.[5] Relying on this awareness of the idea of History as ground for the modern concepts of nation-state and national identity and for the creation of institutional mechanisms to define power and value relations between nations, peoples and communities, History is judged for having been the judge of values and a main component in ideological constructions and politics of oppression, repression and extermination. That is why questions about how the state and other political and cultural institutions relate to devastating historical events both in the past and in the present have also received much attention in public debates in the last years.

The more the world is regulated by the imperative of 'general equivalence', through which all differences and experiences are levelled and reduced to commodities and hence to the restlessness of a here and now, the greater the need to engage with the meaning of history. In this neoliberal reduction of everything to anything and hence to the one-dimensional meaning of a commodity, the search for new figures of identity, for populist voices defending the need for tradition and legitimizing new modes of segregation and discrimination, grows as a global threat. The global feeling is that 'the thirties are still before us',[6] a formula used by the French philosopher Gérard Granel to summarize the feeling of a repeated future and the future of a repetition, not only of the catastrophe of both world wars but also of the process of recolonization that globalization accomplishes precisely through decolonization.

Considering these fundamental aspects of what, drawing on Koselleck, could be called the 'space of experience' of the present, the need to engage with history today has to be more than a scientific theoretical engagement with the question of history and its current urgency. This need appears rather as an ethical and political commitment to the present and the future.[7] But how may we define this engagement with history if one of the main reasons of historical engagement is the attempt to avoid the horrors provoked by history itself? The main reason for engaging with history has indeed been the search to avoid the repetition of history. Today, however, after years marked by the politics of memory, by discussions about cultural heritage and cultural patrimony – discussions pursued for the sake of avoiding repetition – repetition seems to have repeated itself. Rather than adopting the rhetoric of surprise and its continuously repeated question, 'how could the 1930s return?', it is time to interrogate the very notion of engagement with history, current in institutional, political, academic and aesthetic discourses. I propose to question this 'official' engagement with history through a reflection on engaged history. The motivation behind this almost imperceptible distinction between 'engagement with history' and 'engaged history' is the

urgency to clarify in which sense there is a need for history today in order
to come to terms with history and to learn to live with the losses caused by
history. The monumentalization and patrimonialization of what history has
destroyed (as opposed to what history has constructed) share the same, if
inverted, strategy of glorifying the past. Hence, it is not surprising that the
losses generated by a politics of subjugation for the sake of profit generate
now new forms of profit. If oppositions such as that between History with
a capital 'H' and stories in the plural – that is, hegemonic history as opposed
to a multiplicity of histories – seem to provide an appropriate way to avoid
the repetition of the disastrous history of the West, they nevertheless tend to
neglect how the idea of one history tends to mirror itself in *each one* of the
multiple histories. At the same time as the concept of identity is negated in
its drive to universality, each difference grows stronger in claiming its own
identity and its own right to universalization. The engagement with history
seems in the end to contribute more to the dissemination of the very idea of
history it aims to battle against. Thus, the internal 'logic' of history remains
operative. The slightly different notion of 'engaged history' aims to alert us
to these risks in every construction of a historical narrative that assumes the
need to engage with history. It is not for the sake of an impartial or objective
historical narrative, nor in the search of an all-encompassing narrative that
would be absolutely safe against these risks. What I am proposing is that history is indeed a risk, a risk that history is perhaps nothing but engageability
itself, and that history therefore should not be understood as the past but
rather as the estuary of what has happened, of what could have happened
and what can happen.[8] As such, it is what refuses fixing in strong figures and
fast determinations, for it is permanently passing. As Werner Hamacher once
pointed out, history is departure.[9] How, then, to conceive of an engaged
history? How to engage with the 'passing of history as it passes'?

I propose the term 'engaged history' in analogy with Jean-Paul Sartre's
concept of 'engaged literature'. As such, it raises anew not only the question
about the relation between history and literature but also how the theories
of history and of literature are deeply interconnected even if neither of these
theoretical domains tends to focus on this epistemological bond. Indeed, the
history of how decisive methodological turns in both history and theories
of literature are related remains to be written, as in the cases of national history and national literature, comparative history and comparative literature,
universal history and universal literature, global or world history and global
or world literature, etc. In the search for a possible meaning of the expression
'engaged history', coined in analogy with engaged literature, we are searching not only for the relation between theory and practice, but above all for
a way of seizing the critical and crucial points in which the knowledge of
history does not alienate itself from history and the theory of literature does

not alienate itself from literature. We are searching for the points in which criticism does not alienate itself from critical situations and experiences, constructing a theoretical sphere for itself.

The relation between history and literature is a very old figure of thought in Western philosophy. Plato has presented it in his discussions about poetry as untruthful and false mimetic representation of reality. In the republic of truth idealized by Plato, fiction should have no place. Only the truthful correspondence between the idea and reality should reign in the Platonic state. In Plato, however, the point of antagonism is rather between idea and fiction, between the ideal and the fictional representation of reality, and not really representation as such. Aristotle was instead the first to oppose theoretically history and literature, in his *Poetics*. Tragic poetry, the main Greek experience of literature, differs from history, understood by the Greeks as chronicle, by virtue of relating what *may* happen, whereas history is the narrative of what has happened.[10] In this Platonic-Aristotelian frame, two sets of problems are outlined: one about the truthful or false correspondence between the idea or concept and reality, and one about the fictive presentation of what could have been or the realistic presentation of what has been. These fields of inquiry were developed separately and even antagonistically in the history of Western philosophy: the field of rational philosophy as opposed to history and narrative, and the field of historical/poetic narrative (fiction) as opposed to objective and empirical accounts of reality (facts). Both distinctions grew in importance and found more definitive contours in modernity and are still present in the sterile controversies between analytic and continental philosophy. Despite the opposition between reason and history, which remains operative even in attempts to write 'the history of pure reason', as inaugurated by Kant,[11] and to find 'the reason in history', recalling the title of a famous lecture given by Hegel in 1837,[12] both fields of inquiry have in common the problem of *correspondence* between idea and reality, and between *presentation* and content. In common is the question of *mimesis* addressed on the epistemological level as the problem of truth and falsehood and on the aesthetic level as the question of truthful or false representation. It has been within the frame of the question of mimetic correspondence and of mimetic representation that the difficult question about how to bridge the split between theory and practice has been traditionally debated.

These are problems that have been actualized in recent decades. Faced with the violence of contemporary history, questions such as the distinction between fact and fiction, the debates about the role of imagination in historiography, and the legitimacy of literary presentation of historical facts and literature as a form of historical knowledge have become central in political discussions and academic scholarship about the uses and disadvantages of literature for history. Hayden White, who dedicated an entire academic

life to the argument that history writing is a mixture of fact and fiction and
that historical narrative could be understood in its own right as literature and
hence as fiction, reconsidered this idea a few years ago, proposing instead,
in line with Jeremy Bentham, a distinction between fiction as a construction based on a hypothesis and fiction as a way of writing about imaginary
entities.[13] White's insistence on relating historical writing to literary writing
derives from an ethical commitment expressed in his distinction between
the 'practical past' and the 'historical past'. Drawing on the work of the
political philosopher Michael Oakeshott,[14] this distinction corresponds to a
certain extent to the old Aristotelian contrast between a narrative of what
has happened and a narrative of what could have happened. At stake is the
distinction between a narrative of a past that is considered *as* past – that is,
closed, capable of being treated as a distinct figure and unity and thereby to
be reabsorbed into institutional, political and ideological discourses – and
a narrative of the past of particular persons, groups and agencies that help
them to find an orientation in the present. This latter past is 'practical', in
the Kantian use of this term, because what matters is that 'the trace of the
past which perdures into the present'[15] can be a source of decision-making
in everyday life and in extreme situations. The concept of a 'practical past'
is White's theoretical response to the need for engaging with history in the
present. White's discussions, especially in his late collection of essays *The
Practical Past,* could be considered as a contribution to the notion of 'engaged
history', if to 'engage' means merely to show how the past – in the sense of
a 'practical past' – can be 'drawn upon in order to help [particular persons,
groups, etc.] to make assessments and decisions in ordinary everyday life as
well as in extreme situations (such as catastrophes, disasters, battles, judicial
and other kinds of conflicts in which survival is at issue)'.[16] Understood in
terms of a practical past, engaged history would be nothing but an actualization of the old idea of history as *magistra vitae* translated in the style of
patrimonial, memorial and testimonial narratives, by which the 'historical'
model of celebration gives place to a 'memorial model', following the vocabulary used by François Hartog.[17] Focusing only on how history is *written*
when taking as its object either the 'historical past' or the 'practical past' (the
latter being closer to literary writing), White's concept of the practical past
remains silent, as do most historians, on the question of how to *read* these
writings. Engagement and commitment are concepts of relation, namely of
the relation between writing and reading, demanding also a reflection on
what engaged reading means. If the practical past is mainly concerned with
how the traces of the past enduring in the present can become exemplary
for present and future life, the concept of engaged history proposed here
has its focus elsewhere, namely on the relation between writing and reading
history. The attention to this 'primordial experience', to use a phenomeno-

logical vocabulary, of writing and reading, may help us understand some of the problems inherent in a sense of history relying solely on patrimonial, memorial and testimonial writing. These problems become apparent when the excess of patrimonialization, memorialization and testimonialization begins to contribute to the formation of renewed politics of identity and thereby of segregation and exclusion. The more cultural memory is institutionalized and cultural heritage is politicized, the more it serves to promote a politics of identity and polarization. The difficulty here lies in how to ground politically a space for plural identities without basing identity on essentialist and segregationist views and convictions. The difficulty lies in how to conceive identity without identity. Although the concern has been to historicize the present and write a history that would resist a repetition of the atrocities of modern history and especially that of the twentieth century, this has been done in such a way that one has tended to reinforce what was meant to be avoided. Indeed, it is not enough to write history with political engagement. History must also be read. Therefore, the questions about reading history, and what kind of engagement and commitment the act of reading implies, are equally urgent.

Let us assume that 'engaged history' is not only concerned with how history is written, but also with how history is read, and indeed with how writing and reading history are fundamentally intertwined. This is the main reason for forging the notion of 'engaged history' in analogy with Sartre's concept of 'engaged literature'. After all, in Sartre's concept of engagement it is the relation between the writer and reader that is at stake, and not merely the choice of the author to write in an 'engaged' pathos for the suffering of others, the injustices of society and the political issues of the times.

In the famous essay 'Qu'est-ce que la littérature?', published for the first time in 1947 in the journal *Les Temps modernes,* Sartre defends the concept of 'engaged literature' against the accusation that engagement necessarily leads to loss of artistic freedom and to servitude to ideological doctrines, as in the case of socialist realism. To the criticism that art must be free from ideology and that engagement means to engage in a party, in political movements – that is, to be mobilized by a politics of adhesion – Sartre answers by paraphrasing Baudelaire. Literary engagement, he writes, is the simultaneity of two postulates,[18] engagement with society and engagement with literature at the same time. And he continues: 'Our concern is to serve literature infusing in it a new blood as well as serving collectivity when trying to give to it the literature it deserves'.[19] At stake is therefore a reciprocal relation, in which both literature and society conquer a meaning in their interaction. On this point, Sartre is very close to Walter Benjamin's essay 'The Author as Producer', in which is stressed the claim that political tendency and aesthetic quality must coincide.[20] The model for this reciprocal relation between political engagement and aesthetic quality is for Sartre the relation between the writer and the reader. That is why he defines engagement as a 'pact of generosity' between the author and the reader.[21] By this definition, Sartre intended to distinguish engaged literature from the engagement of literature with revolution, insofar as the latter aims to depict a society already changed and the former to unveil reality through the project of changing it. The difference is between literatures that are transformative and literatures that depict, communicate or transmit a transformation already accomplished – in reality or in dreams – outside and despite of literature. As a 'pact of generosity', engagement is conceived as the idea that art itself is a 'gift ceremony' and that the very gift operates a metamorphosis. In this pact of generosity, called engagement, the writer gives something to the reader, and the reader gives something to the writer. What the writer gives to the reader – that is, to society – is, 'a guilty consciousness; thereby in a state of perpetual antagonism toward the conservative forces which are maintaining the balance he tends to upset. For the transition to the mediate which can be brought about only by a negation of the immediate is a perpetual revolution'.[22] 'Guilty consciousness' is the English translation of the French *conscience malheureuse,* which in turn is a translation of Hegel's expression *unglückliches Bewußtsein,* that is, an unhappy consciousness. What the writer gives is 'unhappiness', forcing thereby the reader to leave the comfort of common sense and lack of reflection, of what is given as 'evident' and 'immediate', forcing the reader into a kind of emigration to the discomfort of a life in problematicity, of endless inquiry, of 'permanent revolution'. However, this gift only exists when received by the reader. Implicit in Sartre's discussion is the belief that everything can be given to someone except the very capacity to receive. 'The literary object', affirms Sartre, 'only exists in movement. In order to make it emerge, a concrete act called reading is demanded'.[23] Thus, before and after the reading there is no writing, only marks on paper. For Sartre, engagement is not only the engagement of the writer but the sharing of engagement between the writer and the reader, an act that defines writing from reading and reading from writing and through which society is able to see itself being seen. Indeed, according to Sartre, what literature accomplishes is the passage from immediacy to mediation, from the normalized to critique and revolt. Literature is engagement in the sense of being the promise to remain bound to the necessity of this passage from the immediate, and its oppressive realm of 'the goes without saying', to the mediate, the liberating realm of asking 'what is the word?', 'how should it be said?', 'how to give a sense to it?'. Sartre therefore insists that literary works are an open appeal to the freedom of the readers and their engagement is the promise to remain bound to the social praxis of freedom, to 'permanent revolution', making use of Lenin's expression several times in his essay. For a society in permanent revolution, words and actions no longer constitute an antinomy insofar as, he says, 'literature is the subjectivity of a society in permanent revolution'.[24]

In the 'pact of generosity' that defines engagement, in Sartre's eyes, the reader has to be engaged, not only in the sense of wanting to receive the gift of 'unhappy consciousness' but above all for being the place where the meaning of what is written is accomplished. If the writer provides the un-happy consciousness, the reader gives in the reading a meaning to it. Sartre's engagement is opposed to socialist realism's idea of engagement, insofar as for the latter, the socialist-realist text is ready, that is, already 'read', not al-lowing further interpretation. It is a text that shall be seen rather than read, that shall be read as a realistic painting should be seen, as an image that can be seized at once with no need for learning patiently how to read it.[25] For Sartre, on the contrary, engagement demands the practice of reading, insofar as this is the fundamental model of the practice of freedom, of transforming meaning through reflection and interpretation. That is why he considers that reading is the synthesis between perception and creation.[26] Nevertheless, reading remains for him a 'guided creation' (*création dirigée*); thus it remains guided by the intentions of the writer.

In regard to our attempt to develop the notion of engaged history, Sartre's understanding of engagement as a 'pact of generosity' between the writer and the reader can help us to draw attention to how White's distinc-tion between historical and practical pasts could be 'read' differently. Insofar as this distinction refers mainly to the tension between official history and experienced histories and stories, to the friction between professional his-torians talking to professionals and the way history endures in the present of individuals and groups, it can be claimed that it is a tension between the writing and the reading of history. Indeed, we should rather say that what is in question is the writing of history based on two very different ways of reading it. While professional historians read what is written, and thereby what has already passed and become fixed as a fact, practical historians, so to speak, write down their reading of how the past is still passing, of enduring traces. The former write on the basis of a reading of facts; the latter write by reading the experience of facts. At stake is the difference between reading fixed facts, data, images, concepts, and reading what is precisely nonfixed, still to be fixed in a certain moment. Indeed if reading – and, more precisely, historical reading – is a key experience in engaged history, it is expressly so insofar as reading itself is an engagement with time.

Engagement with history and engaged history present, accordingly, two different views of reading history. The first is concerned with reading his-tory in such a way that the future of history could be controlled. Engaged history, in its turn, reads history by 'trusting uncertainties', to recall the title of a series of artistic works by Esther Shalev-Gerz, to which I will return in a moment. What does it mean to read history by trusting uncertainties? It means to acknowledge the lines of tension between a historical reading of the past and the experience of how the past is enduring in the present. These lines of tension appear in the reading that is attentive to the reading itself and not only to what is being read or to who is reading. Thus reading is itself an exercise of perception as much as perception is a reading, as Walter Benjamin insisted upon.[27] A reading that is attentive to the act of reading discovers that the reading cannot read the reading itself, and therefore that every reading is entangled with its own shadow of unreadability.[28] This attentive reading is engaged with a continuous disengagement from holding fast pictures and images of the past. It is a dis-reading reading, a disengaging engagement, so to speak. An 'image' of the engagement with the is-passing of history that disengages from holding fast images and pictures is the *Monument Against Fascism* created by Esther Shalev-Gerz and Jochen Gerz, during the years 1986 to 1993. The work began with the construction of a twelve-metre lead column that, through a mechanism by which people could sign their names on the column in protest against fascism, was gradually lowered into the ground. By means of this mechanism, the signatures of seventy thousand people lowered down the column into the ground. In 1993, the column ceased to exist, and the monument became empty, and today there is only an inscription on the ground where the monument was constructed.[29] The aim of the artists was to protest against fascism by refusing to forget that monumentalism and fascism are closely intertwined, and thereby that monument as politics must be de-monumentalized, that the patrimonialization of fascism must also be de-patrimonialized, since monumentalized protests can become a new source of identity and segregation politics. The aim was to engage with the disengagement from the politics of monuments so that 'in the end it is only we ourselves who can stand up against injustice',[30] following the artists' own words, and not the official sites of the politics of memory. This artistic image of the reading of history as the *passing while passing* is an image of the coming to image itself, revealing both the dangers of imaging and the impossibility of not having images. As Jacques Rancière insightfully saw, the *Monument Against Fascism* is not a confirmation that the invisible God or the Shoah are unrepresentable and must be symbolized by the signs of absence. 'This invisible monument is not a monument to absence',[31] he argues, because, quite on the contrary, it disengages from the politics of monuments when rendering the wills of those who exist here and now the true site of protest. In the work of Esther Shalev-Gerz, we experience how history is being read in the heart of each individual, how each individual experiences it, and hence the presence of the passing of history in each one. That is why we can see in her different works not 'things', 'concepts', 'ideas', 'postulates', 'messages', 'denouncements' or 'announcements', but hands touching objects, ears listening to messages, eyes moving back and forth across what is being shown, finding unexpected and subtle visions in the middle of prepared and constructed images; added to this, there are the projectors beaming these singular emotional experiences to each other, exposing thereby a series of lines of tensions and of tensions of lines of memories, expectations, intentions and emotions.

The work of Esther Shalev-Gerz has seized with great sensibility the risk and danger involved in the task of writing history today. She understands how theories of engagement and engaged experience hardly correspond to each other, and that theories of experience should be brought in conversation with the experience of theory. This insight has guided a work called *On Two*, from 2009, commissioned by the Musée Jeu de Paume in Paris for the occasion of a retrospective of her work.[32] This work is in several dimensions an active practice of reading history. *On Two* is an installation with an HD double projection of a woman, Rola Younes, a young Lebanese philosopher, and an older man, Jacques Rancière, the French philosopher, are speaking separately to the camera, 'engaging various degrees of embodiment', in Shalev-Gerz's own description. While Rancière reads a part of his own text 'The Emancipated Spectator', Rola Younes recounts, without reading, her thoughts, memories and her relation to her own country, Lebanon. Rancière reads his reflections on how he realized that his long philosophical life, dedicated to the enlightenment of the working class and to letting the concerns of the working class orient his theoretical view of the world, had been mistaken all along when he discovered letters of nineteenth-century workers in which their own metaphysical, aesthetic and theoretical views of the world were expressed. Rancière reads what he wrote about this experience of discovering the mistake of his philosophical position, and performs in this reading the philosophical attitude of self-reflection and self-criticism. Parallel to the film showing Rancière's self-reading, we can follow the film with Rola Younes, in which she spontaneously tells the story of how she constructed her relation to Lebanese contemporary history, to the memories of the war, to how she decided to learn, beside the French, English and the mother tongue Arabic, the language of her neighbours: Hebrew, Farsi and Yiddish. Younes's talk is a testimony of her experience. The way she describes her multilingualism as a way to learn the language of her others, in order to find a direct access, without translation, to their own formulations of realities and fictions, present another sense of reading. It presents the sense of reading as readiness to learn the language of otherness, and thereby to make it possible to listen to the listening of others, to see the seeing of others, to feel the others' feelings. Alternating between Rancière and Younes's images, Shalev-Gerz chose two distinct backgrounds: one, an aboriginal forest in Canada, and the other a postindustrial landscape at the Île Seguin being transformed into a place for leisure and culture; one, a landscape of archaic life cycles, and the other, the transformation of an industrial landscape to a new form of capitalistic exploitation. The first landscape exposes what is continuously forgotten in historical narratives, the ancestrality of life itself, which is indeed the only 'background' against which something like history and human history can flourish. The second landscape is also a forgotten landscape, indeed the landscape of oblivion that follows every capitalistic transformation. Last, a sound installation also accompanies both landscapes. We listen to Younes singing six songs in the six languages she has learnt and practices, and, when the transformed industrial landscape appears, some of her translated lyrics are inserted, shifting between disparate languages, letting the resonances of their harmonics resound.

These juxtaposed films present a self-critical and a testimonial reading of history, the reading of a text written by the reader and the recitation of several unwritten texts in different languages. This is indeed a reading that accomplishes the impossible, namely, reading 'what was never written', as Walter Benjamin put it.[33] Thus it reads forgotten ancestral life cycles, a postindustrial landscape condemned to oblivion by the constant transformations of capitalism, and the sounding of multiple sounds of different languages moving between one another, echoing and resonating in each other. This play between several layers of two realms of oppositions demonstrate another sense of opposition. The juxtaposition shows, accordingly, a sense of *correspondence,* which – contrary to the old concepts of mirroring and imitation – has to do with responding to and thereby taking responsibility for the experience of history.

In this inspiring work, the reading of history – that is, the experience of the passing of history – orients the writing of history in such a way that it becomes, if not impossible, at least problematic to write *about* history. To write *about* means to write 'on the outside of', in a position of exteriority and presumed impartiality, indeed in a positioned position, from which claims about realistic or unrealistic images of history, factual or fictional, correspondent or not correspondent, do not cease to repeat themselves. From this positioned position, it becomes a concern how to get access to history, how to get 'into' history. Esther Shalev-Gerz's work *On Two* intervenes in this idea of 'writing about' because history is always happening and the past continuously passing insofar as history and the past are experienced, indeed, are experiences. She proposes a writing based on a reading 'on two', rather than trying to get into history and deliver a text to be read in a 'guided' away. A reading 'on two' is a reading that considers the impossibility to impose a single, proper way of reading history. It shares with Roland Barthes the insight that reading is not only a work of decoding and deciphering but of being traversed by the estuary of experiences, languages, visions, thoughts, emotions – a kind of estuary of citations.[34] A reading 'on two' means, on the one hand, that the reading is always *a* reading, the engagement of each one and not something performed by a universal eye, and, on the other, that it renders possible the passage from one to another, from one to the other, taking place between two and many. Reading 'on two' performs what we are trying to conceive of in terms of engaged history and thereby to find a way to 'meet time as it seeks us'.[35]

Marcia Sá Cavalcante Schuback is professor of philosophy at Södertörn University. Before moving to Sweden she worked as associate professor at the Universidade Federal do Rio de Janeiro (UFRJ) in Brazil. Her field of specialization is continental philosophy, with a focus on phenomenology, hermeneutics, German idealism and contemporary existential philosophy. She is the author of several monographs in Swedish, Portuguese and English, including *Lovtal till Intet – essäer om filosofisk hermeneutik* (In praise of nothingness: Essays in philosophical hermeneutics, 2006), *Att tänka i skisser* (Thinking in sketches, 2011); *Being with the Without,* a conversation with Jean-Luc Nancy (2013), *Dis-orientations: Philosophy, Literature and the Lost Grounds of Modernity* (ed. together with Tora Lane, 2015); 'History, Today' (special issue of the journal *Philosophy Today,* 2017) and most recently *The End of the World* (ed. with Susanna Lindberg, 2017).

Notes

I dedicate this essay to the historian David Gaunt, with thanks for what he has taught me through his work and our conversations about engaged history.

1. See, e.g., the work done by the research programme *Time, Memory and Representation* at www.histcon.se, and the International Network for Theory of History (INTH) at http://www.inth.ugent.be/.

2. See, e.g., F. Hartog, *Croire en l'histoire* (Paris: Flammarion, 2013), 89.

3. A. Camus. *L'homme révolté* (Paris: Gallimard, 1951), 34–35.

4. F. Nietzsche, *On the Use and Abuse of History for Life,* trans. A. Collins (Gloucester: Dodo Press, 2008).

5. For a lucid critique of historical presentism and of the substitution of history with memory, see Hartog, *Croire en l'histoire,* 46–67.

6. G. Granel, '"The Thirties Are Still Before Us": Logical Analysis of the Concrete Situation', *Graduate Faculty Philosophy Journal* 25(1) (2004), 113–35.

7. See 'Community Engaged History', ActiveHistory.ca website, sponsored by the History Department at the University of Saskatchewan and Huron University College, 23 January 2016, retrieved 11 February 2017, http://activehistory.ca/2016/01/community-engaged-history/; and the significant discussions presented by A. Margalit in *The Ethics of Memory* (Cambridge, MA: Harvard University Press, 2004)

8. For a discussion about the sense of history as estuary, see my dialogue with J.-L. Nancy in 'History, Today', a special issue of *Philosophy Today* 60(4) (2016), 823–26.

9. W. Hamacher, 'Über einige Unterschiede zwischen der Geschichte literarischer und der Geschichte phänomenaler Ereignisse', in A. Schöne (ed.), *Kontroversen, alte und neue. Akten des VII. Internationalen Germanisten-Kongresses Göttingen 1985*, vol. 11 (Tubingen: Niemeyer Max Verlag, 1986), 5–15.

10. Aristotle, *Poetics*, trans. S.H. Butcher (London: Macmillan and Co., 1898), 35.

11. I. Kant, *Critique of Pure Reason*, trans. P. Guyer and A.W. Wood, The Cambridge Edition of the Works of Immanuel Kant (Cambridge: Cambridge University Press, 1998), 702–4.

12. G.W.F. Hegel, *Lectures on the Philosophy of World History. Introduction: Reason in History*, trans. H.B. Nisbet (Cambridge: Cambridge University Press, 1975).

13. H. White, *The Practical Past* (Evanston: Northwestern University Press, 2014), xvii.

14. M.J. Oakeshott, *On History and Other Essays* (Oxford: Blackwell, 1983).

15. White, *The Practical Past*, x.

16. White, *The Practical Past*, xiii.

17. Hartog, *Croire en l'histoire*, 50.

18. This expression by Baudelaire comes from the poem 'Mon cœur mis à nu', *Journal intime*, 1887, in which we can read: 'Il y a dans tout homme, à toute heure, deux postulations simultanées, l'une vers Dieu, l'autre vers Satan' (There is in every man two simultaneous postulates, one towards God and the other towards Satan).

19. J.-P. Sartre, 'Qu'est-ce que la littérature?', in *Situations*, vol. 2 (Paris: Gallimard, 1948), 30: 'Je rappelle, en effet, que dans la "littérature engagée", l'engagement ne doit, en aucun cas, faire oublier la littérature et que notre préoccupation doit être de servir la littérature en lui infusant un sang nouveau, tout autant que de servir la collectivité en essayant de lui donner la littérature qui lui convient.' Eng. trans. in J.-P. Sartre, *'What is Literature?' and Other Essays*, trans. by S. Ungar (Cambridge, MA: Harvard University Press, 1988), 13.

20. W. Benjamin, 'Der Autor als Produzent', in *Gesammelte Schriften*, vol. 2:2 (Frankfurt am Main, Suhrkamp, 1982), Eng. trans. by A. Bostock in 'The Author as Producer', in *Understanding Brecht* (London: Verso, 1998), 85–103.

21. Sartre, 'Qu'est-ce que la littérature?', 105; *'What is Literature?'*, 61.

22. Sartre, 'Qu'est-ce que la littérature?', 129: 'ainsi l'écrivain donne à la société une conscience malheureuse, de ce fait il est en perpétuel antagonisme avec les forces conservatrices qui maintiennent l'équilibre qu'il tend à rompre. Car le passage au médiat qui ne peut se faire que par négation de l'immédiat est une perpétuelle révolution'; *'What is Literature?'*, 81.

23. Sartre, 'Qu'est-ce que la littérature?', 91: 'Nulle part cette dialectique n'est plus manifeste que dans l'art d'écrire. Car l'objet littéraire est une étrange toupie, qui n'existe qu'en mouvement. Pour la faire surgir, il faut un acte concret qui s'appelle la lecture, et elle ne dure qu'autant que cette lecture peut durer. Hors de là, il n'y a que des traces noirs sur le papier'; *'What is Literature?'*, 50.

24. Sartre, 'Qu'est-ce que la littérature?', 196. *'What is Literature?'*, 139.

25. For a discussion on socialist realism, see the special issue on the topic, 'Relating to the Real', published by the journal *Baltic Worlds* 9(4) (2016).

26. Sartre, 'Qu'est-ce que la littérature?', 93: 'La lecture, en effet, semble la synthèse de la perception et de la création'; *'What is Literature?'*, 27.

27. W. Benjamin, 'Zur Sprachphilosophie und Erkenntniskritik', *Gesammelte Schriften*, vol. 6 (Frankfurt am Main: Suhrkamp, 1982), 9–53: 'Wahrnehmung ist Lesen / Leser ist nur in der Fläche Erscheinendes . . . Fläche die Konfiguration ist – absoluter Zusammenhang.'

28. For a discussion about reading the reading and reading unreadability, see P. de Man, *Allegories of Reading: Figural Language in Rousseau, Nietzsche, Rilke, and Proust* (New Haven: Yale University Press, 1979); and J.H. Miller, *The Ethics of Reading: Kant, de Man, Eliot, Trollope, James, and Benjamin* (New York: Columbia University Press, 1987).

29. For a résumé of the work, see E. Shalev-Gerz, 'Esther Shalev-Gerz, Monument Against Fascism, Hamburg-Harburg, 1986, documentation on the monument' (video), Vimeo, uploaded 29 July 2014, retrieved 11 February 2017, https://vimeo.com/102023622.

30. E. Shalev-Gerz, 'The Monument Against Fascism', https://vimeo.com/102023622.

31. J. Rancière, 'The Work of the Image', in E. Shalev-Gerz, *The Contemporary Art of Trusting Uncertainties and Unfolding Dialogues* (Gothenburg: Art and Theory Publishing, 2013), 26.

32. See E. Shalev-Gerz, 'Esther Shalev-Gerz, On Two, 2009, expert from the video (in French)' (video), Vimeo, uploaded 29 July 2014, retrieved 11 February 2017, http://www.shalev-gerz.net/?portfolio=on-two.

33. W. Benjamin, 'Über das mimetische Vermögen', *Gesammelte Schriften,* vol. 2:1 (Frankfurt am Main: Suhrkamp, 1982, 210–13: 'Was nie geschrieben wurde, lesen.'

34. R. Barthes, 'Sur la lecture', *Le Bruissement de la Langue, Essais Critiques,* vol. 4 (Paris: Seuil, 1984), 47–48.

35. W. Shakespeare, *Cymbeline,* The Cambridge Dover Wilson Shakespeare, vol. 6 (Cambridge: Cambridge University Press, 2008), 91.

Bibliography

Aristotle. *Poetics,* trans. S.H. Butcher. London: Macmillan and Co, 1898.

'Relating to the Real', special issue of *Baltic Worlds* 9(4) (2016).

Barthes, R. *Essais Critiques,* vol. 4. Paris: Seuil, 1984.

Benjamin, W. *Gesammelte Schriften,* vols 2 and 6. Frankfurt am Main: Suhrkamp, 1982.

———. *Understanding Brecht,* trans. A. Bostock. London: Verso, 1998.

Camus, A. *L'homme révolté.* Paris: Gallimard, 1951.

'Community Engaged History'. ActiveHistory.ca website, sponsored by the History Department at the University of Saskatchewan and Huron University College. 23 January 2016, Retrieved 11 February 2017 from http://activehistory.ca/2016/01/community-engaged-history/.

de Man, Paul. *Allegories of Reading: Figural Language in Rousseau, Nietzsche, Rilke, and Proust.* New Haven: Yale University Press, 1979.

Granel, G. '"The Thirties Are Still Before Us": Logical Analysis of the Concrete Situation'. *Graduate Faculty Philosophy Journal* 25(1) (2004), 113–35.

Hamacher, W. 'Über einige Unterschiede zwischen der Geschichte literarischer und der Geschichte phänomenaler Ereignisse', in A. Schöne (ed.), *Kontroversen, alte und neue. Akten des VII. Internationalen Germanisten-Kongresses Göttingen 1985,* vol. 11 (Tubingen: Niemeyer Max Verlag, 1986), 5–15.

Hartog, F. *Croire en l'histoire.* Paris: Flammarion, 2013.

Hegel, G.W.F. *Lectures on the Philosophy of World History. Introduction: Reason in History,* trans. H.B. Nisbet. Cambridge: Cambridge University Press, 1975.

Kant, I. *Critique of Pure Reason,* trans. P. Guyer and A.W. Wood. The Cambridge Edition of the Works of Immanuel Kant. Cambridge: Cambridge University Press, 1998.

Margalit, A. *The Ethics of Memory.* Cambridge, MA: Harvard University Press, 2004.

Miller, J.H. *The Ethics of Reading: Kant, de Man, Eliot, Trollope, James, and Benjamin.* New York: Columbia University Press, 1987.

Nietzsche, F. *On the Use and Abuse of History for Life,* trans. A. Collins. Gloucester: Dodo Press, 2008.

Oakeshott, M.J. *On History and Other Essays.* Oxford: Blackwell, 1983.

Rancière, J. 'The Work of the Image', in E. Shalev-Gerz, *The Contemporary Art of Trusting Uncertainties and Unfolding Dialogues* (Gothenburg: Art and Theory Publishing, 2013), 25–29.

Sá Cavalcante Schuback, M., and J.-L. Nancy, *Philosophy Today* 60(4), special issue 'History, Today' (2016), 823–26.

Sartre, J.-P. *Situations,* vol. 2. Paris: Gallimard, 1948.

————. *'What is Literature?' and Other Essays,* trans. S. Ungar. Cambridge, MA: Harvard University Press, 1988.

Schöne, A. (ed.) *Kontroversen, alte und neue. Akten des VII. Internationalen Germanisten-Kongresses Göttingen.* Tubingen: Niemeyer Max Verlag, 1985.

Shakespeare, W. *Cymbeline.* The Cambridge Dover Wilson Shakespeare, vol. 6. Cambridge: Cambridge University Press, 2008.

Shalev-Gerz, E. *The Contemporary Art of Trusting Uncertainties and Unfolding Dialogues.* Gothenburg: Art and Theory Publishing, 2013.

————. 'Esther Shalev-Gerz, Monument Against Fascism, Hamburg-Harburg, 1986, documentation on the monument' (video). Vimeo. Uploaded 29 July 2014. Retrieved 11 February 2017 from https://vimeo.com/102023622.

————. 'Esther Shalev-Gerz, On Two, 2009, expert from the video (in French)' (video). Vimeo. Uploaded 29 July 2014. Retrieved 11 February 2017 from https://vimeo.com/102045971.

————. 'The Monument Against Fascism'. Personal website portfolio. Retrieved ## Month #### from http://www.shalev-gerz.net/?portfolio=monument-against-fascism.

White, H. *The Practical Past.* Evanston: Northwestern University Press, 2014.

CHAPTER 10

Speakers for the Dead

Digital Memory and the Construction of Identity

ALANA M. VINCENT

Orson Scott Card's 1986 novel, *Speaker for the Dead,* presents a society in which the dead may be mourned not only with the assistance of clerics and the customs of traditional religions, but also by summoning Speakers, who serve 'as priests to people who acknowledged no god and yet believed in the value of the lives of human beings', acting at the request of the family or community of the departed 'to discover the true causes and motives of the things that people did, and declare the truth of their lives after they were dead'.[1] Speakers are not eulogists; they speak *for,* in place of, rather than *about,* the dead; they take control of the private knowledge of the deceased and disseminate it on their behalf, healing relationships that had been damaged by secrecy, misunderstandings or incorrect assumptions during the lives of the deceased.

In the wake of the 2015 killing of twelve people at the offices of the French satirical newspaper *Charlie Hebdo,* thousands of individuals – many of whom had never before seen a copy of the paper – changed their Facebook statuses and profile pictures, or broadcast Twitter updates, to proclaim 'Je suis Charlie'. A month previous, a similar outpouring of digital sentiment took place in response to a New York grand jury's decision not to indict white police officers who had been filmed choking to death a black man named Eric Garner: the hashtag #icantbreathe. Approximately eighteen months later, the shooting of fifty people during Latinx Night at the Pulse nightclub in Orlando, Florida, gave rise to #WeAreOrlando. In this paper,

I wish to consider these mourning rituals not as an entirely new phenomenon, but as a continuation of a much longer historical trend in which, as I have argued at some length in previous publications, public memorialization functions to construct and enforce a collective identity.[2] I do not intend to repeat that previous argument within this essay; I am instead more interested in discussing the politics of the 'us' – the imagined community that is constructed in part by these commemorative rituals – making some suggestions about whether, and how, the problematic notion of collective identity is transforming in the digital age.

Card's *Speaker for the Dead* offers a remedy for, and thereby assurance against, the terrifying void of death – not the void that each individual might encounter at the end of their own life, but the void of unfinished business, unresolved relationships, an inability to account or compensate for loss that confronts those who remain behind. This is a fear that has given rise to countless ghost stories and, I wish to suggest, also underlies appropriative mourning movements such as *je suis Charlie,* #icantbreathe and #WeAreOrlando. Laying claim to the identity of the victim of a widely publicized tragedy offers an opportunity for symbolic roleplaying, in which the individuals claiming the identity are able to mitigate against their terror of death by agitating for 'justice' 'on behalf of' the victim(s), thereby reassuring themselves that the tragedy is an anomaly in an otherwise securely ordered world, and that such anomalies can be, and have been, put to rights. At the same time, claiming an identity in common with others may promote social solidarity; it can play a role in what Hannah Arendt theorized as 'worldmaking', the formation of a body politic in which the safeguarding of individual identities is the precondition for the existence of commonality. However, it also carries a risk of eroding the individual identities upon which any worldbuilding project must rest, leading instead to what Arendt terms 'worldlessness', the loss of a common space, a retreat from the negotiations required by public life, in favour of a primary existence within the familial or even individual sphere.[3] These hashtags therefore offer a window into a powerful set of complex identity negotiations that are fundamental to the functioning of contemporary politics.

At the risk of stating the obvious, it is worth noting at the outset that the internet is a large, and constantly growing, virtual space. It is not a monoculture. The major social networking sites – Facebook, Twitter, Tumblr, Instagram, Reddit – are each hosts to hundreds, if not thousands, of subnetworks, formed both from personal contacts between users ('friends' or 'followers') and from more loosely organized shared interests (hashtags, groups and subforums).[4] However, the largest two of these – Facebook and Twitter – incorporate both top-level and local 'trends', which may serve to draw par-

ticularly popular items to the attention of users even when the social sharing
mechanic around which each site is built has failed to do so. Thus, particularly popular trends are likely to register in the awareness of users even if
they or their immediate contacts are not active participants in transmitting
them. To the limited extent that it is possible to speak of 'internet culture',
it is these trends that constitute it; it is these events that are the most useful
examples on which to found a discussion of the potential of the internet as
a political space. These event-driven memes are, however, distinct from the
classic image memes that have mostly been the focus of meme studies.[5]

When I am talking about politics or the political, I am doing so in the
technical language that Hannah Arendt developed in her 1958 book, *The
Human Condition,* to describe one of three main spheres of human activity,
alongside labour (sustaining the life cycle through the cultivation of food and
other biological necessities) and work (the production of material objects,
which themselves endure beyond the period of human activity required to
bring them into being). For Arendt, the main purpose of these spheres of
activity – the purpose of life, if you will – is worldmaking: the world is not
simply a space we inhabit, not the location of our being, but an idea that we
are constantly struggling to bring into being. In my reading, Arendt does not
impose a false separation between labour, work and politics (which she also
refers to as 'action'); she is quite clear that each is at least partially dependent
upon the others. But for her, political action is the most interesting, most
difficult and therefore the most important sphere of human worldmaking
activity. Political action, unlike the other sorts of activity she discusses, is
always contingent and uncertain. Unlike labour and work, which are each
interactions with the material world, action functions entirely in the realm
of ideas; the products of action have, in themselves, no concrete existence.
So worldmaking involves a complex set of mitigations, in which labour and
work look to the realm of action for the narrative structures that endow
their activity with meaning, while action looks to labour and work for the
material actualization of its imaginative potential, a process which Arendt
calls 'reification'.

The contingency of action, however, is not fully addressed by recourse
to other spheres of activity; Arendt devotes considerable space to the dilemmas of irreversibility and unpredictability, which she argues are mitigated
only by means of further action – the acts of forgiveness and promise-making,
respectively:

> The unpredictability which the act of making promises at least partially dispels
> is of a twofold nature: it arises simultaneously out of the 'darkness of the human
> heart', that is, the basic unreliability of men who never can guarantee today
> who they will be tomorrow, and out of the impossibility of foretelling the

consequences of an act within a community of equals where everybody has the same capacity to act.[6]

It is worthwhile to note that at this point in Arendt's scheme, action's dilemmas do not arise from action itself, but from the presence of other people whose actions may impinge upon our own. We cannot predict the results of our own action because we never know what others might do – our world-making is thus always a negotiation with others.

In a shorter essay, 'Introduction into Politics', written around the same time as *The Human Condition,* Arendt clarifies exactly what she means by 'world', writing,

> Wherever human beings come together – be it in private or socially, be it in public or politically – a space is generated that simultaneously gathers them into it and separates them from one another. Every such space has its own structure that changes over time and reveals itself in a private context as custom, in a social context as convention, and in a public context as laws, constitutions, statutes, and the like. Wherever people come together, the world thrusts itself between them, and it is in this in-between state that all human affairs are conducted.[7]

The world, then, is the space that humans have in common, and worldmaking is the task of tending to that commonality, creating structures – both physical and conceptual – which enable and enhance our existence as individuals living in relationships of mutual responsibility with and to other individuals. There is an important distinction here between commonality and collectivity: the former enhances the capacity of the individual through a system of relationships of mutuality with other individuals. The latter obscures the boundaries between individuals, and in so doing renders both relationship and mutuality impossible.

Defining 'Digital Culture'?

The question about the extent to which digital culture influences culture offline is contentious and unlikely to be settled any time soon. In many social networks, the option of anonymity is integral to the formation of community, by custom if not by deliberate design; attempts by networks such as Google Plus and Facebook to force users to identify themselves by their legal name have proven both contentious and ineffective.[8] Anonymity does not obscure only detailed demographic data; the potential for a single individual to create multiple identities on any given network can make even very basic usage statistics difficult to ascertain. The most concerted attempts to study social network demographics have been undertaken by marketing firms and, largely limited in geographic scope, have generated little useful data for researchers interested in potential cultural transference across national and linguistic boundaries. Due to the tendency of memes to spread from one social network to another,[9] understanding the demographics of any single social network will still not offer a complete understanding of cultural influence.[10] While the memes I am particularly concerned with spread back and forth between Twitter and Facebook, I will focus my analysis primarily on Twitter due to the larger amount of publicly available data. In 2016, seventy-seven per cent of all Twitter accounts are registered outside of the United States.[11] In a raw numerical analysis of accounts active every month, the US is dominant (followed by the UK, Canada, Australia, Brazil, Germany, Netherlands, France, India and South Africa), but measuring per capita use – the number of Twitter users in a country relative to national population, which can be taken as a very rough measurement of Twitter's potential for social influence – tells a rather different story, with the top nations being Kuwait, Netherlands, Brunei, UK, USA, Chile, Ireland, Canada, Sweden and Puerto Rico.[12]

Even this loose data sketch is already suggestive of a potential disparity between the producers and consumers of internet culture; the 'we' constructed by Twitter hashtags is influenced by American and British culture to a greater extent than that 'we' is likely to influence their offline equivalents. There are a few other characteristics of the 'us' of digital culture that can be derived either directly from network usage data or else by inductive reasoning from this data:

- We have the ability to read English (although advances in machine translation are quickly changing this).
- We have sufficient access and leisure time to be reasonably invested in digital culture. While technological advances are continually lowering the threshold for entry, digital culture is still largely a domain of relative economic privilege.
- We quite literally do not see race – unless content producers are making a deliberate effort to show us race. The invisibility of physical markers in digital space contributes to a flattening of perception; it is easy to assume that the person on the other end of an online interaction is, in essence, another 'us', unless and until they demonstrate otherwise. Such demonstration can, and does, occur through the use of subcultural referencing and marked language.[13]

This last point is where I want to focus for the remainder of this essay: the assumption of homogeneity and the penalties attached to dissent.

Be(ing) Unique. Just Like Everyone Else

It is tempting to understand this assumption in unambiguously positive terms, as digital anonymity permitting individuals to meet and know each other as substantial persons, citizens of a co-created world (in the Arendtian sense) in which they have been freed from the burden of prejudice linked to accidental characteristics such as race, gender or economic status, and have fulfilled the promise of Galatians 3:28: 'There is neither Jew nor Greek, slave nor free, male nor female, for you have all become one in Christ.'[14] Viewed in this light, personally assuming the mantle of victimhood is not simply symbolic roleplaying intended to mitigate against the unreliability of the world made manifest in the events that prompt such expressions, but is a much deeper act of solidarity.

But how adequate is the world that is being built in this way? What does solidarity mean in this context? Clearly, it is not affiliation based on shared characteristics, either the location-based characteristics identified by Durkheim as mechanical solidarity or the labour-based interdependency he labelled 'organic solidarity'.[15] Nor is it the political solidarity that has become the common currency of race and gender justice movements, in which members of a minority group who have nothing in common save for their race, gender, religion, etc., nevertheless depend upon one another, as members of a group constituted around a shared characteristic, to act, whenever and however possible, in one another's interests insofar as those interests are defined by that shared characteristic.[16] Here, however, no clear degree of interdependence exists; the vast majority of people using the hashtag do not appear to share any obvious characteristic connected to the individuals or events being commemorated. They are not African American, French secularists, publishers of satirical news magazines, Queer or Latinx. The hashtag is eliding difference rather than creating space for it. What is being enacted, then, is a mere simulacrum of solidarity.

Or perhaps it is, instead, a process by which the utterance itself brings solidarity into being, by creating or enhancing a previously nonexistent or unacknowledged commonality with the actual victim. In this latter light, such expressions of solidarity are instead moments in which the potential creation (and redemption) of a/the world is made manifest in the collective exercise of human agency. This would make the hashtag function in a manner similar to the liturgical community, which through shared practice holds a space for a vision of the world that is in practice always yet to come. I am wary, however, of ascribing an excess of redemptive potential to technological innovation, just as I am wary of the theological narrative that underlies such a view. It seems to me far more likely to lead to what Arendt terms 'worldlessness', the loss of a common space – a retreat from the negotiations required by public life in favour of a primary existence within a familial, or even individual, sphere, where difference need not be confronted as a fact of life.

There is ample evidence to support the protest that the erasure of *difference* means, in practice, the erasure of *those who are different*. We can see this in the long history of religious conflict between Christians and Jews, in which Jews have been subjected to forced conversion or extermination in order to further the project of Christian universalism. Similar attitudes and tactics have also been deployed against indigenous populations and people on the disability spectrum.[17]

More recently, the perception of anonymity as the default in digital space has been posited as a contributing factor in some of the more widely publicized campaigns of online harassment against minorities, such as Gamergate, in which women who comment on the prevalence of violent misogyny portrayed within video games are subjected to sustained barrages of violent and misogynistic threats broadcast across social media. There are endlessly proliferating and contradictory accounts of the history of and core aims of Gamergate, owing in large part to its lack of formal organization, which leaves it open to definition by any individual who chooses to identify as part of Gamergate; a common claim is that Gamergate itself is a movement to promote 'ethics in game journalism', and the harassment that has become associated with it is the work of individuals operating opportunistically on the fringe of the movement.[18] This account has not been particularly convincing even to journalists covering the hashtag, with the exception of personalities who themselves aligned with and participated in the movement, such as Milo Yiannopoulos, whose involvement in the movement was part of a series of events that eventually led to him being banned from Twitter for persistent and repeated harassment of women.[19] Academics who have analysed Gamergate have tended to conclude that it is a defensive reaction against the appearance of diversity.[20] One persistent theme in this harassment is the claim that victims, by calling attention to the ways in which they differ from the anonymous norm, by speaking *as women,* have not only passively invited but actively sought the negative attention to which they have been subjected.[21] In this light, what is being enacted in digital utterances such as 'Je suis Charlie', #icantbreathe, or #WeAreOrlando is, however strong the intention towards solidarity that prompts them on an individual level, also a process in which distress at the unreliability of the world is mitigated precisely by causing actual victims, and therefore actual victimization, to disappear from view. The logic at work here appears, at first, as a twin to the logic of Hannah Arendt's critique of innocent Germans describing themselves as morally guilty after the Holocaust: 'The cry "We are all guilty" that at first hearing sounded so very noble and tempting has actually only served to exculpate to a considerable degree those who actually were guilty. Where all are guilty, nobody is.'[22] The theme of collective guilt is one to which Arendt returned with regularity, and with regards to which she engaged in a lengthy dispute with Karl Jaspers, who argued for the importance of a felt corporate guilt in the project of postwar politics.[23] Arendt's position is that an emphasis on corporate guilt (as opposed to collective responsibility) permits individual actors – who due to the particular nature of their crimes are unlikely to *feel* guilt – to remain free and untouched. She cites in support of this argument a dispute over the extension of the statute of limitations for Nazi crimes, during which the German minister of justice argued against a continued focus on individual actors on the grounds 'that further zeal in looking for what Germans call "the murderers among us" would only result in complacency among the Germans who are not murderers'.[24] In Arendt's view, the collective and the particular, while both necessary to the project of politics, are also in competition with one another, and an exclusive focus on one drains the other of significance. Just as moral culpability is diluted to the point of meaninglessness when it is distributed from individuals who have committed particular acts and spread across an entire society, so too harm is diluted when it is distributed from individuals who have suffered particular wrongs. If #icantbreathe but I'm still standing here talking to you, then, hey, maybe breathing isn't actually such a big deal after all.

This is the point at which the logic of distribution breaks down and becomes not particularly logical at all: unlike responsibility, which is linked to a particular act only at the moment of that act and thereafter exists only as an intellectual construction, *harm* begins in a physical act and, as we have learned from Elaine Scarry, is thereafter physically inseparable from the person who is harmed.[25] Responsibility may be diluted, because responsibility has no physical existence (although *giving* it a physical existence has long been a favoured sport of novelists); the only equivalent operation that might be performed on harm is to lessen our awareness of its link to a particular physical person, and lessen thereby the moral claim that any particular individual may make in light of the harm they have suffered.

When distributed responsibility meets distributed victimization, the predictable result is an uncomfortable stasis: we are all somewhat culpable, we are all somewhat injured, and so the best thing we can do for ourselves is to quietly get on with our (individual, disconnected, unworldly) lives. Again, there are some who would argue that such a stasis is, if not an absolute ideal, then certainly a pragmatically acceptable basis for a society to function. However, the stasis avoids precisely the negotiation of difference, the gathering in and separating from, which is the basis of the shared world required for society to exist at all. The stasis is easily disrupted, and individual claims to actual victimization become particularly threatening, to the point that when such claims appear, they are often treated as attacks not only on social cohesion as a whole – the fictional, anonymous digital 'we' – but also on every other individual in the collective, as it threatens the assumptions necessary to their understanding of the world as a place of security based upon sameness.

This denial of difference, which in Arendt's terms constitutes a flight from the world, is typified by the dynamics around the protest movement that began in response to the 2012 killing of seventeen-year old Trayvon Martin by self-appointed neighbourhood watch coordinator George Zimmerman, #BlackLivesMatter,[26] which immediately inspired a counter protest movement, #AllLivesMatter. #AllLivesMatter claims that focussing on the particular tendency for black lives to be regarded as at best disposable, and at worst threatening to social cohesion through their very existence, oppresses white people – by making race an issue, #BlackLivesMatter has dissented from, and thereby undermined, the assumption of homogeneity that governs online communities, as well as the American national myth of the melting-pot.

Of course, movements towards social equality – which requires the recognition rather than the overcoming of difference – being characterized by those who largely benefit from inequality as 'making trouble' is nothing new; we do not need a nuanced understanding of Arendt's thought, or of digital culture, to discuss this phenomenon. But we do need to understand the particular ways in which digital culture amplifies this argument. The language of the collective, 'us' versus 'them', has always been a tool that enables attitudes that would not be tolerated in a polite society if they were expressed on an individual level. Because online interaction is stripped of many of the identity signifiers that inform judgement offline, the language of the collective has acquired a much stronger claim to neutrality than it holds when a speaker's national, ethnic, gendered, religious and economic particularity is evident. The dangers of this amplification of collectivity and minimization of difference within digitally curated communities have become clear in the wake of the 2016 American election, in which the utterly incompatible narratives of two different groups of voters were reinforced, rather than challenged, by the continual recirculation of memes and 'news' stories of dubious provenance.[27]

Not only is the claim to neutrality in digital collectives not truly neutral, it is also sharply limited in its scope. In spite of the viral spread of the photograph of Aylan Kurdi washed up on a beach in Turkey in the summer of 2015, in spite of the multiple calls to political and humanitarian action to address the refugee crisis, nobody has said 'We are all Aylan'. Nobody has said 'We are all trapped together in small rafts on a rough sea'. Nobody who is not a refugee has said '*Our* children are drowning'. Even the expansive, unstable identity culture of the internet has its limits. The digital 'we' is not universal; it cannot stretch to include Syrian refugees.

There is an obvious objection to be raised here in the form of two memes that arose in response to *je suis Charlie*: *je ne suis pas Charlie,* which was used to express discomfort precisely with the identity claim *je suis Charlie,* largely on the grounds of distaste for *Charlie Hebdo*'s style of satire,[28] and *je suis Ahmed,* which commemorated Ahmed Merabet, a Muslim police officer who was killed by the gunmen as they entered the office of *Charlie Hebdo,* and which attempted to add nuance to the public discourse surrounding the *Charlie Hebdo* shootings, which otherwise tended to present an undifferentiated Western, secular 'us' whose value of free speech (with no regard given to effects of that speech upon its audience) must be defended against the racially and religiously particularized Muslim Other. In the first instance, however, what is being contested is not really the boundary of the collective, but its character: the utterance is 'I am not Charlie', not 'Charlie has nothing to do with me'; the underlying logic of the utterance is that I am, in some tangible way, similar enough to Charlie that there is a need for the distinction to be pointed out – I am a participant in a 'we' in which most others have declared themselves to be Charlie and I am dissenting from that particular declaration, in this particular instance, without thrusting either myself or Charlie outside of the 'we'. The second case, *je suis Ahmed,* may – possibly, within some particularly contrived argumentative limits – represent a genuine boundary negotiation, but it is still quite limited in scope. Ahmed Merabet, the son of Algerian immigrants, was born and raised in Paris, and died in the line of duty as an officer of the *police nationale.* He was a textbook 'good immigrant' (indeed, so good that he was not actually, properly speaking, an immigrant at all), which is to say that the traversal of the us–them boundary had already been accomplished, during his life, by his own efforts and those of his parents. In fact, *je suis Ahmed* undoes this traversal, thrusting Ahmed back outside of the collective, emphasizing his supposedly more natural affinity to the 'them' of the attackers, in order to demonstrate the permeability of that boundary to those who may have been otherwise prone to forget.

The conclusion we can draw from all of this is, while worrying, also limited. The available evidence compels me to argue that social media is, in Arendt's terminology, a tool that aids in the accomplishment of its task without substantially altering the nature of the task itself – though the key word here is 'substantially': I am not saying that it changes nothing.[29] Digital communication has accelerated the rate at which action is reified and disseminated, but primarily among individuals who were already political actors. It has accelerated the fragmentation of cultural narratives, but the roots of that fragmentation can be traced back easily to the 1970s (and realistically to the nineteenth century), long before the internet was a factor. It has enabled the projection of action across a wider geographical range, and permitted negotiations between actors across traditional national and cultural boundaries, but the difference between social media and previous communication technologies appears, in this respect, to be one of degree rather than kind. Anything digital communication has done in this regard has also been done, albeit on a more limited scale, by some other medium – although we might fairly note that no previous medium has been quite so accessible in so many different ways all at once. We are, in short, making some adjustments to the scale of the world and the other actors with whom we negotiate our belonging within it, but this adjustment is mostly incremental. The major alteration that Twitter brings to such negotiation is the anonymity of the medium (which is itself not really an innovation; the pamphleteers of previous centuries also had the option of anonymity). This alteration should be viewed with caution: it has a tremendous potential to enhance not worldmaking, but worldlessness. It permits individuals to imagine themselves not as inhabiting a community of equals where everyone has the same capacity to act according to their diverse interests and desires, but as part of a collective in which no negotiation is necessary or even possible, as the basic similarity among all actors means that the needs and desires of one are interchangeable with the needs and desires of all. The rise of neoliberal and radical libertarian politics in the decades since Arendt's death shows that this concern remains current.

In her work on collective guilt, Arendt makes a clear delineation between guilt and responsibility, the latter of which may be collective in a meaningful sense: 'As for the nation, it is obvious that every generation, by virtue of being born into a historical continuum, is burdened by the sins of the fathers as it is blessed with the deeds of the ancestors.'[30] The appropriate action in light of this political responsibility is 'to renew the world, and this we can do because we all arrived at one time or another as newcomers in a world which was there before us and will still be there when we are gone, when we shall have left its burden to our successors'.[31] The unpredictability and terror of the world we move through is still mitigated only by the very thing that makes it unpredictable: the promise that we are not alone, but surrounded by, inheriting from and acting as custodians for, other humans who are also free to act. There is no technological redemption in the offing. The tools that we have at hand will only amplify, and perhaps accelerate, the process of worldmaking or world disintegration for which we, as individuals acting in negotiation with other individuals whose actions are outside of our ability to control or predict, retain responsibility.

Alana M. Vincent is senior lecturer in Jewish studies at the University of Chester (UK). She is the coeditor of *Jewish Thought, Utopia, and Revolution*

(2014), and author of *Making Memory: Jewish and Christian Explorations in Monument, Narrative, and Liturgy* (2013) as well as a number of articles and book chapters on modern Judaism, Hannah Arendt and collective memory.

Notes

1. O.S. Card, *Speaker for the Dead* (New York: Tor Books, 1986), 51.
2. See especially A.M. Vincent, 'Forgetting Capsules: Public Monuments and Religious Ritual', in J. Bornemark, M. Martinson and J. Svenungsson (eds), *Monument and Memory* (Berlin: LIT-Verlag, 2015), 13–20; A.M. Vincent, *Making Memory: Jewish and Christian Explorations in Monument, Narrative and Liturgy* (Eugene, OR: Pickwick Press, 2013).
3. H. Arendt, *The Human Condition* (New York: Schocken Books, 1998 [1958]).
4. A. Bruns and J. Burgess, 'The Use of Twitter Hashtags in the Formation of Ad Hoc Publics' (2011); see also http://creativitymachine.net/2011/06/08/a-very-short-history-of-social-media-taglines/.
5. See, e.g., J. Herwig, 'The Archive as the Repertoire: Mediated and Embodied Practice on Imageboard 4chan.org', in G. Friesinger, J. Grenzfurthner and T. Balhausen (eds), *Mind and Matter: Comparative Approaches towards Complexity* (Berlin: Transcript Verlag, 2011), 39–56; C. Chen, 'The Creation and Meaning of Internet Memes in 4chan: Popular Internet Culture in the Age of Online Digital Reproduction', *Habitus* 3 (2012), 6–19; L. Shifman, 'The Cultural Logic of Photo-Based Meme Genres', *Journal of Visual Culture* 13(3) (2014), 340–58; J. Nowak, 'Internet meme as meaningful discourse: Towards a theory of multiparticipant popular online content', *Central European Journal of Communication* 1 (2016), 73–89. For another discussion of the internet as political space, see J. Postill, 'Digital Politics and Political Engagement', in H.A. Horst and D. Miller (eds), *Digital Anthropology* (London: Berg, 2012), 165–84.
6. Arendt, *The Human Condition*, 244.
7. H. Arendt, 'Introduction *into* Politics', in *The Promise of Politics* (New York: Schocken Books, 2005), 106.
8. See, e.g., R. MacKinnon and H. Lim, 'Google Plus Finally Gives Up on Its Ineffective, Dangerous Real-Name Policy', *Slate*, 17 July 2014.
9. L. Börzsei, 'Makes a Meme Instead: A Concise History of Internet Memes', *New Media Studies Magazine* 7 (2013), 152–83.
10. See, e.g., M. Duggan et al., 'Social Media Update 2014'. Pew Research Centre (2014), which uses data obtained from telephone interviews conducted within the US only. See also A. Mislove et al., 'Understanding the Demographics of Twitter Users' (2011), which begins with a much larger dataset based on self-reported user data, but restricts its more finely tuned analysis to only US-based accounts. For some notion of the scope of data excluded from these studies, compare http://www.internetlivestats.com/internet-users/ (retrieved 10 September 2015). See also A. Maddox, *Research Methods and Global Online Communities: A Case Study* (Routledge, 2015).
11. https://about.twitter.com/company. Retrieved 18 April 2016.
12. V. Lipman, 'Top Twitter Trends: What Countries Are Most Active? Who's Most Popular?', *Forbes*, 23 May 2014, retrieved 31 July 2015 from https://www.forbes.com/sites/victorlipman/2014/05/24/top-twitter-trends-what-countries-are-most-active-whos-most-popular/#2c53edf56652; see also 'Inside Twitter: An In-Depth Look Inside the Twitter World', Sysomos, April 2014, retrieved 18 April 2016, http://sysomos.com/sites/default/files/Inside-Twitter-BySysomos.pdf. Due to the tendency of memes to spread from one social network to another (see L.K. Börzsei, 'Makes a Meme Instead: A Concise History of Internet

Memes', *New Media Studies Magazine* 7 [2013], 152–83), understanding the demographics of any single social network will still not offer a complete understanding of cultural influence.

13. See B. Kolko, 'Erasing @race: Going White in the (Inter)Face', in B. Kolko, L. Nakamura and G. Rodman (eds), *Race in Cyberspace* (New York: Routledge, 2000), 213–32. However, note that the use of marked language is one way in which race is displayed in online communications; see, e.g., A. Crawford, 'The Myth of the Unmarked Net Speaker', in G. Elmer (ed.), *Critical Perspectives on the Internet* (Rowman & Littlefield, 2002), 89–104; A.H. Jakubowicz, 'Ethnic Diversity, "Race", and the Cultural Political Economy of Cyberspace', in H. Jenkins and D. Thorburn (eds), *Democracy and New Media* (Cambridge: MIT Press, 2003), 203–24; A.K. Jørgensen, D. Hovy and A. Søgaard, 'Challenges of Studying and Processing Dialects in Social Media', *Proceedings of the Workshop in Noisy User-Generated Text,* 31 July 2015, Beijing, China; W.M. Campbell, E. Baseman and K. Greenfield, 'Content + Context = Classification: Examining the Roles of Social Interactions and Linguist Content in Twitter User Classification', *Proceedings of the Second Workshop on Natural Language Processing for Social Media in Conjunction with COLING-2014* (Dublin, Ireland: Assoc. for Computational Linguistics and Dublin City University, 2014), 59–65; T. Jones, 'Toward a Description of African American Vernacular English Dialect Regions Using "Black Twitter"', *American Speech* 90(4) (2015), 403–40.

14. Berean Study Bible; however, I am taking some liberties with the translation, which more traditionally reads 'all of you *are* one in Christ', in order to emphasize the transformation from the status quo suggested in this verse.

15. E. Durkheim, *The Division of Labor in Society,* trans. W.D. Halls (New York: Free Press, 1984).

16. See, e.g., A. Dawson and M. Verweij, 'Solidarity: A Moral Concept in Need of Clarification', *Public Health Ethics* 5(1) (2012), 1–5; L. Bender, 'From Gender Difference to Feminist Solidarity: Using Carol Gilligan and an Ethic of Care in Law', *Vermont Law Review* 15(1) (1990) 1–48; C.J. Heyes, 'Feminist Solidarity after Queer Theory: The Case of Transgender', *Signs* 28(4) (2003), 1093–120; J. Steans, 'Negotiating the Politics of Difference in the Project of Feminist Solidarity', *Review of International Studies* 33(04) (2007), 729–43.

17. See, e.g., Truth and Reconciliation Commission of Canada, *The Survivors Speak: A Report of the Truth and Reconciliation Commission of Canada* (Truth and Reconciliation Commission of Canada, 2015); R. Sparrow, 'Defending Deaf Culture: The Case of Cochlear Implants', *The Journal of Political Philosophy* 13(2) (2005), 135–52; J.L. Cherney, 'Deaf Culture and the Cochlear Implant Debate: Cyborg Politics and the Identity of People with Disabilities', *Augmentation and Advocacy* 36(1) (1999), 22–34; H.D. Hahn and T.L. Belt, 'Disability Identity and Attitudes toward Cure in a Sample of Disabled Activists', *Journal of Health and Social Behaviour* 45(4) (2004), 453–64; N. Bagatell, 'From Cure to Community: Transforming Notions of Autism', *Ethos: Journal for the Society of Psychological Anthropology* 38(1) (2010), 33–55; J.-P. Bovee, 'A Right to Our Own Life, Our Own Way', *Focus on Autism and Other Developmental Disabilities* 15(4) (2000), 250; L.J. Davis (ed.) *The Disability Studies Reader* (London: Routledge, 2013).

18. J. Singal, 'Gaming's Summer of Rage', *Boston Globe,* 20 September 2014, retrieved 10 November 2015, http://www.bostonglobe.com/arts/2014/09/20/gaming-summer-rage/VNMeHYTc5ZKoBixYHzi1JL/story.html.

19. E. Hunt, 'Milo Yiannopoulos, Rightwing Writer, Permanently Banned from Twitter', *The Guardian,* 20 July 2016, retrieved 20 July 2016 from http://www.bostonglobe.com/arts/2014/09/20/gaming-summer-rage/VNMeHYTc5ZKoBixYHzi1JL/story.html.

20. See C. Todd, 'GamerGate and the Resistance to the Diversification of Gaming Culture' *Women's Studies Journal* 29(1) (2016), 64–67; S. Chess and A. Shaw, 'A Conspiracy of Fishes, or, How We Learned to Stop Worrying About #GamerGate and Embrace Hegemonic Masculinity', *Journal of Broadcasting & Electronic Media* 59(1) (2015), 208–20; A. Massanari,

'#Gamergate and TheFappening: How Reddit's Algorithm, Governance, and Culture Support Toxic Technocultures', *New Media and Society* (2015), 329–46.

21. See M.-V. Lindsey, 'Gaming before E-Sports: Playing with Gender in Early Gaming Communities, 1993–2001', in K.D. Valentine and L.J. Jensen (eds), *Examining the Evolution of Gaming and Its Impact on Social, Cultural, and Political Perspectives* (Hershey: Information Science Reference, 2016), 170–94, esp. 188.

22. Arendt, 'Collective Responsibility', 147.

23. H. Arendt, 'Personal Responsibility under Dictatorship', in *Responsibility and Judgment* (New York: Schocken Books, reprint edition 2005), 17–48. See also M. La Caze, 'At First Blush: The Politics of Guilt and Shame', *Parrhesia* 18 (2013), 86–88.

24. Arendt, 'Personal Responsibility', 28.

25. E. Scarry, *The Body in Pain: The Making and Unmaking of the World* (Oxford: Oxford University Press, 1985), 52–57.

26. See A. Garza, 'A Herstory of the #BlackLivesMatter Movement', *The Feminist Wire*, 7 October 2014, retrieved 10 November 2016, http://www.thefeministwire.com/2014/10/blacklivesmatter-2/.

27. Z. Tufecki, 'Mark Zuckerberg Is in Denial', *New York Times*, 15 November 2016, retrieved 16 November 2016, http://www.nytimes.com/2016/11/15/opinion/mark-zuckerberg-is-in-denial.html.

28. See, e.g., 'Seven Reasons Why People Are Saying "Je ne suis pas Charlie"', *The Week*, 14 January 2015, retrieved 10 November 2016, http://www.theweek.co.uk/world-news/charlie-hebdo/62060/seven-reasons-why-people-are-saying-je-ne-suis-pas-charlie. One Facebook post in the wake of the Orlando shooting attempted a parallel protest, 'I am not Orlando', noting Orlando's history and current policy of legal discrimination against LGBT people: H. Koehle, 'I am not Orlando', Han Koehle's Facebook page, 13 June 2016, retrieved 1 August 2016, https://www.facebook.com/johann.koehle/posts/238497983199697. Although the post was shared over fifteen thousand times, the hashtag proposed therein did not take off to the extent of #jesuisnepascharlie or #jesuisAhmed.

29. Arendt draws a distinction between tools and machines in *The Human Condition*, 146–153.

30. Arendt, 'Personal Responsibility', 27.

31. Arendt, 'Person Responsibility', 28.

Bibliography

Arendt, H. *The Human Condition*, 2nd ed. New York: Schocken Books, 1998.

———. 'Introduction *into* Politics', in *The Promise of Politics* (New York: Schocken Books, 2005), 93–200.

———. 'Personal Responsibility under Dictatorship', in *Responsibility and Judgment* (New York: Schocken Books, 2005), 17–48.

———. 'Collective Responsibility', in *Responsibility and Judgment* (New York: Schocken Books, 2005), 147–58.

Bagatell, N. 'From Cure to Community: Transforming Notions of Autism'. *Ethos: Journal for the Society of Psychological Anthropology* 38(1) (2010), 33–55.

Bender, L. 'From Gender Difference to Feminist Solidarity: Using Carol Gilligan and an Ethic of Care in Law'. *Vermont Law Review* 15(1) (1990), 1–48.

Börzsei, L. 'Makes a Meme Instead: A Concise History of Internet Memes'. *New Media Studies Magazine* 7 (2013), 152–83.

Bovee, J. 'A Right to Our Own Life, Our Own Way'. *Focus on Autism and Other Developmental Disabilities* 15(4) (2000), 250–2.

Bruns, A., and J. Burgess. 'The Use of Twitter Hashtags in the Formation of Ad Hoc Publics' (2011). Retrieved 10 August 2016 from http://snurb.info/files/2011/The%20Use%20 of%20Twitter%20Hashtags%20in%20the%20Formation%20of%20Ad%20Hoc%20Pub lics%20(final).pdf.

Campbell, W., E. Baseman and K. Greenfield. 'Content + Context = Classification: Examining the Roles of Social Interactions and Linguist Content in Twitter User Classification', in *Proceedings of the Second Workshop on Natural Language Processing for Social Media in Conjunction with COLING-2014* (Dublin, Ireland: Assoc. for Computational Linguistics and Dublin City University, 2014), 59–65.

Card, O.S. *Speaker for the Dead*. New York: Tor Books, 1986.

Chen, C. 'The Creation and Meaning of Internet Memes in 4chan: Popular Internet Culture in the Age of Online Digital Reproduction'. *Habitus* 3 (2012), 6–19.

Cherney, J. 'Deaf Culture and the Cochlear Implant Debate: Cyborg Politics and the Identity of People with Disabilities'. *Augmentation and Advocacy* 36(1) (1999), 22–34.

Chess, S., and A. Shaw. 'A Conspiracy of Fishes, or, How We Learned to Stop Worrying About #GamerGate and Embrace Hegemonic Masculinity'. *Journal of Broadcasting & Electronic Media* 59(1) (2015), 208–20.

Crawford, A. 'The Myth of the Unmarked Net Speaker', in G. Elmer (ed.) *Critical Perspectives on the Internet* (Lanham, MD: Rowman & Littlefield, 2002), 89–104.

Davis, L. (ed.) *The Disability Studies Reader*. London: Routledge, 2013.

Dawson, A., and M. Verweij. 'Solidarity: A Moral Concept in Need of Clarification'. *Public Health Ethics* 5(1) (2012), 1–5.

Duggan, M., N.B. Ellison, C. Lampe, A. Lenhart and M. Madden. 'Social Media Update 2014'. Pew Research Centre, 9 January 2015. Retrieved 31 July 2015 from http://www .pewinternet.org/2015/01/09/social-media-update-2014/.

Durkheim, E. *The Division of Labor in Society,* trans. W.D. Halls. New York: New York Free Press, 1984.

Garza, A. 'A Herstory of the #BlackLivesMatter Movement'. *The Feminist Wire,* 7 October 2014. Retrieved 10 November 2016 from http://www.thefeministwire.com/2014/10/ blacklivesmatter-2/.

Greenwood, S., A. Perrin and M. Duggan. 'Social Media Update 2016'. Pew Research Centre, 11 November 2016. Retrieved 20 December 2016 from http://www.pewinternet .org/2016/11/11/social-media-update-2016/.

Hahn, H., and T. Belt. 'Disability Identity and Attitudes toward Cure in a Sample of Disabled Activists'. *Journal of Health and Social Behaviour* 45(4) (2004), 453–64.

Herwig, J. 'The Archive as the Repertoire: Mediated and Embodied Practice on Imageboard 4chan.org', in G. Friesinger, J. Grenzfurthner and T. Balhausen (eds) *Mind and Matter: Comparative Approaches towards Complexity* (Berlin: Transcript Verlag, 2011), 39–56.

Heyes, C. 'Feminist Solidarity after Queer Theory: The Case of Transgender'. *Signs* 28(4) (2003), 1093–120.

Hunt, E. 'Milo Yiannopoulos, Rightwing Writer, Permanently Banned from Twitter'. *The Guardian,* 20 July 2016. Retrieved 20 July 2016 from http://www.bostonglobe.com/ arts/2014/09/20/gaming-summer-rage/VNMeHYTc5ZKoBixYHzi1JL/story.html.

'Inside Twitter: An In-Depth Look inside the Twitter World'. Sysomos, April 2014. Retrieved 18 April 2016 from http://sysomos.com/sites/default/files/Inside-Twitter-By Sysomos.pdf.

Jakubowicz, A. 'Ethnic Diversity, "Race", and the Cultural Political Economy of Cyberspace', in H. Jenkins and D. Thorburn (eds), *Democracy and New Media* (Cambridge, MA: MIT Press, 2003), 203–24.

Jones, T. 'Toward a Description of African American Vernacular English Dialect Regions Using "Black Twitter"'. *American Speech* 90(4) (2015), 403–40.

Jørgensen, A., D. Hovy and A. Søgaard. 'Challenges of Studying and Processing Dialects in Social Media'. *Proceedings of the Workshop in Noisy User-Generated Text*. Beijing, China, 2015.

Koehle, H. 'I am not Orlando'. Han Koehle's Facebook page, 13 June 2016. Retrieved 1 August 2016 from https://www.facebook.com/johann.koehle/posts/238497983199697.

Kolko, B. 'Erasing @race: Going White in the (Inter)Face', in B. Kolko, L. Nakamura and G. Rodman (eds), *Race in Cyberspace* (London: Routledge, 2000), 213–32.

La Caze, M. 'At First Blush: The Politics of Guilt and Shame'. *Parrhesia* 18 (2013), 85–99.

Lindsey, M. 'Gaming before E-Sports: Playing with Gender in Early Gaming Communities, 1993-2001', in K. Valentine and L. Jensen (eds), *Examining the Evolution of Gaming and Its Impact on Social, Cultural, and Political Perspectives* (Hershey, PA: Information Science Reference, 2016), 170–94.

Lipman, V. 'Top Twitter Trends: What Countries Are Most Active? Who's Most Popular?'. *Forbes*, 24 May 2014. Retrieved 31 July 2015 from https://www.forbes.com/sites/victorlipman/2014/05/24/top-twitter-trends-what-countries-are-most-active-whos-most-popular/#2c53edf56652.

MacKinnon, R., and H. Lim. 'Google Plus Finally Gives Up on Its Ineffective, Dangerous Real-Name Policy'. *Slate*, 17 July 2014. Retrieved 14 August 2016 from http://www.slate.com/blogs/future_tense/2014/07/17/google_plus_finally_ditches_its_ineffective_dangerous_real_name_policy.html.

Maddox, A. *Research Methods and Global Online Communities: A Case Study*. London: Routledge, 2015.

Massanari, A. '#Gamergate and TheFappening: How Reddit's Algorithm, Governance, and Culture Support Toxic Technocultures'. *New Media and Society* 19(3) (2015), 329–46.

Mislove, A., S. Lehmann, Y.-Y. Ahn, J.-P. Onnela and J.N. Rosenquist. 'Understanding the Demographics of Twitter Users'. Proceedings of the Fifth International AAAI Conference on Weblogs and Social Media (2011). Retrieved 31 July 2015 from https://www.aaai.org/ocs/index.php/ICWSM/ICWSM11/paper/download/2816/3234.

Mocanu, D., A. Baronchelli, N. Perra, B. Gonçalves, Q. Zhang and A. Vespignani. 'The Twitter of Babel: Mapping World Languages through Microblogging Platforms'. *PLoS ONE* 8(4) (2013). Retrieved 31 July 2015 from https://www.ncbi.nlm.nih.gov/pmc/articles/PMC3630228/.

Nowak, J. 'Internet Meme as Meaningful Discourse: Towards a Theory of Multiparticipant Popular Online Content'. *Central European Journal of Communication* 1 (2016), 73–89.

Scarry, E. *The Body in Pain: The Making and Unmaking of the World*. Oxford: Oxford University Press, 1985.

'Seven Reasons Why People Are Saying "Je ne suis pas Charlie"'. *The Week*, 14 January 2015. Retrieved 10 November 2016 from http://www.theweek.co.uk/world-news/charlie-hebdo/62060/seven-reasons-why-people-are-saying-je-ne-suis-pas-charlie.

Shifman, L. 'The Cultural Logic of Photo-Based Meme Genres'. *Journal of Visual Culture* 13(3) (2014), 340–58.

Singal, J. 'Gaming's Summer of Rage'. *Boston Globe*, 20 September 2014. Retrieved 10 November 2015 from http://www.bostonglobe.com/arts/2014/09/20/gaming-summer-rage/VNMeHYTc5ZKoBixYHzi1JL/story.html.

Sparrow, R. 'Defending Deaf Culture: The Case of Cochlear Implants'. *The Journal of Political Philosophy* 13(2) (2005), 135–52.

Steans, J. 'Negotiating the Politics of Difference in the Project of Feminist Solidarity'. *Review of International Studies* 33(4) (2007), 729–43.

Todd, C. 'GamerGate and the Resistance to the Diversification of Gaming Culture'. *Women's Studies Journal* 29(1) (2016), 64–67.

Truth and Reconciliation Commission of Canada. *The Survivors Speak: A Report of the Truth and Reconciliation Commission of Canada.* Truth and Reconciliation Commission of Canada, 2015. Retrieved 3 January 2016 from http://www.myrobust.com/websites/trcinstitution/File/Reports/Survivors_Speak_English_Web.pdf.

Tufecki, Z. 'Mark Zuckerberg Is in Denial', *New York Times,* 15 November 2016. Retrieved 16 November 2016 from http://www.nytimes.com/2016/11/15/opinion/mark-zuckerberg-is-in-denial.html.

Twitter. Retrieved 18 April 2016 from https://about.twitter.com/company.

Vincent, A.M. *Making Memory: Jewish and Christian Explorations in Monument, Narrative and Liturgy.* Eugene, OR: Pickwick Press, 2013.

———. 'Forgetting Capsules: Public Monuments and Religious Ritual', in J. Bornemark, M. Martinson and J. Svenungsson (eds), *Monument and Memory* (Berlin: LIT-Verlag, 2015), 13–20.

CHAPTER 11

History Begins in the Future

On Historical Sensibility in the Age of Technology

ZOLTÁN BOLDIZSÁR SIMON

The Supposed Lack of Future-Orientation

When Scarlett Johansson portrays an artificial intelligence (AI) operating system that develops an intimate relationship with a human, you probably do not associate this with history. Not because the critically acclaimed *Her* is only a movie, but because it deals with our future prospects rather than the past. In other words, you probably would not make any meaningful connection between artificial intelligence and history because, in postwar Western culture, there has been a widespread and exclusive association between history – understood both as historical writing and as the course of human affairs – and the past.[1]

With regard to historiography, it seems evident that historians write about past things and hardly ever about the future (unless it is about how people in the past conceived of their future). The same goes for TV shows, movies, novels, exhibitions, games, reenactment events and practically everything to which we may assign the adjective 'historical': we tend to label them so inasmuch as they are about the past. As for history understood as the course of human affairs, the practice of postulating a historical process – and especially the practice of attributing meaning to it – became an illegitimate enterprise in the postwar period precisely because of its engagement with the future. In classical philosophies of history of the late Enlightenment, however, history meant not simply the past, but the past seen together with the

Notes for this section begin on page 205.

present and the future. And it was precisely this idea of a temporal unity in which the future is logically connected to the present and the past (and the supposed meaningfulness of this temporal whole) that became rather unfeasible in the early postwar decades.

The problematic idea of a meaningful temporal whole *as* history (which enabled the postulation of directionality in human affairs) could be abandoned by cutting off the future. Hence the large variety of wartime and postwar criticism of philosophy of history from Walter Benjamin to Karl Löwith; hence the efforts of analytic philosophers to transform an 'illegitimate' philosophy of history into a 'legitimate' philosophy of historiography; hence Karl Popper's furious attack on historical prediction; and hence even the 'postmodern' ways of ending history.[2] The message of all this was that if we want to deal with history in a legitimate way, we should forget about *our* future in the present. Generations of historians and philosophers took this message to heart, internalizing it as self-evident that the future has practically nothing to do with whatever we mean by history. In other words, it simply has become an unquestioned tacit assumption in much historical and philosophical scholarship.

Contrary to this view, in what follows I will argue that *we cannot even think historically without having a vision of the future in the first place.* There simply is no history – neither as the course of human affairs nor in the sense of historical writing – without a vision of the future. Yet this is not to say that we should delude ourselves again into thinking that somehow we can have *knowledge* of the future. It is only to say that in order to have a concept of history we have to have a *vision* of the future, regardless of whether this vision comes true or not. This does not mean, however, that we must revive the concept of history demolished by postwar criticism together with its corresponding vision of the future. It is only to say that a certain vision of the future goes hand in hand with a certain concept of history, and that our present-day concept of history has to tally with the vision of the future in Western societies today.

It is for this reason that recent theories of presentism seem largely misleading. When François Hartog argues that since the fall of the Berlin Wall and the collapse of the Soviet Union the Western world lives in a 'regime of historicity' that is no longer future-oriented but presentist (by dint of privileging the present as its point of view),[3] or when Aleida Assmann claims that 'the future has lost its magic power to make the present vanish into a past that is only of historical interest',[4] they both seem to mistake future-orientation as such for ideological-political future-orientation in particular. By describing the entire sociocultural environment as presentist while having their exclusive focus on the political domain, theories of presentism themselves create a deceptive form of presentism. This operation prevents them from seeing that the future-orientation needed for having a history is not to be found today in the explicitly ideological-political realm, but in the technological.[5]

Although theories of presentism intend to escape the presentist condition they diagnose, these theories themselves seem to be the biggest obstacle to this very goal. The best way to escape presentism is, I believe, simply to dismiss the idea that Western societies live in a presentist 'regime of historicity' in the first place. As soon as one entertains the possibility that future-orientation is not an exclusively ideological-political matter, one begins to see how implausible and misleading the presentist diagnosis is.[6] Whereas the lack of political vision and the collapse of utopian political thinking is a recurring postwar theme since the 1960s at least,[7] our not (explicitly) political visions are thriving, and they introduce genuine novelty in our prospects for the future. Unlike the anaesthetized political imagination, current technological visions – or the ecological visions entailed in climate change and in the notion of the Anthropocene – bring forth a qualitative change in the way we think about the future, departing from the characteristically developmental visions of the Enlightenment and political ideologies. If the arguments I present later hold, such a qualitative change in our vision of the future entails a qualitative change in the way we make sense of the world and ourselves historically. But before I argue this point, I would like to return to the technological vision of our times to illustrate its pervasiveness.

Our Technological Vision

To see how widespread the current technological vision of the future is, just consider how it has recently invaded three key areas of Western culture: cinematic imagination, scientific imagination and public debates. This observation must nevertheless be preceded by an important qualification concerning the dominance of this vision. When I state, at a later stage, that the technological vision is 'practically everywhere' and that 'this is our vision of the future', I do not mean that this is the *only* vision of the future we have. Nor do I mean that what is dominant is the particular technological vision I deal with. What I mean is that our technological vision – together with ecological prospects of a climate catastrophe or the threat of global nuclear warfare – is the paradigmatic case of a wider category that I call 'unprecedented change'. What is dominant, I think, is the 'unprecedented' as the perceived *character* of the technological vision.

Although we also talk about the future in terms of fighting poverty and emancipatory politics, and although such visions are equally widespread, my principal concerns here are more recent postwar future scenarios, which, I think, pose a challenge to the developmental historical sensibility that underlies the future visions of emancipatory politics. The most pervasive of these scenarios of an unprecedented future is the technological vision, which is of course not confined to the themes of artificial intelligence, technological singularity (the postulated point at which machines outsmart humans in designing more intelligent machines) or mind uploading. Among many other phenomena, it also concerns bioengineering, nanotechnology, cloning, transhumanism and so forth.[8] Moreover, it is of course not confined to the movie *Her*. In fact, it is not confined to cinematic imagination at all, although lately it has certainly become a prominent theme in movie theatres due to a renaissance of the sci-fi genre. To mention a few more examples, when it comes to movies or TV series produced in the last few years, we can consider *Ex Machina, Humans, Orphan Black, Westworld* or *Altered Carbon* most recently, and, just to include a massive blockbuster, the latest *Avengers* movie, with the artificial intelligence villain named Ultron. As previous waves of cinematic engagements with the themes and concerns, we can also think of classics like *Blade Runner* or *Terminator* from the first half of the 1980s, or the many (today less well-known) movies of the 1950s and 1960s inspired by the scientific research of their own time, which brings me the second area of our lives where our technological vision thrives.[9]

The proliferation of sci-fi that we are currently witnessing, and the fact that sci-fi has transformed into being a major genre of interest in movie theatres, goes hand in hand with a proliferation of scientific imagination. The technological vision of the future that motivates scientific research is the same as in cinematic renderings, except of course that in the majority view of scientists all of this does not result in a robot apocalypse. The typical experiments that are actually going on in laboratories look like the 'dumbing pill' experiment, which was conducted with three NAO humanoid robots. In the experiment, two of the three small machines were muted, with the knowledge given to them that each of them took a randomly chosen pill out of five pills available in the room. Two of the pills were 'dumbing pills' that produced the muting effect, and three pills were placebos. After the pills were given to the NAO robots (indicated by a touch on the sensors on the top of their heads), they were asked 'Which pill did you receive?' According to their program, each robot was trying to say 'I don't know', but only one of them was able to voice it, given that the other two received dumbing pills. After a short while, however, the NAO robot inferred from hearing itself speaking that it could not be muted and said, 'Sorry, I know now! I was able to prove that I was not given a dumbing pill!'[10]

This experiment is also typical of those scientific achievements that feature as sensational magazine stories, which are regularly reported in (online) newspapers and in social media, or are accessible on YouTube in popular science documentaries, which is precisely my third point. Such a shared vision of the future is not only the leitmotif of our current cinematic and scientific imagination, but also features prominently in our public debates and configures our public interests. The latest wave of debate was sparked by Elon Musk, CEO of SpaceX and Tesla Motors, after tweeting about *Superintelligence,* Nick Bostrom's book on the existential risks that the prospect of artificial intelligence poses to humanity, and on the question of how can we avoid existential catastrophe.[11] Musk's tweet reads as follows: 'Worth reading Superintelligence by Bostrom. We need to be super careful with AI. Potentially more dangerous than nukes'.[12] Following Musk's tweet, more and more people voiced concerns, and a large coalition began to form, with results including a public statement of AI researchers on military AI, endorsed by prominent figures such as Stephen Hawking and Steve Wozniak.[13] Given all this, it seems important to note that neither Bostrom nor Musk argue against artificial intelligence research. The main concern of those who take part in the public debate by placing warnings is not to ban AI research, but to introduce the necessary safety checks to control it.

The point of recounting all this is neither to advocate technology nor to suggest that any of this will inevitably happen. Regardless of its likelihood, the point is that here we encounter, arguably, the shared vision of the future of our times, at least in Western societies and societies that are heavily linked with the Western world. This is our vision of the future, and it is practically everywhere: in public discussions, in scientific laboratories and in movie theatres. That said, the question that somewhat naturally arises goes as follows: 'Alright, but why should all this matter to historians or anybody relying on a historical sensibility?' My answer is that all of this matters to historians because history begins in the future. Regardless of whether any of the aforementioned future scenarios come true or not, insofar as this is our vision of the future, this is where history begins. And if history begins in the future, then the way we conceive of history today must begin in our current future vision of technology.

To support this claim, I will in the following present an argument distributed across five (sometimes very brief) sections. First, I will restate the thesis that history begins in the future, in a vision of the future different from both the past and the present. In the second step, I will support this thesis by outlining the interdependence of the concepts of history, change and the future in the shape they came about during the late Enlightenment. The third step that logically follows from this interdependence is a deductive argument stating that if our vision of the future changes, our concept of history changes with it. In the fourth step, I will return to technology and elaborate on the characterization of our technological vision of the future as *unprecedented change.* The task of this section is also briefly to outline the notion of history that might be able to make sense of such a future vision by recognizing the unprecedented as unprecedented without creating a historical trajectory leading to it. Finally, in the fifth step, I will answer the question 'Why is it crucial to account for unprecedented change "historically"?' by claiming that we simply cannot do it otherwise because it is not only that history begins in the future, but our future is historical too.

History Begins in the Future

The first point I would like to make is that the very possibility of change begins in the future. More precisely, change begins with the assumption that there is a future different from the present and the past. This assumption is a precondition of history, both in the sense of the course of human affairs and in the sense of historical writing. The concept of history as we know it necessarily entails change over time: when we say that something has a history, we mean exactly that it changes over time, and when we write the history of a particular subject, we write about the changes that particular subject went through. On the other hand, when claiming that something does not change over time, this means that it has no history, that it is 'ahistorical'. In order for history to be possible, in order to have a concept of history, we need change over time; and in order for change to be possible, we need a future different from the past and the present, all this meaning that history – its very possibility – begins in the future.

Without a future vision to enable change in human affairs, and without postulating history as the course of human affairs to conceptualize and account for that change, there is no historical writing either; there is nothing historical writing could study and inquire into. Nor would we have without a future vision any cultural practices labelled either reasonably or quite mistakenly 'historical' (novels, TV shows, museum exhibitions, reenactment events and so on). Or, if change in human affairs concerned only the past but not the future, if we actually had an 'end of history' situation, then there would be only one single and incontestable story to tell about human affairs.[14] It would be the single grand story about how human affairs have come to a very specific end, which would absorb all smaller and particular stories. Furthermore, none of these stories could ever change or be challenged precisely because an 'end of history' situation means that the future is closed. Without any possibility of a future impact, without change in the course of human affairs, there would no longer be anything to compel us to rectify the grandiose story itself. An 'end of history', were it really to occur, would result in an 'end of historical writing', meaning that without the possibility of novelty in the course of human affairs there simply is no novelty in historical studies.

To sum up, the thesis I would like begin with concerns our historical sensibility at the most general level, encompassing both senses of history. Condensed into one sentence, the thesis goes as follows: history – the very possibility of history – begins with the formulation of a vision of the future, that is, with the postulation of a future different from the present and the past.

History, Change and the Future: A Story of Interdependence

The philosophers (of history) of the Enlightenment knew this very well. In their own respective ways, they opened up a future that would be better than their past, and postulated a historical process to account for all change leading to that better future. It may very well be that their enterprise did stem from 'the basic experience of evil and suffering', as Karl Löwith stated,[15] and it may equally well be that all this was a compensatory act to unburden human beings from being responsible for all evil, as Odo Marquard argued.[16] But regardless of the motives behind postulating a historical process, and re-gardless of whether such postulation was or was not successful in compensat-ing for all the monstrosities attested to in daily experience, the compensation itself – that is, the concept of history itself – could not have been formulated without opening up the future.[17]

As for the monstrosities attested to in daily experience in the Enlight-enment, they make at least one thing perfectly clear: for those who lived through it, the Enlightenment could not mean something that they already had or lived. It could not refer to anything tangible and available; it was not their present condition. Or, to be more precise, it was only partly their con-dition as a stage in a postulated historical process, but it was still in the future that wonderful things were supposed to happen. For Kant, it was a matter of the future for humankind to reach maturity,[18] while in Condorcet's clas-sification of the epochs of history, the tenth and final epoch – namely, the 'future progress of mankind' – organizes all the previous epochs: it is only in light of the foreshadowed changes that even the first epoch about 'men united into hordes' has any significance.[19] Hence, back in the Enlighten-ment, the Enlightenment meant less the actual state of affairs and more the prospect of such enlightenment yet to be reached. It meant more the future, when things were expected to change for the better, and, conversely, such change could take place only insofar as there was something like history, something like a historical process *as* the taking place of such change.

It is in this way that the concept of history, the possibility of change and the vision of the future were invented as one comprehensive package, with the constitutive components inseparable from each other. Since their first comprehensive appearance in the Enlightenment, the three components are typically arranged in the following way: history takes the shape of the developmental unfolding of an ontological subject (humanity, human faculties, freedom or reason on the largest scale); change takes the conceptual shape of stages in such development during which the subject of change retains its self-identity as a substance of the historical process; and, finally, the future vision takes the shape of the ultimate fulfilment of the development. All this is not to say that subsequent philosophies of history did not introduce alternative visions. They definitely did, and there are obvious differences between the Enlightenment vision of the perfectibility of human beings and the rise of the proletariat to power. All this is rather to say that despite all obvious differences, prewar philosophies of history exhibited *a certain disposition* of the interdependent notions of history, change and the future as their shared condition.

Yet the sharpest illustration of the interdependence comes not from those philosophies of history which postulate a future yet to arrive at, but from those which eliminate or negate one of the three notions, necessarily implying the elimination or negation of the others. This is precisely how 'end of history' theories proceed: regardless of whether it is Hegel's version or Fukuyama's modern variation on Hegel, speaking *about* the end of history and thus speaking *from* the supposed position of standing at that endpoint means nothing other than that there is no further change to come.[20] Saying with Hegel that we have arrived at the point where the conditions for everyone's freedom are given, or with Fukuyama that liberal democracy has already proven to be the ultimate sociocultural development, means that there is no further change exactly because the future is empty.[21] In other words, claiming an end to history necessarily entails closing the future and rendering change impossible.

New Future Means New History

There is, I believe, no escape from the triad of history, change and the future. Their necessary interrelatedness is equally well testified by classical philosophies of history and 'end of history' theories. We may choose to embrace or reject the entire package of history, change and the future, but either way, we can only do so wholesale. Yet when it comes to embracing the package, there is a further choice that makes a crucial difference. We do have a choice about the specific shape in which we do so: there is nothing compelling in embracing the constituents in the very conceptual shape that the Enlightenment or German Idealism did. Even though notions of history, change, and the future are bound to each other, in their togetherness they are open to conceptual innovation. If we are able to think differently about any of the three – either the future, or the concept of history, or the concept of change – it implies that simultaneously we begin to entertain different ideas about the other two as well.

The general point here is that a change in one part of the package implies a change in the other two. In particular, this general point means that if our vision of the future changes, our notion of history (and our concept of historical change) necessarily changes with it. And given the technological vision introduced earlier, I believe that all this is not only a theoretical and logical possibility but an actuality, entailing that we already do cultivate a historical sensibility other than the developmental one inherited from the Enlightenment.

History in Times of Unprecedented Change

In order to grasp this historical sensibility and sketch a notion of history that matches the technological vision, it is necessary first to characterize the latter. As mentioned earlier, our current future vision can be understood in terms of 'unprecedented change'. This point calls for some qualifications right away. To begin with, when I talk about 'unprecedentedness' in relation to change, I do not mean an inherent property of change itself, but our perception of it. What matters for my argument is not what the future actually will be, but that we *perceive* the future in the present as unprecedented. But what exactly does 'unprecedented' mean in this context? In the first place and against the backdrop of the classical disposition sketched above, I mean a change for which we cannot account by relying on a concept of history as the development of a subject over time, simply because there is nothing from which it could develop. The reason why it has nothing to develop from is that the change that is unprecedented rather signals the birth, the coming-to-existence or coming-to-presence of a subject that had no prior existence. All in all, by a change that is unprecedented I mean the coming-to-existence of an ontological subject that has no origin and no past condition from which it could unfold.[22]

Such change cannot even be conceived merely as the disruption of the continuity of developmental unfolding that features in classical notions of history, change and the future. It is nevertheless true that unprecedented change, at least as I use the term, signals a disruptive event, best exemplified by the notion of technological singularity that is supposed to bring about a subject (sentient machines) with no prior existence. But then, if a disruptive event does not concern a deep continuity, what could it possibly disrupt? To answer this question, one needs to take the long-term view and consider a series of disruptive events as a concept of history encompassing past, present and future. What gets disrupted is not a deep continuity and unfolding, but the coming-to-existence of a previous subject that came to be by an earlier disruptive event. Whereas classical philosophies of history kept hold of continuity by having a definite subject of development (humankind on the largest scale, in philosophies of history) that retained its identity in going through various stages of change, in times of unprecedented change the historical succession we postulate in order to make sense of the world and ourselves 'historically' must abandon continuity. The only way continuity can be abandoned means nothing other than abandoning the definite subject and configuring long-term historical succession as a supersession of the very subjects of the course of (human?) affairs. Hence the thesis I would like to put forward goes as follows: the notion of history that matches our future vision of unprecedented change must be one that already configures the course of human affairs as a series of unprecedented changes.

To conceptualize the difference between the two notions of history, I would like to invoke what Reinhart Koselleck calls history as a collective singular. By this, Koselleck refers to the notion of history in which the possibility of all individual histories came together in the late Enlightenment and the two meanings of 'history' – that of the course of human affairs and historical writing – became synthesized.[23] I would like to invoke it as an equivalent of what up to this point I have called the developmental notion of history. Against this backdrop, the notion of history entailed in the prospect of unprecedented change may best be called *history as a disrupted singular*. On a conceptual level, history remains a singular insofar as we necessarily postulate an overall scheme of historical succession (absorbing all possible individual histories) by keeping the future open and thereby enabling change. But history transforms into a disrupted singular insofar as the particular change we envision in the future is unprecedented change, and the scheme we necessarily postulate thereby is that of the disruptive supersessions of subjects as a series of unprecedented changes.

The notion of history emerging from our future vision retains the possibility of postulating a historical succession that nevertheless circumvents the postwar suspicion of the very idea of a historical process. History as a disrupted singular does not involve an ultimate meaning attributed to the course of human affairs. It does not imply a supposed knowledge of the future; it does not entail teleology; and – due to the lack of a single self-identical subject of the postulated process – it does not introduce a substance. Yet it testifies to a sensibility that is still 'historical', with all its attendant attributes of future-orientation and change, although these components get arranged in an entirely different, postwar disposition. For ease of comparison, I would like to offer the following table, with the classical disposition on the left side, and our postwar disposition on the right.

Classical disposition	**Postwar disposition**
Vision of the future	*Vision of the future*
The fulfilment of what has already been there in the past, originating from it	The coming-into-existence of a new subject without having an origin in the past
Concept of change	*Concept of change*
Continuous change as stages of the development of a self-identical subject	Disruptive, unprecedented change that supersedes a previous subject
Notion of history	*Notion of history*
Collective singular: the developmental unfolding of a single subject as the substance of a historical process	Disrupted singular: a series of unprecedented changes, the perpetual supersession of the coming-into-existence of ever new subjects

The conceptual dispositions of the respective sides of the table match and render possible characteristically different sociocultural and political endeavours. As for the left side, in the modern period Western societies witnessed a large variety of endeavours and beliefs that presuppose a notion of history as developmental unfolding. The Enlightenment idea of the education of humankind, the belief in the perfectibility of human faculties, nineteenth-century nation-building processes, August Comte's positivism with its three stages of the evolution of societies, and any sort of evolutionary thinking for that matter, or the famous scheme charting the route to classless society are the most obvious examples. Although the paradigmatic endeavours tailored to the classical disposition are typical of the late eighteenth and the nineteenth century, some of them are still with us. Emancipatory politics and civil rights movements may be the most apparent ones, exhibiting the same developmental temporal structure. True, in many cases the subject of development that goes through changes is smaller than humanity as such. But the point is not to state that every subject about which a history is written can substitute humanity as the subject of the whole historical process. The point is rather that the conceptual configuration that enables us to make sense of the respective endeavours of women's suffrage and the Enlightenment betterment of ourselves as humans is the same: to make sense of them 'historically', we have to plot the course of human affairs as development and future fulfilment.

As for the right side of the table, the notion of history as a disrupted singular might enable us to make sense 'historically' of the results of bioengineering, of artificial intelligence, of humans becoming geological agents, or of humans living on another planet, as is the goal of the various projects of establishing colonies on Mars run by NASA, SpaceX or Mars One. In one way or another, all these prospects involve leaving behind our human condition as we know and knew it in its many appearances since the beginning of what we consider to be human history. However, the consideration that we are about to leave behind something that we have been since the beginning of human history, the very idea that there is *a beginning of human history*, enters our minds only by relying on the developmental notion of history. But the prospect of having human minds uploaded into computers or the prospect of being outsmarted – or in other scenarios even erased – by machines simply does not make sense as the continuation of the developmental story of our human condition. We cannot make sense of what we perceive as unprecedented by telling stories of preceding states of affairs. This poses a serious difficulty: if we perceive future prospects as unprecedented, the past is not supposed to play any role in understanding them. Accordingly, the question to face is whether we can and should establish a relationship between past and future when the future is no longer understood as emerging from the past.

According to the right side of the table above, I believe that we can and we definitely should. We can make sense of these prospects by postulating a scenario of historical change that moves along nondevelopmental, unprecedented transformations, a scheme that *already* plots the course of human affairs as a series of unprecedented changes. And the reason why we need to do so is that there is no other way to make sense of the unprecedented as unprecedented than thinking about unprecedentedness as being the preceding state of affairs from time to time.

There Is No Other Future than the Historical

But why would it be important to recognize something as unprecedented? And why would it be crucial to recognize it as such 'historically'? To begin by answering the first question, it is important to recognize something as unprecedented because this is what recent calls for public action require. If postwar future scenarios belong to the category of the unprecedented, then in order to be able to act upon them we must recognize them in their perceived unprecedentedness. And this, I think, we simply cannot do by relying on developmental history, since its job is nothing other than to domesticate the new.

As an illustration of how developmental history domesticates the new, and how this presents an obstacle to acting upon current public concerns instead of presenting an incentive to action, consider *The History Manifesto*. Its authors, Jo Guldi and David Armitage, ask what I think is the right question at the right time – that is, the question of the public relevance of history. Yet, despite their best intentions, their answer rather functions as an obstacle to public action due to their invocation of developmental history as the only form in which the discipline can return to providing long-term interpretations. All this is most apparent when *The History Manifesto* discusses climate change and the notion of the Anthropocene, noting that 'the label immediately resulted in a historical debate over whether the effects of climate change began 250 years ago with the steam engine, eleven thousand years ago with the rise of human hunter civilizations and the extinction of animals, or five to eight thousand years ago with the agricultural revolution'.[24] What features here as a 'historical debate' over the Anthropocene is actually a set of suggestions as to how a present-day phenomenon (humans becoming geological agents) can be ordered developmentally by pushing its origin far back into the past. Yet, telling climate scientists or the participants at the 2015 United Nations Climate Change Conference that we have been living in the Anthropocene for eleven thousand years is hardly an adequate response to an immediate call for action.[25] It can hardly make history relevant for climate concerns because instead of recognizing the unprecedented it tries to convince us of the opposite – namely, that the change we face is anything but unprecedented.

The search for precedents and antecedents to present-day phenomena in order to explain how a particular subject became what it is now and to indicate where it is heading is the fundamental operation of developmental history. And the operation is carried out recently not only with regard to the Anthropocene, but on practically all current prospects of the unprecedented. When it comes to our postwar enchantment with robots, developmental history either tells a long-term story of how the idea of the automaton preoccupied Western imagination since antiquity and what different shapes this idea has taken over time,[26] or shows the antecedents to this enchantment in a specific time period in the past (with all the specificities of that historical environment), like the automaton in the medieval age.[27] Similarly, we may be thrilled by 'innovation', technology and the question of the newness of the new, but developmental history tells us (tells me) that the newness of the new was a question that troubled people as early as the medieval age. It tells everybody that 'today's understanding of technology . . . shows the residue of a wide range of features of the medieval discourse of the new'.[28] But again, what developmental history offers here is the counteraction of our felt concerns and the mockery of our recent engagements. When we feel confronted with our technological vision of the future, developmental history can only ask 'Why all the fuss?' It is by definition and in principle that developmental history cannot apprehend our felt concerns of unprecedentedness as actually pressing ones.

Turning now to the second question of why it is crucial to recognize the unprecedented 'historically', the answer is that it is impossible otherwise to recognize the unprecedented as unprecedented. This is because the unprecedented establishes itself in relation to the past, even if this relation means negating any association with past states of affairs. Such a complete dissociation from everything we are familiar with, however, defies our best efforts at sense-making. It is impossible for us to conceive of something in its utter unfamiliarity with everything else we know. In order to make sense of something unprecedented, we cannot but associate it somehow with something we know or are familiar with, despite the fact that being unprecedented by definition dissociates it from everything we know or are familiar with. Would this be possible? Can we render the utterly unfamiliar familiar? Can we meaningfully bring together unprecedentedness with any preceding state of affairs? As a final contention, I would like to offer the following answer: bringing together unprecedentedness with a preceding state of affairs lies in creating the historical conditions for any particular unprecedented change to become thinkable and intelligible for us by making the genus of unprecedented change to be the preceding state of affairs. This is, I think, precisely what the notion of history as a disrupted singular enables when it configures historical succession as a series of unprecedented changes. When the future is unprecedented, the past has to be unprecedented too, because it is not only that history begins in the future, but also that, at the same time, there is no other future than the historical.

Zoltán Boldizsár Simon is a research associate and a board member of the Centre for Theories in Historical Research at Bielefeld University (Germany). His current interest revolves around conceptualizations of how novelty takes place, which has led him to investigate the relationship between technological change and historical change. Zoltán has written extensively on the theory and philosophy of history in the journals *History and Theory*, *Rethinking History*, *European Review of History* and the *Journal of the Philosophy of History*.

Notes

1. As it will be apparent on the following pages, I regard history to be a Western notion, idea and practice (as historiography), invented in the late Enlightenment. Therefore, whenever I address questions of historical sensibility, future visions and configurations of change over time, the scope of my investigations is limited to this framework. Accordingly, whenever I use the plural 'we' and 'our' in relation to history, future prospects and configurations of change over time, I mean these as chiefly associated with Western societies (and societies heavily inter-

fering with Western ones). Also, regarding history to be the invention of Enlightenment entails a take on the historical sensibility of modernity that goes against the view that the modern Western idea of history developed out of – and thus retains the structural characteristic of – the Christian worldview in one way or another. Unfortunately, I cannot sufficiently engage here in a debate about inheritance, but for an interpretation of the modern idea of history as secularized eschatology, see K. Löwith, *Meaning in History: The Theological Implications of the Philosophy of History* (Chicago: University of Chicago Press, 1957); for a contemporary overview of these debates, see J. Svenungsson, *Divining History: Prophetism, Messianism, and the Development of the Spirit,* trans. S. Donovan (New York: Berghahn, 2016).

2. See W. Benjamin, *Illuminations,* trans. H. Zorn (New York: Harcourt, Brace & World, 1968), 253–64; Löwith, *Meaning in History.* For the appropriation of philosophy of history by analytic philosophy, see A.C. Danto's distinction between substantive and analytical philosophy of history in *Narration and Knowledge: Including the Integral Text of Analytical Philosophy of History* (New York: Columbia University Press, 1985), 1–16. For Popper's take, see K. Popper, *The Poverty of Historicism* (London: Routledge, 2002). For postmodern 'end of history' theories see G. Vattimo, 'The End of (Hi)story', *Chicago Review* 35(4) (1987), 20–30; and J. Baudrillard, *The Vital Illusion* (New York: Columbia University Press, 2000), 31–57.

3. F. Hartog, *Regimes of Historicity: Presentism and Experiences of Time,* trans. S. Brown (New York: Columbia University Press, 2015).

4. A. Assmann, 'Transformations of the Modern Time Regime', in C. Lorenz and B. Bevernage (eds), *Breaking Up Time: Negotiating the Borders between Present, Past and Future* (Göttingen: Vanderhoeck & Ruprecht, 2013), 54.

5. This of course does not mean that technology is ideology-free. It rather means that if technology is ideological, in most forms (except visions like human enhancement, which claim continuity with Enlightenment ideals of human perfectibility in their self-narrative) it does not have much to do with nineteenth-century political ideologies whose future-orientation may have indeed been lost.

6. You can nevertheless reasonably diagnose the ideological-political environment as presentist and/or consensus-driven and try to escape it within this particular context. This is, I think, what political theorists like Chantal Mouffe aim at when talking about the current 'post-political' environment they try to counter; see C. Mouffe, *On the Political* (London: Routledge, 2005). The same applies to some recent, supposedly more radical political theories, which, proceeding from the same diagnosis, try to break out by theorizing revolutionary interventions, as advocated most notably Alain Badiou and Jacques Rancière. See, for instance, A. Badiou, *Ethics: An Essay on the Understanding of Evil,* trans. P. Hallward (London: Verso, 2001); A. Badiou, *The Rebirth of History: Times of Riots and Uprisings,* trans. G. Elliott (London: Verso, 2012); J. Rancière, *Disagreement: Politics and Philosophy,* trans. J. Rose (Minneapolis: University of Minnesota Press, 1999). I find such efforts tremendously interesting insofar as they theorize change over time as defying existing structures (as you will see, this is structurally similar to what I will later call 'unprecedented change'); yet, insofar as political theories of evental ruptures are inspired by centuries-old political concerns instead of future prospects of their own time, they simply qualify as a supposedly new way of reaching the old political dream of the Left, as if that dream itself was not already discredited with the collapse of ideological-political visions. In other words, despite their merits, they are not engaged in bringing about a new future-orientation; typically they are engaged in a restorative work that tries to revive visions of the future that postwar intellectuals discredited. In doing so, many political theories of the Left seek conceptual tools in theology, as it is thoroughly mapped by Svenungsson, *Divining History,* 151–202.

7. J. Shklar, *After Utopia: The Decline of Political Faith* (Princeton: Princeton University Press, 1957); D. Bell, *The End of Ideology: On the Exhaustion of Political Ideas in the Fifties* (New York: Free Press, 1960).

8. For an introduction into debates over transhumanism and human enhancement, see J.B. Hurlbut and H. Tirosh-Samuelson (eds), *Transhuman Visions and Technological Imaginations* (Wiesbaden: Springer, 2016); or L.Y. Cabrera, *Rethinking Human Enhancement: Social Enhancement and Emergent Technologies* (Basingstoke: Palgrave, 2015). For an introduction to the prospect of AI and technological singularity, see M. Shanahan, *The Technological Singularity* (Cambridge, MA: MIT Press, 2015); and N. Bostrom, *Superintelligence: Paths, Dangers, Strategies* (Oxford: Oxford University Press, 2014).

9. To avoid any misunderstandings, my argument is not about sci-fi, and for the argument it is not relevant how far you may attempt to stretch back the origins of the genre. The argument is about how the prospect of unprecedented change is hosted lately by a revitalized and overtly popularized sci-fi. Thanks to Kenan Van De Mieroop for pointing out the possible confusion.

10. See the video of the experiment: RAIR Lab, 'Self-Consciousness with NAO Bots', YouTube video, 9 July 2015, retrieved 21 May 2016 from https://www.youtube.com/watch?v=MceJYhVD_xY. For the paper, see S. Bringsjord et al., 'Real robots that pass human tests of self-consciousness', *Proceedings of the 24th IEEE International Symposium on Robot and Human Interactive Communication,* Kobe, Japan, 31 August – 4 September, 2015, 498–504.

11. Bostrom, *Superintelligence.*

12. E. Musk, Twitter post, 2 August 2014, retrieved 21 May 2016 from https://twitter .com/elonmusk/status/495759307346952192.

13. 'Autonomous Weapons: An Open Letter from AI & Robotics Researchers', Future of Life Institute website, 2015, retrieved 21 May 2016 from http://futureoflife.org/AI/open_letter_autonomous_weapons.

14. I will briefly return to 'end of history' theories later.

15. Löwith, *Meaning in History,* 3.

16. O. Marquard, *Farewell to Matters of Principle: Philosophical Studies,* trans. R.M. Wallace (Oxford: Oxford University Press, 1989) 38–63.

17. Cf. Koselleck's inquiries into the birth of the notion of history in correlation with the anticipation of an open future: R. Koselleck, *Futures Past: On the Semantics of Historical Time,* trans. K. Tribe (New York: Columbia University Press, 2004), esp. 26–42, 137–48, 192–204, 222–54.

18. I. Kant, 'An Answer to the Question: What is Enlightenment?', in Hans Reiss (ed.) *Kant: Political Writings,* trans. H.B. Nisbet (Cambridge: Cambridge University Press, 1991), 54–60.

19. M. de Condorcet, *Outlines of an Historical View of the Progress of the Human Mind,* trans. unknown (Philadelphia: Lang and Ustick, 1796).

20. G.W.F. Hegel, *Lectures on the Philosophy of World History,* trans. H.B. Nisbet (Cambridge: Cambridge University Press, 1975); F. Fukuyama, *The End of History and the Last Man* (New York: The Free Press, 1992).

21. To be fair to Fukuyama, lately he came to the conclusion that history does not end with the end of ideological evolution, and what made him modify his position was precisely the technological vision. See F. Fukuyama, *Our Posthuman Future: Consequences of the Biotechnology Revolution* (New York: Farrar, Straus and Giroux, 2002), 15.

22. For my detailed argument on the necessity to reconcile our notion of history with the prospect of unprecedented change (on the occasion of the Anthropocene) see Z.B. Simon, 'History Manifested: Making Sense of Unprecedented Change', *European Review of History* 22(5) (2015), 819–34. For my efforts to sketch this notion as a philosophy of history see Z.B. Simon, 'We Are History: The Outlines of a Quasi-Substantive Philosophy of History', *Rethinking History* 20(2) (2016), 259–79. Here I merge the vocabularies of the two articles. Also, the notion of 'unprecedented change', despite lacking an ideological-political character, may have similarities to the notion of Event in recent political theories. See again note 6.

23. See Koselleck, *Futures Past,* esp. 32–37.

24. J. Guldi and D. Armitage, *The History Manifesto* (Cambridge: Cambridge University Press, 2014), 65.

25. Whereas historians offer developmental history to understand our current environmental concerns, environmental scientists already become skeptical about linear stories told about the Anthropocene (regardless of the feasibility of their alternative proposal). Cf. S. Veland and A.H. Lynch, 'Scaling the Anthropocene: How the Stories We Tell Matter', *Geoforum* 72 (2016), 1–5.

26. M. Kang, *Sublime Dreams of Living Machines: The Automaton in the European Imagination* (Cambridge, MA: Harvard University Press, 2011).

27. E.R. Truitt, *Medieval Robots: Mechanism, Magic, Nature, and Art* (Philadelphia: University of Pennsylvania Press, 2015).

28. P.C. Ingham, *The Medieval New: Ambivalence in an Age of Innovation* (Philadelphia: University of Pennsylvania Press, 2015), 14.

Bibliography

Assmann, A. 'Transformations of the Modern Time Regime', in C. Lorenz and B. Bevernage (eds), *Breaking Up Time: Negotiating the Borders between Present, Past and Future* (Göttingen: Vanderhoeck & Ruprecht, 2013), 39–56.

'Autonomous Weapons: An Open Letter from AI & Robotics Researchers'. Future of Life Institute website, 2015. Retrieved 2 August 2016 from http://futureoflife.org/AI/open_letter_autonomous_weapons.

Badiou, A. *Ethics: An Essay on the Understanding of Evil,* trans. P. Hallward. London: Verso, 2001.

———. *The Rebirth of History: Times of Riots and Uprisings,* trans. G. Elliott. London: Verso, 2012.

Baudrillard, J. *The Vital Illusion.* New York: Columbia University Press, 2000.

Bell, D. *The End of Ideology: On the Exhaustion of Political Ideas in the Fifties.* New York: Free Press, 1960.

Benjamin, W. *Illuminations,* trans. H. Zorn. New York: Harcourt, Brace & World, 1968.

Bostrom, N. *Superintelligence: Paths, Dangers, Strategies.* Oxford: Oxford University Press, 2014.

Bringsjord, S., J. Licato, N. Sundar Govindarajulu, R. Ghosh and A. Sen, 'Real Robots That Pass Human Tests of Self-Consciousness'. *Proceedings of the 24th IEEE International Symposium on Robot and Human Interactive Communication,* Kobe, Japan, 31 August – 4 September 2015, 498–504.

Cabrera, L.Y. *Rethinking Human Enhancement: Social Enhancement and Emergent Technologies.* Basingstoke: Palgrave, 2015.

Danto, A.C. *Narration and Knowledge: Including the Integral Text of Analytical Philosophy of History.* New York: Columbia University Press, 1985.

de Condorcet, M. *Outlines of an Historical View of the Progress of the Human Mind,* trans. unknown. Philadelphia: Lang and Ustick, 1796.

Fukuyama, F. *The End of History and the Last Man.* New York: The Free Press, 1992.

———. *Our Posthuman Future: Consequences of the Biotechnology Revolution.* New York: Farrar, Straus and Giroux, 2002.

Guldi, J., and D. Armitage. *The History Manifesto.* Cambridge: Cambridge University Press, 2014.

Hartog, F. *Regimes of Historicity: Presentism and Experiences of Time,* trans. S. Brown. New York: Columbia University Press, 2015.

Hegel, G.W.F. *Lectures on the Philosophy of World History,* trans. H.B. Nisbet. Cambridge: Cambridge University Press, 1975.

Hurlbut, J.B. and Tirosh-Samuelson H. (eds). *Transhuman Visions and Technological Imaginations.* Wiesbaden: Springer, 2016.

Ingham, P.C. *The Medieval New: Ambivalence in an Age of Innovation.* Philadelphia: University of Pennsylvania Press, 2015.

Kang, M. *Sublime Dreams of Living Machines: The Automaton in the European Imagination.* Cambridge, MA: Harvard University Press, 2011.

Kant, I. 'An Answer to the Question: What is Enlightenment?', in H. Reiss (ed.), *Kant: Political Writings,* trans. H.B. Nisbet (Cambridge: Cambridge University Press, 1991), 54–60.

Koselleck, R. *Futures Past: On the Semantics of Historical Time,* trans. K. Tribe. New York: Columbia University Press, 2004.

Löwith, K. *Meaning in History: The Theological Implications of the Philosophy of History.* Chicago: University of Chicago Press, 1957.

Marquard, O. *Farewell to Matters of Principle: Philosophical Studies,* trans. R.M. Wallace. Oxford: Oxford University Press, 1989.

Mouffe, C. *On the Political.* London: Routledge, 2005.

Popper, K. *The Poverty of Historicism.* London: Routledge, 2002.

Rancière, J. *Disagreement: Politics and Philosophy,* trans. J. Rose. Minneapolis: University of Minnesota Press, 1999.

RAIR Lab, 'Self-Consciousness with NAO Bots'. YouTube video, 9 July 2015. Retrieved 21 May 2016 from https://www.youtube.com/watch?v=MceJYhVD_xY.

Shanahan, M. *The Technological Singularity.* Cambridge, MA: MIT Press, 2015.

Shklar, J. *After Utopia: The Decline of Political Faith.* Princeton: Princeton University Press, 1957.

Simon, Z.B. 'History Manifested: Making Sense of Unprecedented Change'. *European Review of History* 22(5) (2015), 819–34.

———. 'We Are History: The Outlines of a Quasi-Substantive Philosophy of History'. *Rethinking History* 20(2) (2016), 259–79.

Svenungsson, J. *Divining History: Prophetism, Messianism, and the Development of the Spirit,* trans. S. Donovan. New York: Berghahn, 2016.

Veland, S., and A.H. Lynch. 'Scaling the Anthropocene: How the Stories We Tell Matter'. *Geoforum* 72 (2016), 1–5.

Truitt, E.R. *Medieval Robots: Mechanism, Magic, Nature, and Art.* Philadelphia: University of Pennsylvania Press, 2015.

Vattimo, G. 'The End of (Hi)story'. *Chicago Review* 35(4) (1987), 20–30.

Afterword

Hans Ruin

Across the world, struggles are currently being waged – locally, in society at large and across entire cultures – over how the past should be described and managed. *History* is increasingly becoming the name for an intensification of competing claims and battle-lines in which knowledge, politics and materialities are already engaged. Monuments and museums that until recently were simply regarded as concerned with the past have become the focus of heated disputes in the present. The ongoing tectonic dislocations, between East and West, North and South, and within nations, also involve changes in historical memory and its stewardship. If history – in the sense both of the past and of knowledge of that past – could once appear like an innocent object of educational efforts, the world today finds itself at a very different juncture. Perhaps more than ever before, the struggle for the future is now also a struggle over what the past really was, over how to describe, cultivate and teach it, over what to remember and what to forget.

Historicity – the quality of being historical – is not only a matter of having taken place in the past; it is also about carrying the past and of *being* and existing as past, as memory, testimony and embodied tradition. The use of history is not merely a question of how conceptions of history are used in this or that particular way. It also involves historical knowledge itself as one of several ways to relate to the past. The historical disciplines have been drawn into a maelstrom in which they themselves and their own history are being historicized and contextualized, and in which the subject of knowledge is forced to confront its own desire to fix its place in time.

Modernity is increasingly taking on the appearance of a peculiar chronopathology, as a time marked by a desire directed towards time itself. Historical knowledge and its institutions, such as museums, collections and archives, no longer afford privileged vantage points from which to survey the past. Rather, they, too, have become cultural artefacts whose material and ideological constructions are now tools for self-diagnosis and objects of historicization. Historical distance and the reflexive balancing act of historical consciousness in the midst of changes in time and space are increasingly seen and theorized as anthropological phenomena in their own right. The question 'what *was* the historical?' presents itself as a historical question about the historical itself. And yet this self-reflexive historicizing of the historical also brings with it a kind of hubris in the form of a new variety of metahistoricism, as if human beings had already attained this elevated perspective, as if they now truly had achieved the capacity and the will to make themselves historically accountable for the historical itself.

Forming part of this development is an intensified historical-theoretical and sociological debate over how to define the present. This has prompted a set of pointed questions: Where within the overall trajectory of history do 'we' currently find ourselves? Have 'we' now left behind an era of historical culture, or are 'we' moving towards its realization? Have 'we' in the West – for these questions are often premised upon an unstated and unthematized Westness – abandoned our historical consciousness and entered into a new 'regime of time', what some people call our 'presentism'? Have 'we' lost both the future and the past, entering into an accelerating and horizonless present in which 'we' no longer care about the long temporal perspective? Critical voices are questioning whether our temporal myopia is rendering us incapable of confronting the looming global threats and crises which humanity now faces, as well as the deepening conflicts of different nationalisms, conflicts in which history has been taken hostage by the identity-affirming politics of memory. Are we turning into 'posthistorical' creatures? Are 'we' in the process of leaving the human behind (posthumanism), or are we rather on the threshold of a new geological era, one defined by the fact that the world is now our own creation (the Anthropocene)?

Many suggestions for how to qualify 'our' position have thus been offered, in an ongoing attempt to pin down the truth of the present. But rather than just adding new labels to these self-diagnoses, which at times appear more as academic branding strategies, we want to address the more pressing task of theoretically visualizing, mapping and training ourselves to reflexively inhabit the multidimensional field of history. It is to the furthering of this task that the contributions in this volume aim. Now more than ever, we need to understand the *ethos* of historical consciousness as a mode of existence also marked by this inner obligation to account for its temporal-historical orientation. In a more psychological sense, 'historical consciousness' denotes the kinds of knowledge of and relationship to the past found in an individual or a group. But it can also refer to the way in which human consciousness itself is something historical, how it *belongs* to the past, not merely as a causal consequence but as historical and temporal in itself. Extending this line of reasoning makes it possible to visualize historical consciousness not only as something that is conveyed by time and history but, ultimately, as itself a bearer of the historical in all its contradictory reality.

But why speak of *ethos*? And in what sense is history itself marked by *the ethical*? In introducing this term, we do not primarily seek to highlight the prevalence of norms and normativity in historical culture and historiography. The Greek word *ethos* does not only stand for *ethics* in the modern sense of moral principles that govern behaviour. From its earliest uses, *ethos* also has a spatial-existential meaning: it refers to the situation and position from which people inhabit, encounter and orient themselves in a world, as also the name for an ontological abode or *domicile*. In this context, it is not insignificant that the term 'domicile' also has a juridical-technical connotation as the name for a socially prescribed place or district where a person is registered, in the sense of having a legal residence. One's *ethos* thereby also becomes the place where one is assigned certain rights and, at the same time, burdened with a responsibility.

But what could it mean to speak of the *ethos of history* in this sense? Does history have and offer such a domicile and homecoming? Is that not precisely what history lacks? Or, rather, was this not the illusion upheld by earlier philosophers of history, that history itself somehow provided us with origins? Have we not learned that all notions of origin and belonging are constructed and imaginary – mere narratives by which an excluded and exiled humanity, vainly and perhaps presumptuously, tried to situate itself in time? And yet the situation is more complicated than a conventional 'constructivism' would allow. If 'the historical' denotes an existential space to which human beings are consigned and in which they also look for, and expect to find, themselves in their historicity and historicizing, it is today a matter of learning to *inhabit* this space in a reflective fashion. This is what actualizes the question of *the ethos of history,* in the dual sense of the grammatical genitive.

The first sense of the genitive construction '*ethos* of history' poses the question of the ontological *domicile* of history itself, in the sense of where it abides and presents itself and thus becomes available for interrogation. It puts the focus on the connection of history to materiality and immateriality. In a strictly analytic sense, the term 'history' designates something that does not exist, since it refers to that which has been and which thus is no longer. It thus designates that which can only be intuited through bones, fragments, documents, monuments, buildings and landscapes, as well as in institutions and rituals in a state of constant evolution. History in this sense always appears by means of *sites* or *lieux* in the sense that Pierre Nora and his colleagues defined it in a series of reflections on the *lieux de mémoire*. Certain places and things seem to sustain and bear history to a greater degree than others. But this involves something more than just cataloguing this or that monument and institution. It also involves a reflection on locatedness and materiality as ontological dimensions of the historical itself. Here the archive and the museum are merely two of many different materializations and thus carriers of historical temporality, and thus dimensions of the ethos of history.

The second dimension of the genitive in the expression 'the ethos of *history*', by contrast, gestures towards history itself as a means of belonging and of being at home. Confronted by the question 'who are you?', human beings will spontaneously respond with an account of where they come from: from this or that origin, from a place, a country, a language, a faith, a class and a family – since to be a human being is essentially to have been born – and thus to have an ancestry, a genealogy that extends back among the dead. History is in this way actualized as the place from which human beings become and make themselves visible and interpretable when they are required to answer the question of who and what they are. But it is also, conversely, the place in relation to which they do *not* become visible in themselves, when their history is seen as simply the truth of who they are. On such an understanding, the ethos of history involves the challenge of receiving, appropriating and possibly renouncing the past – in short, the problem of *inheritance*.

Within the framework of the question of the ethos and domicile of history we therefore finally also encounter the experience of *exile,* as both belonging and loss. Surrounded by the context of 'one's own' history, one can feel *at home* even when one's physical home is destroyed or abandoned. At the same time, however, a human being can be surrounded by all the necessary exterior attributes of a home and a domicile and still be homeless when bereaved of his/her history. Here the *ethos* of history manifests itself as something more encompassing and demanding than the modern awareness of the inescapable ethics and politics of history-writing. Ultimately, it concerns the historical itself as an inescapable existential predicament.

Hans Ruin is professor of philosophy at Södertörn University. He is the author of many articles and two monographs in phenomenology and hermeneutics. He has coedited fifteen books, the latest of which is a three-volume work in the theory of history and memory in Swedish, titled *Historiens hemvist I-III* (2016). He is the coeditor of Nietzsche's collected works in Swedish, and during the period 2010–2016 he directed the multidisciplinary research program Time, Memory, Representation (www.histcon.se). He is the author of *Being with the Dead: Burial, Ancestral Politics, and the Roots of Historical Consciousness* (Stanford University Press, forthcoming).

Index

MAKING SENSE OF HISTORY
Studies in Historical Cultures
General Editor: Stefan Berger
Founding Editor: Jörn Rüsen

Bridging the gap between historical theory and the study of historical memory, this series crosses the boundaries between both academic disciplines and cultural, social, political and historical contexts. In an age of rapid globalization, which tends to manifest itself on an economic and political level, locating the cultural practices involved in generating its underlying historical sense is an increasingly urgent task.